How to Build a
High-Performance
Mazda Miata MX-5

By Keith Tanner

First published in 2010 by Motorbooks, an imprint of MBI Publishing Company, 400 First Avenue North, Suite 400, Minneapolis, MN 55401 USA

Motorbooks titles are also available at discounts in bulk quantity for industrial or sales-promotional use. For details write to Special Sales Manager at MBI Publishing Company, 400 First Avenue North, Suite 400, Minneapolis, MN 55401 USA.

To find out more about our books, visit us online at www.motorbooks.com.

Library of Congress Cataloging-in-Publication Data

Tanner, Keith, 1971-
  How to build a high-performance Mazda Miata MX-5 / Keith Tanner.
    p. cm.
  ISBN 978-0-7603-3705-9 (pbk. : alk. paper)
  1. Miata automobile--Performance. 2. Miata automobile--Motors--Modification. 3. Miata automobile--Customizing. I. Title.
  TL215.M45T355 2010
  629.28'722--dc22
                        2010014422

Editor: Chris Endres
Creative Director: Michele Lanci-Altomare
Design Managers: Brad Springer, Jon Simpson, James Kegley
Designer: Kathleen Littfin

Printed in the USA

On the cover: Carefully selected modifications can make a great car even better!

Inset: A well-modified Miata can make for an affordable, competitive race car.

On the title page: Few cars are as fun to drive as a V-8–powered Miata.

About the author
Keith Tanner first started working on Miatas 17 years ago and has been one of the techs at Flyin' Miata for over 9 years. He spends his days modifying, repairing, dismantling, and providing technical support for Miatas. He's authored two other Miata books in the Motorbooks Workshop series—*Mazda Miata MX-5 Performance Projects* and *Mazda Miata: Find It, Fix It, Trick It*—and is a contributor to and technical resource for a number of magazines. When he's not playing with cars, he's out on skis or a bike.

Contents

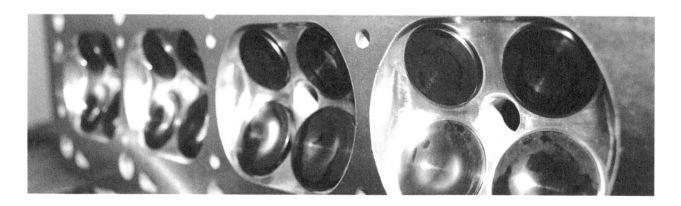

Acknowledgments

There are hundreds of people who should be thanked for helping to bring this book into reality. I owe a debt to anyone who's ever spent the time to explain something to me, to correct a mistake, or simply to ask a question that caused me to do some research and learn more about the Miata and high-performance cars. This book is the result of more than a decade and a half of fooling around with these little cars. I learn something new every day, often in response to a question someone else asked me.

Of course, there are a few specific individuals I need to thank: Bill Cardell, the owner of Flyin' Miata, has taken the time to educate me on just about every system in a car. We've built a few cars together, and it's always a learning experience. Even better, it's a lot of fun. My other co-workers at Flyin' Miata, Jeremy Ferber and Brandon Fitch, are an invaluable resource that I rely on every day. Brandon spent a lot of time proofreading this book, asking questions that helped me improve it. Moti Almagor, Emilio Cervantes from 949 Racing, Jim Langer at Racing Beat, the guys at Integral Cams, and Lance Schall all chipped in with some of their experience and knowledge. Kevin Lakkis at Toyo Tires was especially helpful, working for more than a year to obtain the Toyo Tire data shown in Chapter 7 and, more important, to secure the permission to use it. I'm sure I've forgotten someone, and if that someone is you, I apologize. It was not intentional.

Of course, the biggest thanks are reserved for my wife, Janel. She's my favorite co-pilot on the street, the track, and the rally stage. She supports me regardless of whatever mad project is underway, whether it's writing a book, building a mutated car, or traveling all over the country to various racetracks.

Introduction

It's not that the Miata is a bad car. It's just that it's mass-produced. That means its design is the result of a series of compromises. The suspension had to give precise handling and a good ride over a wide variety of pavement. The engine had to be reliable, inexpensive, fuel-efficient, smooth, powerful, and based on an existing powerplant. Light weight was a goal but not at the expense of a reasonable interior. The car had to be inexpensive to build so that it could be sold at a low price. And so on.

Naturally, these design decisions weren't for everyone. Oh, the engineers did a great job. The stock Miata is a fun, forgiving, nimble little car that has made a million drivers very happy. But there are those who have different priorities. They might prize light weight over civility or wish to bias the suspension more toward handling. Or maybe they want to take advantage of the strides in automotive technology since the Miata was introduced in 1989.

This book is for those people.

For as long as there have been Miatas, there have been people modifying Miatas. In fact, there was a modified Miata on the stand at the Chicago auto show in 1989 when the car was unveiled. Even the original development team couldn't resist the urge to tweak their new baby before it was released to the public.

We hope the information you find here will help you get the most out of your Miata, whether you're simply looking for a fun back-road toy or you want to set the fastest time at a track day. It'll let you make decisions on what will suit you best, and possibly suggest some improvements you hadn't considered. In the end, I hope it helps make your car more fun. That's rather the point of all this, isn't it?

This book isn't a "how–to." It's more of a "why–to." It's intended to help you make decisions on how best to modify your Miata. So instead of telling you how to install a new set of springs and shocks, you'll learn what they do, how they affect the ride and handling of the car, how to select the components, and how to adjust them. It's also not going to be a "cookbook," telling you which parts to modify and in which order. The best way to do that will depend on your final goals. Again, you'll learn how it all interacts so that you can make these decisions yourself.

If you want more information on how to actually carry out some of these modifications, I'd recommend picking up a copy of one of my other books, *Mazda Miata MX-5 Performance Projects*. It's a sister volume to this one and contains 42 projects such as how to change shocks and install a roll bar.

While writing this book, I wasn't sure if I should identify the sources of some of the components or not. The Miata aftermarket is always changing, with new suppliers appearing and old standbys disappearing as the years roll on. I'd hate to have someone hunting around for a part or manufacturer that has disappeared since the book was published. By giving the source at the time of writing, I figure you'll at least have a fighting chance of tracking down the parts or finding out what's replaced it.

I should also make it clear that I work at Flyin' Miata. Because of this, I have easy access to parts from FM, as it's often called. You'll see quite a few of them in the pictures. Again, this isn't intended as an endorsement, it's simply a matter of what's available to me.

A word about nomenclature: the Miata—at the time of writing—has been through three generations. The first generation, known as the NA, was available from 1990 until 1997. From 1998 until 2005 was the NB, and the NC appeared in 2006. For more details on exactly what changed over this time, check out *Mazda MX-5 Miata: Find It. Fix It. Trick It.* I'll cover some of the changes in this book, but it's important to know the NA-NB-NC terminology at least. Another common acronym is MSM, referring to the 2004–2005 Mazdaspeed MX-5 turbo model.

If you're interested in any of the ongoing projects, I invite you to visit **www.slowcarfast.com**. Not only will it have any updates and corrections to this book, but there are detailed build diaries on some unusual Miatas and variants thereof.

Chapter 1
The Philosophy of Modification

The secret to knowing how to modify a car well is to know just what it is you're building. This seems obvious enough, of course, but you've seen the results. Some modified cars just work for some reason, while others never rise above the sum of their parts. Some, of course, don't even get that far. What makes the good ones stand out is a clarity of vision. Before starting out, the builder had an idea of what the end result would be. Every change made to the car was made in the goal of achieving that result. Next time you're standing in front of a car with a good spec sheet that just doesn't seem to gel, see if you can figure out what the goal was. Same with the car that has that cohesive feel. It'll be a lot easier for the latter.

This doesn't mean you have to sit down and write out a full parts list before you start to modify a car. It simply means

you need to define what it is you want. It's fairly easy to do when you're building a competition car. Simply read the rule book, and see what it is you're allowed to do. Even without that constraint, it's not too difficult. Chances are you already know. Just think about what you like about the car and how you want to be able to use it. Use this description of your perfect car as a filter as you consider each modification. Does the change take you closer to your goal?

For example, if your goal is to build a lightweight autocrosser, installing a chrome double-hoop "style bar" behind the seats probably isn't going to work in your favor. If you want a fun Sunday back-road car suitable for cross-country trips, a stiff track-biased suspension may not be what you need. It can be tempting to simply tear through an

accessory catalog and order one of everything, but you won't be happy in the long run.

Another advantage to knowing your final destination is that you can avoid dead ends, or at the least, they won't take you by surprise. If you're planning on putting a turbocharger on the car down the road, do you want to spend money on a header now? You'll just have to replace it. If you *are* planning to go to a high-power turbo, maybe it makes sense to install a programmable ECU now. It's not a great power gain for the cost, but it's something you'll be doing eventually and this gives you the chance to work out the bugs and learn how to use it. This can mean you'll make some choices that seem a bit odd at first, but it'll all come in to focus down the line.

You're going to find a lot of talk in this book about compromises. Over and over again, actually. That's because we're limited by the laws of physics, and gaining some ability in one area will often mean giving up something else. It's an unfortunate situation, but with careful selection and setup you can minimize the downsides of any compromises you have to make.

As mentioned, competition cars are great examples of a clear vision. They are purpose-built to the limit of the regulations, sometimes even a little bit beyond that point. On top of this, they are engineered to avoid any failure. If they do fail, it has to be gracefully. This means they're a fantastic source of ideas and little tricks. A good racing Miata is a fascinating device.

It's important to keep in mind that some race cars are set up the way they are because of the rules, however, not necessarily because it's the best choice. A perfect example of this in the Miata world is the Spec Miata suspension. Spec Miatas are fast and excellent handling little cars, so it's reasonable to want to duplicate their suspension—especially as it's available in a nice, complete package. But ask a fast Spec driver if this is a good idea, and he or she will immediately say no. By working hard over the years, builders have learned how to overcome the limitation of this particular suspension setup. Given a bit more latitude, they'd go faster. Because you are not constrained by the rules, you can easily build a more effective suspension for less money. Race cars also tend to show extreme compromises: creature comforts tossed out for light weight, stiff suspensions that only work on smooth surfaces, alignment settings that make the car a challenge to drive in a straight line but very responsive to steering inputs.

Because it's fun, let's take a look at a few cars that are good examples of well-modified Miatas. In every case, it's easy to tell what the owner was thinking.

7

TARGA MIATA

The Targa Miata was built for competition. Like any competition car, it's defined in large part by the class rules. But the rules were fairly liberal and the event is not a usual one for a Miata, so it's an interesting car.

The Targa Newfoundland is a week-long race on 1,400 miles of public roads. About 20 percent of that is closed stages, where the cars are sent off one at a time to cover the distance as fast as possible. The roads vary from fast, flowing ones along the coast and through the woods to tight, narrow blasts through town. The road surface could be freshly paved, or it could be hammered and battered. The teams have never seen the stages before. The navigator has the basic information about the road, but both members of the team need to be able to deal with all sorts of surprises.

So, in order to do well at the Targa, a car has to be nimble and agile but forgiving and stable at speed. Speeds are limited to 120 miles per hour, but when you're blasting down a bumpy road that you've never seen before and there's a rock wall on one side and miles of woods on the other, 120 miles per hour seems pretty quick. Because every corner is a new one, an engine with a wide powerband is needed. The friendly nature of the Miata makes it a good choice for this race, but a stock one wouldn't quite have what it takes. Still, a good Targa car makes for a competent street car.

The Targa Miata build started with a 1994 Miata that had been completely stripped down to the frame. It was seam-welded for stiffness, the required safety cage was welded in, and every effort was made to take weight out of the car. The dashboard, for example, came from a 1990 because of the light construction, and it was disassembled and cut down until it weighed less than 15 pounds, including the substructure.

Because the team would have to spend more than 12 hours a day in the car, the Corbeau FX-1 Pro race seats were chosen for their comfort and then modified with some memory foam to improve them further. A lot of attention was paid to ergonomics, making sure everything fell close at hand in the heat of competition. Nets were installed on the transmission tunnel for holding books, snacks, and paperwork in place, and Camelbak water bladders were fitted behind the seats so that both driver and navigator would stay hydrated and fresh.

Forced induction wasn't allowed in the car's class. So the engine was bored and stroked to 2,020 cubic centimeters with a Flyin' Miata stroker kit and ran 11.4:1 compression. The head came from a 1999 Miata and was given oversize valves, ported and polished, and had a more aggressive set of cams from Integral Camshaft installed. Partly for fun, a complex header was built. The end result was more than 160 horsepower at the wheels, but more important, a wide band of torque and the ability to run on 91 octane fuel at full power.

Once the engine performed reasonably well and was healthy, development on the powertrain was stopped. After all, power is only good if you can use it. Far more time was spent on the suspension and handling. The front subframe from a 2003 was fitted for its improved steering geometry and better steering rack. A full year was spent on testing a wide variety of suspensions, concentrating on enough travel to absorb anything, and finally ending up on a customized setup put together by AFCO. Testing revealed that this long travel also contributed greatly to stability on the track, as the car rarely hit the bumpstops. A lot of testing was done to get the balance of the car set up, and everything was adjustable in case alterations had to be made mid-race.

The bottom of the car was also fitted with a number of braces, not just to make it stiffer but also to act as armor for the inevitable smacks against the road. A big brake kit with Wilwood calipers and two-piece rotors was fitted because it was lighter and also allowed quick pad changes. The whole car was designed to be tough and easily serviced if required, and it was all built in a home garage, right down to spraying the Martini paint job.

The end result did quite well, finishing 1st in class and 16th overall out of more than 60 starters and coming in ahead of two of the factory teams in the race. Looking over it now, you can spot many small touches that help make the car just that much more effective. The wires for the intercom, for example, are run through the harness pads to keep the cords out of the way but easy to access. The tubes for the hydration system run down the opposite harness strap so it's a simple matter to take a sip. The brake bias can be adjusted easily through a proportioning valve placed just behind the shifter. There are quick releases on the sway bar end links, so the car's balance can be quickly adjusted without tools. The dashboard is painted flat black to prevent reflections on the dash. There's even an anti-skid pad on the transmission tunnel where the driver braces himself to get out of the car.

Good competition cars are like this: The more you look, the more tricks you'll find. You'll find pictures of it throughout this book. The entire build and the race can be found at www.targamiata.com.

Because road conditions can change quite a bit over the course of a rally, the car had to be easily adjustable. Here, the car's getting a quick ride height change.

RICK WELDON'S *SUPERSPORT* AND *RAKUZA*

Rick Weldon owns P R Motorsports near San Francisco, a shop that specializes in Mazdas, Hondas, and Toyotas. He's also a former professional racer who spends a lot of time instructing at track days. His car needed to be quick, reliable, and a good handler, as he will usually hand the keys over to his students at the slightest provocation. The intent was to build a track car that could be driven to and from the track, on a budget.

The first iteration was called the *Supersport*. It was a 1990 Miata, stripped down to the elements. Most of the interior was removed in the name of weight savings, including the carpet, the top, the center console, heat and A/C, and even the lower part of the dashboard. The side windows were also removed, and the car had a hardtop that was used in poor weather. A Hard Dog roll bar protected the occupants, and stock seats with reshaped foam and four-point race harnesses kept both driver and passenger in place. Weldon even went so far as to spend hours trimming the excess length from various bolts to save a couple of pounds.

Under the hood, there weren't a lot of changes. The little 1.6 was left pretty much stock, with a Jackson Racing intake, header, and exhaust the only modifications. Suspension was a set of Flyin' Miata springs and sway bars, Tokico Illumina shocks, and some upgraded bumpstops and NB mounts from Fat Cat Motorsports. Wheels were light SSR Competitions with the forgiving and long-lived Toyo

RA-1 competition tire. Brakes were simply stock units with good pads and fluid.

The end result was a light, inexpensive little car that was as reliable as a hammer. Every time it went to the track, it was shared between two to four drivers and only came into the pits for a driver change and a full tank of gas once in a while. A track day was essentially a six-hour endurance race. The light weight and well-sorted handling made up for a lack

The Supersport hard at work.

Rakuza doesn't look exotic from the outside, but it's the care with which all the modifications were made that make it work so well.

in horsepower, and it proved to be an excellent platform for teaching and for chasing "faster" cars.

While the car was still registered on the street and driven to the track, it wasn't exactly luxurious. So after a decade of running the *Supersport* hard, Weldon decided to start over again. This time, he was aiming for a car that wasn't quite so extreme. Instead of a track car that could be driven on the street, the goal was more of a dual-purpose car that

was happier on the street than the original. As a complete coincidence, Weldon had also recently married.

The car was again an early one, a 1991. A bit of weight was pulled from the car, such as power steering and A/C, but the interior was left more intact. A roll bar was installed, of course, along with a couple of race seats to help keep the occupants in place. This meant the car weighed a bit more, so the power-to-weight ratio was addressed with a nicely built-up replacement engine from Rebello along with intake, header, and exhaust modifications that were similar to the original. The suspension was much the same as before, only with a set of Ground Control coil-overs to allow the car to be corner-weighted. A number of braces were added under the car to keep the chassis rigid. The small 1.6 brakes were replaced with those from a 2004. Wheels were again lightweight SSRs, this time with the newer Toyo R888 for increased grip. The differential was pulled out of a 1996 to provide a Torsen LSD and a slightly higher rear-end ratio, and the rear subframe was also swapped to take advantage of improved bracing.

So far, the new car—named "*Rakuza*"—has proven to be right on the money. It's quieter and more comfortable on the street, making the trip out to the track much more civilized. However, it remains quick and nimble on track, with the same sort of bulletproof reliability this sort of car needs. At the 20th anniversary event that took place at Mazda Raceway Laguna Seca, it spent approximately 10 hours tearing around the track at full throttle without missing a beat.

Rick Weldon shows off the extremes of *Rakuza*'s suspension travel on the Corkscrew at Laguna Seca.

It's almost impossible to tell this is an NA.

The engine looks right at home in the 1995 engine bay.

MARK BRANT'S 1995 MSM

Mark Brant's Miata is an excellent example of a nice street car, built with some ingenuity and a lot of parts-bin raiding. From the outside, it looks like a fairly normal 1995. Inside, it's 10 years newer. Brant got his hands on a wrecked 2005 MSM and appropriated the engine, transmission, rear end, exhaust, suspension, steering, and brakes. Most of this simply bolts in place on the earlier car. In fact, because he was able to get the whole drivetrain including subframes, it was literally just a matter of unbolting the original parts and sliding the new ones into their place.

There were a few details that needed to be sorted out, of course. It's not quite *that* easy. Threading the entire wiring harness through the old chassis would have been a lot of work, so Brant used an aftermarket Link ECU and treated it as if he'd simply added a turbocharger to his stock engine, an intelligent choice that saved a lot of trouble. The intercooler routing on the MSM takes advantage of a couple of holes in the chassis that aren't accessible on a 1995, so new piping had to be made. Trying to squeeze an oversize intercooler intended for a 2005 into the nose was the most complex part of the swap. The intercooler interfered with the air conditioning system, so Brant modified the hard lines of the A/C system to make it work. He reports it would have been much easier if he'd used an aftermarket intercooler intended to fit in a 1995 in the first place. Typical performance upgrades to the MSM engine were made at the same time, with an improved intake, intercooler, exhaust, and downpipe installed, all from Flyin' Miata.

Underneath, the only parts that weren't changed out were the steering column and the master cylinder. The ABS from the MSM wasn't wired in; that's planned for the future. Otherwise, the entire suspension and braking setup was updated. He even added a number of the upgraded chassis stiffeners that Mazda worked in over the years.

The interior was also updated. This required more work than the mechanicals did, as there were some changes in the door panel fixings and the lock mechanisms as well as wiring for the more complex instrument cluster. Brant's attention to detail shows with touches such as integrating the programming keyboard for the link into the center console, with a display built into the rearview mirror. He also fitted a Mazdaspeed boost gauge into the stock instrument cluster in the spot originally occupied by the oil pressure gauge. It looks like a factory job. It was definitely not a matter of simply bolting together a few parts.

The end result is a car with the classic looks of the original Miata but the interior quality and driving experience of Mazda's final evolution of the platform. Brant spent a lot of time thinking about what the final result should be, and it shows.

There's no indication from outside that the car is a hybrid.

This is one seriously wide car.

Removable rear supports for the roll bar solve the problem of fitting a bar with the NC's top design.

BRIAN GOODWIN'S CAR

Brian Goodwin runs Good-Win Racing, and this 2006 is his personal toy and laboratory. Goodwin describes his goal as a "super fun dual-purpose NC for street, autocross, or track." As an example, he describes taking the car on a 200-mile pleasure run up the California coast on Saturday, running an SCCA autocross (and winning his class) on Sunday, and then visiting Willow Springs later in the week. Yes, we should all be so lucky!

So instead of a race car that can be driven on the street, as Rick Weldon's original *Supersport* was, this is a street car with strong ability on the track. Because large tires are important to autocross success, he installed a set of AWR fender flares to let him run massive 295/30-18 tires in the rear and 285/30-18 on the front. Around town, he runs 225/45-17s. They're a bit taller than stock, and it gives him some extra ground clearance and a relatively tall sidewall.

After a lot of experimentation, the suspension ended up with some custom-valved Ohlins coil-overs and Eibach sway bars. 728 inch-pounds front and 448 inch-pounds rear springs were chosen to retain a bit of comfort on southern California roads at the expense of ultimate track performance. A big brake kit from Racing Brake was bolted on, although Goodwin reports the stock brakes with a good set of pads and some ducting was sufficient for most use.

A set of Sparco Roadster seats hold him in place while dropping him down 2 inches in the car, and a roll bar with removable rear supports allows full use of both the soft top and the passenger's seat. This is harder than it sounds with an NC. Because Goodwin's a bit of a power junkie, there's a Cosworth supercharger stuffed underhood, and it's currently pushing approximately 230 horsepower at the wheels. RoadsterSport header, midpipe, and exhaust let the engine breathe. There's a good chance this will see some more evolution as time goes on. The car is competitive in autocross and time trial events, even against cars with a much better power-to-weight ratio, so it can be deemed a success on the competition front. It also puts a huge smile on Goodwin's face, so it's a winner on the street as well.

Chapter 2
Engine

When most people look at improving their car's performance, they focus on the engine. There's a certain amount of logic to that, as it's the engine that actually does all the hard work of acceleration.

Over the years, the Miata came with three basic engine designs. The original was the B6-ZE, a high-performance variant of one of Mazda's bread-and-butter econobox engines. It's a 1,597-cc four with a fairly standard specification for the time of dual overhead camshafts, four valves per cylinder, and 9.4:1 compression ratio. A bit of a twist on the usual spec sees cooling oil spray on the bottom of the pistons, possibly a remnant of the engine's history as a turbocharged motor used in rally specials. It put out 116 horsepower and 100 foot-pounds of torque, which was about par for the course in 1989.

In 1994, the BP-ZE was introduced. It's basically a 1,839-cc version of the B6-ZE producing 128 horsepower. However, since the B6-ZE was based on a block that started off as a 1.3, there wasn't any room to punch it out any bigger. The BP was made just a bit bigger in every dimension, including more space between the cylinders. So while the engines are obviously related in terms of designs and detail, there are almost no parts shared between the two others than a few bearings and seals and the rods.

Over the next 11 years, the BP was tweaked and updated. A new head with better intake port design was introduced in 1999 (that makes a BP-4W), and variable valve timing (VVT) was added in 2001 to make the BP-Z3. A turbocharged variant based on the BP-4W made a short appearance in 2004–2005 as well. Compression ratios crept upward over the years, but overall it's the same basic engine design, and most of the parts can be swapped back and forth. The B6-ZE disappeared from the Miata in North America when the BP arrived on the scene, but it stuck around in Europe until 2005 with minor changes.

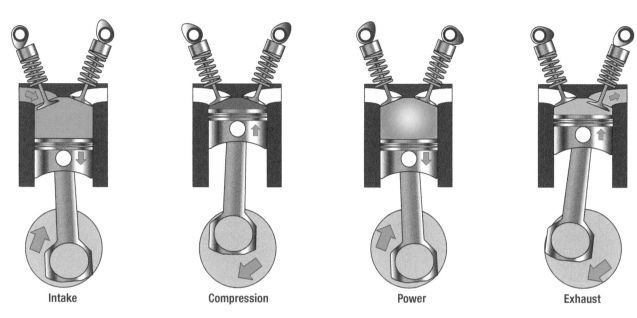

| Intake | Compression | Power | Exhaust |

The four cycles of an internal combustion engine are also known as "suck, squish, bang, and blow."

With the introduction of the NC in 2006, Mazda reworked the entire car. This meant a new drivetrain, and the appearance of the MZR engine in the MX-5. The MZR engine is shared with a number of Fords and is best known as a Duratec. As the Ford engine, it's seen a fair bit of development as a naturally aspirated powerplant. It's a modern 1,999-cc mill that shares absolutely nothing with the earlier cars other than basic specification: four cylinders, 16 valves, overhead cams, and VVT. Europe got a 1,798-cc version of the engine as well. The larger engine got a bit of a refresher in 2009 with the addition of a forged crank and rods for more internal strength.

Okay, that's enough of the history. How do we make these engines perform better? Well, let's go through the life cycle of an oxygen molecule as it is unwillingly involved in the creation of horsepower. Think of it as a guided tour of the engine. Let's call our guide, Oscar.

First, our little molecule will get pulled through a filter, where dust particles and bugs are separated out. Oscar then passes through a device that measures how much air is being sucked into the engine, then continues down the intake piping until he gets to the throttle body. The throttle restricts the amount of air that gets into the engine, but right now it's wide open. Oscar and his friends enter a chamber called the intake plenum to wait for a moment until a pair of intake valves open up. There's some careful timing involved here: The piston is attached to the crankshaft by a connecting rod and goes up and down in the cylinder bore. The valves are opened by the intake camshaft, so when they open the piston is heading down in the bore and creating a powerful suction. Just as Oscar is being sucked into the cylinder, he's doused

in a precisely measured shot of atomized gasoline from the injector at the port.

As the piston reaches the bottom of its travel, the intake valves slam shut. The piston starts to move back up again, which compresses Oscar and friends fairly dramatically. They're all squeezed into a space about 1/10th as big as they had before. Just as the compression gets near its peak, the spark plug sparks and the fuel-oxygen mixture is lit. Poor Oscar. The result isn't an explosion but a controlled burn that forces the piston down in the bore. This is the power stroke of the engine, the whole point of this exercise. Once the power stroke is over and the piston starts to come back up, the camshaft opens up the exhaust valves and the hot exhaust gases get pushed out the exhaust port to eventually escape out the tailpipe. Right as they're leaving, the intake valves open up again and a new shot of air and fuel comes streaming in.

So how can we improve on this process? Think about how Oscar got into the engine. He was sucked in thanks to the vacuum created by the piston dropping down the cylinder. Any restrictions in the intake system will make it more difficult for the engine to pull in the air it needs. The same thing goes for the exhaust: The harder it is for the burnt gases to escape, the less room there is for the fresh air. And it's air that really lets the engine make power. We can deliver all sorts of fuel into the cylinders; that's easy. But without oxygen, the fuel won't burn.

The most obvious way to get more air into the engine is to force it in with some sort of fan or pump. That's what turbochargers and superchargers do. We'll cover them, as well as intakes and exhaust modifications, in later chapters. Right now, let's concentrate on the engine itself.

DYNAMOMETER TESTING

You're going to see many references to "dyno testing" in this book. So what is a dynamometer? It's a device to measure engine power. More accurately, it measures torque and then uses that to calculate horsepower and torque. The measurement is either done by recording the rate of acceleration of a big flywheel—that's an inertial dyno, such as the popular Dynojet—or by measuring the torque applied to overcome a given resistance. A dyno chart typically shows horsepower, torque, and rpm. A fairly flat torque curve will make the car's acceleration even, while one that climbs steeply at some point will accelerate more slowly until that point, then the power will increase quickly. A flatter curve is easier to drive, but a high-power car will often have to give that up in exchange for the increased output.

There are two major types of dynos: engine and chassis. An engine dyno measures an engine mounted on a stand, directly off a crankshaft. This is how Mazda and other manufacturers do it. A chassis dyno, or "rolling road" as it's sometimes known, measures the power at the wheels, after it's passed through the drivetrain.

Obviously, it's a lot easier to measure an engine's power when it's still installed in a car, so that's how most of the aftermarket tuners do their testing. The wheel horsepower number is always lower, as there is some power loss in the transmission and the differential. Unfortunately, there's no accurate way to convert one to the other.

Stock Miatas typically lose around 25 horsepower between measured wheel power and quoted flywheel horsepower. This loss is sometimes quoted as a percentage as a way to inflate gains from modifications, but really it's part percentage and part fixed losses. In Europe, a dyno operator will let the car coast down after a dyno run. This allows the dyno to measure how much power is stored in the drivetrain, and this power is added to the measured power at the wheels to provide a flywheel figure and a certain amount of correction for variances in the drivetrain.

In North America, only the wheel number is used because that's how much power is actually getting to the road. There are good arguments to be made for both ways of doing it. The one technique that doesn't work is to simply pull a "drivetrain loss" figure out of the air and use that to bump up the readings. That's done purely for marketing. I've seen one aftermarket parts vendor claim a flywheel number that was nearly double what had been measured at the wheels, by playing around with a wide variety of imaginary "correction factors."

There are legitimate correction factors, however. The numbers quoted by the manufacturers have to meet a fairly rigid set of conditions by law. All accessories (such as the power steering pump and alternator) have to be installed and the full exhaust system, including cats, needs to be in place. The aftermarket isn't quite so regulated. However, because air temperature, density, and humidity can have a dramatic effect on power output, there is a correction factor developed by the Society of Automotive Engineers (SAE) that is designed to scale the results to take these factors into account. If you want to compare two dyno runs done on different days, or even at different times of day, you need to apply this correction factor. In extreme cases such as dynos being run in high altitudes or very hot or cold temperatures, this correction factor can get as high as 20 percent.

The correction isn't perfect, but it's the best way we have of comparing dyno runs taken under different conditions. In case you're interested, the standard weather conditions are 77 degrees Fahrenheit (25 degrees Celsius), 29.235 inches of vacuum (99 kilopascals) altitude-corrected barometric pressure, sea level, and zero humidity. Unless the car is always tested under these conditions, an SAE correction factor does need to be applied.

There are a lot of things that can affect a dyno reading, especially on a chassis dyno. Because inertial dynos rely upon measuring the rate of acceleration of a given mass, the mass of the drivetrain also has an effect. A light flywheel can give a higher horsepower reading, and even a set of heavy wheels can show a drop in power. If the car is getting hot, power can drop off as the engine computer pulls timing. Tire slippage on the big drums used on Dynojets is a factor, and even tire pressure, the gear chosen in the transmission, and the age of the transmission fluid can have an effect. Then there's the calibration and setup of the dyno, which provides room for error or creative modification on the part of an unscrupulous operator.

As you're probably starting to figure out, it takes a skilled and careful operator to extract meaningful numbers from a dyno. Even with that, there's liable to be a bit of variation between operators and even more between different brands and types of dyno. That doesn't mean they're useless, though. A good before and after test of the same car can be accurate, especially since it gives you a good look at the relative improvement provided by the part.

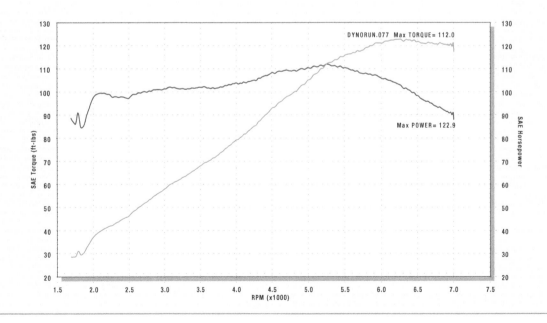

CYLINDER HEAD

Starting from the top, we have the head. The ports and channels in the head are designed to move air in and out of the cylinders as quickly and smoothly as possible. However, the Miata is mass-produced, so the engineers had to trade off their ultimate ports for more rapid production. A bit of attention paid to the shape and finish of these ports can make a big difference. This is called porting.

Proper porting is rather involved. The easiest thing to do is actually "port matching," where the shape and size of the ports on the manifolds and head are matched up. This is done by matching the port to the cutout in the gasket and grinding out any extra material.

But the real magic happens inside the port. There's a lot of science and a bit of art involved in properly porting a head, as it's not just a matter of making the ports as big as possible. The goal is to get as much velocity as possible and to also promote a bit of swirl as the air and fuel mixture enters the combustion chamber to make sure it's well distributed. Most of the work is actually done on shaping the bottom of the port, as this keeps the airflow attached to the edges and promotes smooth flow instead of turbulence. The finish part is easy enough to understand: The rough casting gets smoothed out but not to a mirror finish. A slight bit of roughness is retained to keep a boundary layer of air attached to the port surface. This is usually done with a Dremel or similar tool.

Inside the combustion chamber, all those bumps in the casting will get hotter than the surface of the head and can light off the air and fuel mixture early. Polishing will help avoid this. Also, on a stock head, part of the circumference of the valves is blocked off by the casting. Removing this is called "unshrouding the valves," and it can improve the flow through the head quite nicely.

Porting and polishing is something you can do at home if you want to give it a try. The head does need to be well cleaned when you're done, and the porting should be done with the valves removed so that you can access both sides of the port. It's probably best to take it to a machine shop for final cleaning and a valve job before you install it. Make sure not to cut into the valve seat (where the valve contacts the head) at all, or you'll ruin your head. Err on the side of caution!

A nicely prepared head. The combustion chambers have been polished to remove any roughness, oversize valves are installed, and the valves are not shrouded. The intake valves are the large ones.

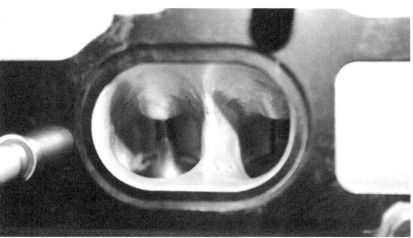

A modified port. You can actually see the back side of the valves here. The gasket is in place to check the gasket-matching work, and it's easy to see how everything is smoothed over. What's not obvious is exactly where aluminum was removed to improve the flow. This sort of art is why ported heads are so expensive.

VALVES

The valves also have a big influence on how much air moves into the cylinder. Because the air has to flow around the edges of the valve, increasing the diameter can make a fairly big difference to the amount of flow. Maximum valve size is based on the size of the combustion chamber. If you go too big, the edge of the valve starts to get heavily shrouded by the side of the chamber, and eventually you simply can't squeeze in a bigger valve. Because there are four valves stuffed into each combustion chamber, there's obviously going to be a limit to just how big the valves can be. A 1-millimeter (0.040-inch) increase is typically as big as you can go, and on engines fitted with VVT this can still cause interference problems with the pistons, which is not good. The shape of the valve seat also has an effect on flow, and a multi-angle seat will work better than one with a single angle. Even the stem of the valve can be narrowed so that it's less restrictive.

CAMS

The camshaft is an important piece. It's what controls the opening and closing of the valves, and thus acts as the traffic cop for airflow. Not only does it decide when each valve is going to open, it also controls how far it opens (referred to as lift), how long it stays open (duration), and the speed at which it opens and closes (the ramp).

Then there's the timing between the two camshafts. Air has momentum. It takes time for it to start moving and to stop. Because of this, the intake valve is opened a bit early to get both the valve and the air moving. It also stays open a bit after the piston reaches the bottom of the stroke to let the momentum of the fuel and air charge ram a bit more into the cylinder. Likewise, the exhaust valve will open a bit early in order to start getting the hot exhaust gas out and stays open after the compression stroke is over. With the intake valve open early and the exhaust valve closing late, there's a period of time when both are open. This overlap will help pull the fresh intake air into the cylinder, but if it's too much then some of the air and fuel mixture goes right out the exhaust port.

Now, because the air velocity is lower at lower engine speeds, the ideal cam design will change, depending on engine speed. Keep the valves open too long and you can push some of the intake charge right out the exhaust or even suck some exhaust back into the combustion chamber. If they're not open long enough, you don't get all your exhaust out or get a full charge of fuel and air. Like so much else, you must compromise.

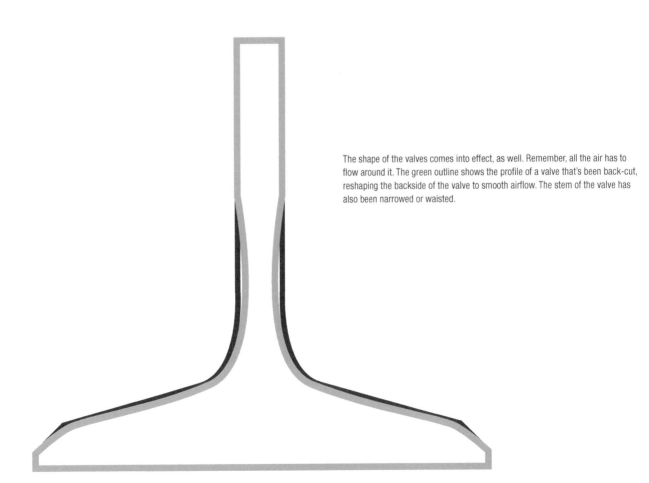

The shape of the valves comes into effect, as well. Remember, all the air has to flow around it. The green outline shows the profile of a valve that's been back-cut, reshaping the backside of the valve to smooth airflow. The stem of the valve has also been narrowed or waisted.

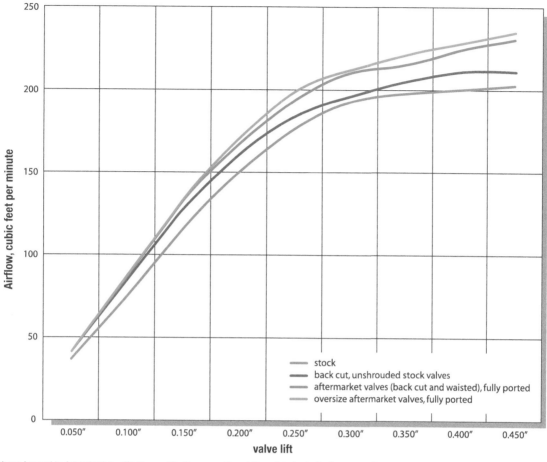

stock
back cut, unshrouded stock valves
aftermarket valves (back cut and waisted), fully ported
oversize aftermarket valves, fully ported

A flow bench can be used to determine how effective modifications are, although it won't test velocity. You can see here that porting had the biggest effect on this 1999–2000 Miata head. The larger valve doesn't make as big a difference as you might think, possibly because it's getting too close to the sides of the cylinder.

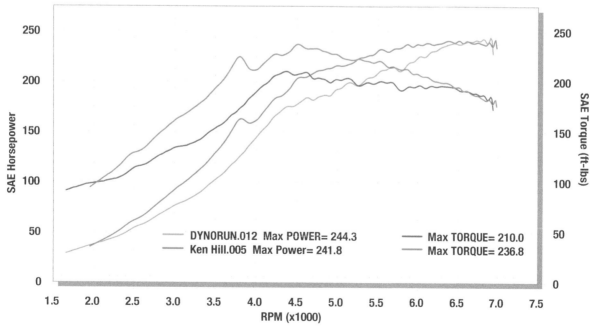

DYNORUN.012 Max POWER= 244.3   Max TORQUE= 210.0
Ken Hill.005 Max Power= 241.8   Max TORQUE= 236.8

The effects of some headwork on a 1.6-turbo Miata. Peak power isn't affected in this case, but the turbo builds boost much faster, creating nearly 50 foot-pounds more at 3,500 rpm. This is a fairly dramatic improvement.

Cam	Duration @ 0.003 inch	Duration @ 0.050 inch	Lift (inches)
1990–1993 intake	236°	192°	0.309
1990–1993 exhaust	250°	204°	0.311
1994–1997 intake	233°	190°	0.318
1994–1997 exhaust	254°	202°	0.338
1999–2000 intake	248°	204°	0.326
1999–2005 exhaust	251°	210°	0.350
2001–2005 intake (WT)	263°	208°	0.370
2004–2005 MSM intake	248°	207°	0.345
2006–2008 intake (WT)	262°	208°	0.371
2006–2008 exhaust	244°	192°	0.322

Here are the lift and duration numbers for a selection of factory camshafts. A big thanks to Integral Camshafts for developing some of this information.

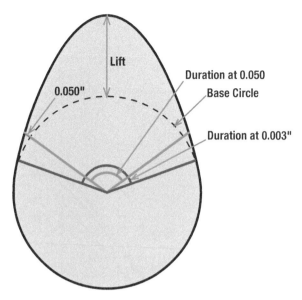

Here's what the numbers mean. The duration numbers are given in crank degrees. Because the cam turns half as fast as the crank does, 180 degrees on the cam is 360 degrees on the crank. The base circle is the diameter of the cam when the valve is closed.

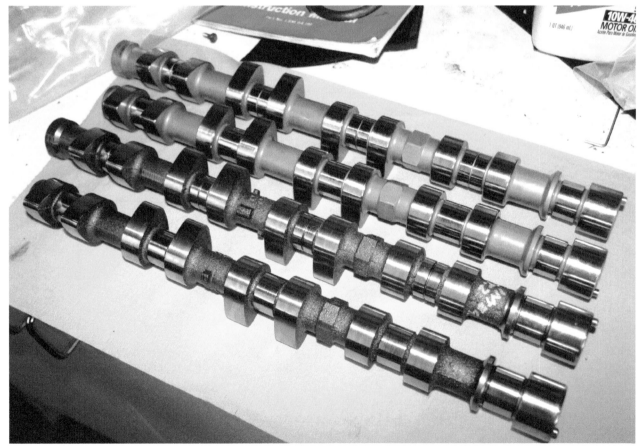

Two sets of aftermarket cams. The golden ones have been finished to a higher standard than the ones cut on a standard Mazda casting. Note the rounded edges to all the surfaces. The longer of the two cams is the one that drives the cam angle sensor, the intake cam on a B6, and the exhaust cam on a BP engine.

The valve springs close the valves when the cam is not opening them. Above a certain engine speed, you can get into the situation where the springs aren't stiff enough to close the valve quickly enough to follow the shape of the cam or allow the valve to bounce when it slaps closed. This is called valve float, and it's something you want to avoid for fairly obvious reasons. Stock valve springs on the NA and NB engines reach valve float at around 7,500 to 7,800 rpm. Stiffer springs will raise this limit but will also add to the amount of drag created by the valvetrain and cost horsepower. A well selected upgraded spring such as this one from Supertech will keep the valve firmly seated up to 9,000 rpm. As an added bonus, it includes a titanium retainer at the top to cut down on valvetrain mass. Stock valve springs will also limit the amount of lift available to around 9 millimeters (0.350 inch). If you want to run a more aggressive cam, you'll need different springs.

This engine is fitted with VVT on the intake cam (closest to the camera) and an adjustable gear on the exhaust cam. The adjustable gear allows the timing of the exhaust cam to be fixed at the ideal location. This usually involves sacrificing some other area of the engine's output. Due to various sensors used over the years or VVT, you cannot use adjustable cam gears on the intake cam of an NB or NC engine. The exhaust side is fine for all models.

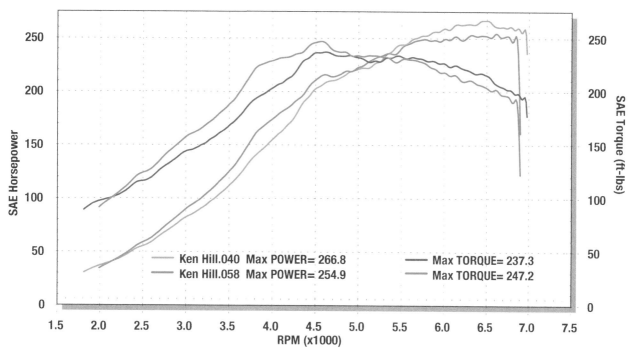

This is the result of some cam gear experimentation. It's no coincidence it looks very much like the VVT comparison on page 22, as it's the same general effect. The difference is that you have to pick one of the two end results, while VVT allows you to adjust the timing of the cam to get the best of both. This is a 1.6 Miata with a healthy turbocharger. A bit of retard (compared to stock) on both cams seems to work pretty well for top-end power and a little bit of retard for low- and mid-range, but dyno time is really the best way to determine the ideal setup.

Typically, cams are identified by their lift and duration. The duration is given in degrees and is often measured from a 0.050-inch lift. In other words, how far does the crankshaft rotate while the valve is open 0.050 inch or more? It's not the only number that matters, of course. A cam that opens the valve rapidly and then tries to keep it open as long as possible will perform differently than a cam that opens the valve more gradually. It's best if you can get a list of durations at different lifts, as that will let you figure out how the engine will behave. One thing to remember is that rapid valve acceleration and high lift mean more wear and tear on the valvetrain, as well as a need for stiffer valve springs to keep the valve under control.

Generally speaking, naturally aspirated cars react well to overlap, as it helps stuff the cylinders full of that all-important air and fuel mixture. Turbo cars don't like as much, as the pressurized intake air can get blown right out the exhaust port too easily. For example, the 1990 Miata engine had 20 degrees of overlap. The similar engine used in the turbocharged 323 GTX had only 6 degrees.

Each cam lobe pushes on a lifter, which then opens the valve. Mazda used hydraulic lifters in the NA engines and mechanical ones in the NB and NC. These two types of lifters require slightly different shapes to the cams, and you'll want to make sure you get a cam that's designed for the correct type.

BUDGET CAM SWAP

One home-brew modification that's shown up in recent years for the 1994–97 BP-ZE is the "exhintake" swap. It involves finding a spare exhaust cam and cutting off the drive for the cam angle sensor, then installing it as an intake cam. The overall shape is very much the same, but the exhaust cam has more duration at all lifts. The extended duration gives you more overlap. The idle gets lumpier, and the power jumps up by around 8 horsepower, according to dyno charts. Adjustable cam gears are required to get the most out of this swap, but given that you can pick up a cam out of a junkyard Ford Escort GT or 1.8 Kia Sephia for peanuts, it's an affordable option for naturally aspirated horsepower.

In 2001, Mazda added variable valve timing, or VVT, to the intake cam. This gives the engine computer the ability to advance and retard the camshaft and thus control the amount of overlap. The lift and duration of the valve opening are still fixed with Mazda's design, however. Still, this means the cam can be less of a compromise, and this improves the efficiency of the engine. Of course, greater efficiency really means greater power. At the time of writing, there weren't a lot of ways to control the VVT system, but one or two aftermarket ECUs did have that ability. There's a lot of rapid development in this area.

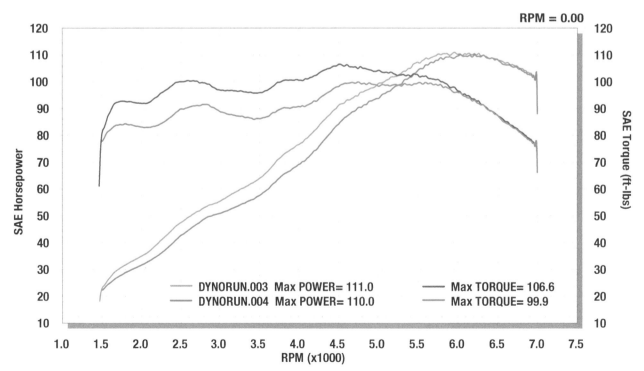

How much effect does the VVT have? Here's a simple test: Unplug it. This is an otherwise stock 2003 Miata. The peak horsepower doesn't change as the cam defaults to its high-rpm position, but look at the loss at the bottom end. There's 10 foot-pounds of torque that have gone missing over a 2,000-rpm range.

COMPRESSION RATIOS

The compression ratio refers to how much the air and gas mixture is compressed in the cylinder. It's the ratio of the maximum volume of the cylinder (when the piston is at the bottom) to the minimum (piston at the top). A 9.0:1 compression ratio means that the mixture is squeezed into a space 1/9th the original volume. The higher the compression ratio, the bigger the bang. Too high a ratio will lead to knock or detonation, when the fuel and air mixture explodes spontaneously from the pressure. That's how a diesel engine works, but it's really damaging to engines that aren't designed for it. Cars with forced induction already introduce the air into the cylinder under pressure, so they generally need a lower compression ratio. If you go too low, then there's no power-off boost. Generally speaking, 9.0:1 works nicely for forced-induction cars.

Stock Miata Compression Ratios over the Years
1990–1993: 9.4:1 manual, 9.0:1 automatic
1994–1995: 8.8:1
1996–1997: 9.0:1
1999–2000: 9.5:1
2001–2005: 10.0:1 (9.0:1 Mazdaspeed)
2006–2010: 10.8:1

THE BOTTOM END

Moving down from the head, we're into what's called the "bottom end" of the engine.

Pistons

Pistons have a rough life. They have to withstand the fuel-air burn that forces them down the bore, and at 6,000 rpm, they have to deal with this 50 times a second. So they have to be tough. Stock pistons are made of cast aluminum, which is brittle and doesn't take the hammering from detonation well.

They'll shatter, obviously not a good thing. But they don't expand much when they get hot, so if treated properly, they last a long time.

Forged pistons are stronger and can withstand higher temperatures and occasional detonation. They also expand more with heat, so they're a bit loose in the bore when cold. Good design can alleviate the effects of this, but generally speaking they will wear more quickly than cast pistons. The extra strength makes forged pistons the choice in the aftermarket.

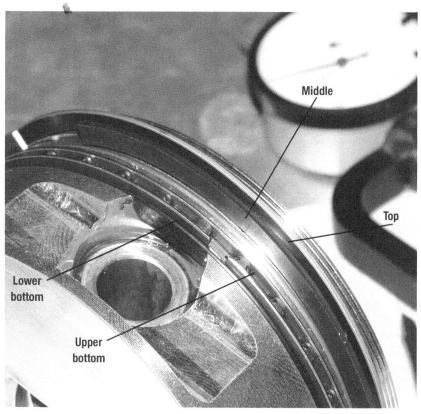

There are a series of rings around the outside of the piston to seal it in the bore. They have to keep oil out of the combustion chamber as well as prevent the expanding combustion gases from blowing by instead of forcing the piston down. Of course, they have to be low friction. They have a gap in them so that they can be installed, and setting the dimensions of this gap is one of the more crucial steps of assembling an engine. The top ring is primarily to keep the combustion gases in place and is known as the compression ring. The bottom ring is actually a three-piece assembly of two thin oil control rings and a spacer. The middle one helps out both the oil control and compression rings.

Middle

Top

Lower bottom

Upper bottom

The shape of the piston plays a part in determining the compression ratio. A piston with a dome on top will have a higher compression ratio than a flattop design. This piston, intended for turbo use, has a dished top to result in a 9.0:1 compression ratio. It's also a strong design with a thick crown and made of a high-strength alloy to deal with abuse. The top ring is farther away from the top of the piston to help protect it from heat. The lower part of the piston, known as the skirt, is coated with a dark gray moly coating to minimize friction.

The dome on the top of these pistons make them a high-compression design. They're from an 11.5:1 race engine. The skirt has been cut away on the sides to minimize friction. This is known as a slipper piston. They also have the wristpin moved as high as possible, to the point where the oil control ring needs an extra support. Not a setup for a daily driver, but at only 260 grams each they are designed for maximum naturally aspirated power and engine speed.

One way to check the health of your engine is to do a compression check. This is a quick and easy way to get an idea of how well your rings and valves are sealing. Simply remove all the spark plugs, unplug the coils, and screw your compression tester into a spark plug hole. Use the starter to spin the engine a few times with the throttle wide open and read the result off the gauge. The actual reading will vary, but generally speaking it should be between 140 and 200 psi. More important, it should be consistent across all four cylinders with no more than a 5 percent variance. A second test is to pour a little bit of oil—no more than a teaspoon—down each cylinder and repeat. If the numbers go up, that means the rings aren't sealing properly. If not, then look at the valves. There's another test that can be done called a leakdown test. In this case, a piston is brought to TDC on the compression stroke, and compressed air is fed into the cylinder at a known pressure. The resulting pressure is measured. If the cylinder pressure is 2 percent lower than the air pressure, then the cylinder has 2 percent leakdown. You'll also be able to tell where the air is escaping by listening to the engine. You'll be able to hear air leaking through the tailpipe (from the exhaust valve), throttle body (intake valve), or oil filler (rings). The tools are more expensive, it takes longer to do, and you will need a source of compressed air, so most people won't perform a leakdown test unless something is shown to be very wrong in a compression test.

Rods

The pistons are connected to the crank by the connecting rods, sometimes called conrods or just rods. These see enormous stresses and are often the cause of catastrophic engine failures. When the piston reaches the bottom of its travel and has to accelerate back up, it's the rod that is pushing it. Also, when the piston is forced down the cylinder by the burning fuel/air mixture, the rod has to transfer this load to the crankshaft. This tries to compress the rod. At the other end, the piston has to change direction again and head down the bore, and again it's the rod that pulls it down. This puts a tensile load on the rod. So it has to be strong in both directions.

How strong? Let's take the example of a 1.8 Miata BP engine spinning at 6,000 rpm. At top dead center, when the piston is at the top of its travel and starting to move down, it's accelerating at 1,246 times the force of gravity, or 1,246 g.

This is the same as hanging 1,246 pistons off the end of the rod, trying to stretch it out. But at the bottom of the travel, it's even worse. There, the peak acceleration is 2,259 g. Ouch. But that's nothing. If we raise the rev limit to 8,000 rpm (we'll have to install some new valve springs for this), the tensile load jumps to 2,215 g and the compression to 4,017 g. That extra 2,000 rpm nearly doubles the load. That's why, if you're going to make a high-performance engine, good rods are almost always on the menu. It's also why piston and rod weights can have an effect on performance, as it takes work to accelerate all that weight up and down. Work that would otherwise be put to use to push your car down the road.

Knock or detonation also puts a big, sharp load on your rods. This is actually what usually leads to the catastrophic failures; the rod simply can't take any more and breaks, which is usually followed by expensive metal parts making a bid

Two common designs of aftermarket rods. The upper one is an "H beam" design, named after its cross-section. The lower is referred to by Carrillo as an "A beam." In the case of these two particular rods from Carrillo, the H beam is approximately 20 percent heavier and 20 percent stronger.

A stock rod that was just asked to do too much. The owner of this engine was lucky that the rod simply bent instead of snapping. When they break, they usually take the rest of the engine with them. The carnage can be spectacular.

The slipper race pistons from earlier mounted on their connecting rods.

25

With regards to performance, about the only thing that you can do to the crankshaft is reshape the thick counterweights (top). See, the crank is spinning around in an atmosphere full of oil mist that's fairly thick, so aerodynamic drag is an issue. A knife-edged counterweight is lighter. This means less inertia, but more important, it's more aerodynamically efficient.

A crank scraper is a flat piece of steel that hugs the shape of the crank. It helps drop the amount of oil mist in the crankcase by literally scraping excess oil off the crank but without touching. This cuts down on the amount of oil flying around in the crankcase, dropping aerodynamic drag and encouraging the oil to return to the sump where it will get put back to work lubricating all the important bits. It's a simple modification but an effective one. It's shown here with just a crank to make it easy to spot, but it's supposed to be bolted to a block.

for freedom through the side of the engine block. Knock is definitely something to be avoided.

Luckily, the B6 and BP engines come with pretty strong rods from the factory. It takes a fair bit of abuse to get one to admit defeat. The MZR in the 2006–08 cars isn't quite as tough, although the 2009 and later cars got forged rods.

Crankshaft

The crankshaft takes all this up-and-down motion and turns it into rotation. In Miatas, they're more than strong enough to handle just about anything you can throw at them, with a cast unit used in the 1.6 and forged cranks found in the 1.8. The 2006—2008 2.0 uses a cast crank, replaced with a forged unit in 2009.

At the back of the crankshaft is the flywheel. We'll talk more about this in Chapter 6, but basically what it does is add momentum to the rotating crankshaft. This smooths out the idle and makes the car easier to drive.

Bolted to the front of the crankshaft is the harmonic damper. Most people think it's just an ordinary pulley for running the water pump, alternator, and other accessories, but it has an important role to play in the health of your engine. Every time a cylinder fires, the power is transmitted into the crankshaft through the connecting rod. That's the whole point, really. But because the rods are spaced out along the length of the crankshaft, these power pulses push on the crank in different places and at different times. At certain engine speeds, these staggered pulses can set up harmonic vibrations in the crankshaft, and they're worst at the front of the engine. The damper absorbs some of this energy, which cuts down on the vibrations.

You see, right behind that harmonic damper is the oil pump. It's obviously a fairly essential piece of equipment, literally the heart of the engine. If the nose of the crankshaft starts to vibrate, the gears can shatter. This is usually followed quickly by a seized engine. It doesn't help that the sintered metal used to make the gears is fairly brittle.

Miatas built in 1990 and early 1991 had a crankshaft with a fairly small nose on it. If the bolt on the front of the crankshaft was allowed to loosen at all, rapid damage would follow even to the point of the crankshaft pulley falling off. Of course, any Miata crankshaft will suffer if the bolt is loose, but the early design is more prone to failures. The crank on the right is a "short nose" with a badly damaged keyway. The crank on the left is the later "long-nose" design, which is much larger and stronger. The short nose will often keep people away from the early cars, but if it's properly maintained and monitored it's nothing to worry about. Details on how to repair a damaged short nose may be found in *Mazda Miata MX- 5 Performance Projects*.

If the power pulses get strong enough thanks to a more powerful engine, the stock harmonic damper can't absorb them and the oil pump can be destroyed. Any BP engine over 300 horsepower should either have stronger oil pump gears installed or, better yet, an upgraded damper.

One tempting upgrade often found on eBay is the "underdrive pulley," which is a crank pulley that's smaller than usual. The idea is that it spins the water pump, alternator, and accessories more slowly, so it cuts down on drag. They're also lighter than the stock part so they cut down on the inertial losses in the engine. But the problem is that they're invariably made out of solid aluminum and delete the harmonic damper. On a mostly stock naturally aspirated car, this doesn't seem to have any ill effects. But removing the harmonic damper on a turbocharged car will lead to oil pump failure before the next oil change. Bad plan. If you really want to run your accessories more slowly, put larger pulleys on the accessories and leave the stock damper in place. If you want a lighter rotating assembly, change to a lighter flywheel. After all, that's exactly what the flywheel is for.

The factory harmonic damper doesn't look like much, but it's critical to the health of your engine.

The result of 350 horsepower, a stock harmonic damper and oil pump, and lots of racetrack time. This is not a healthy oil pump.

SUPPORT SYSTEMS
Cooling

Setting fire to gasoline causes heat. The more power you make, the more heat you generate. The engine takes care of this by pumping coolant through the block and head, then cooling it off in the radiator. A thermostat controls flow to the radiator to keep the temperature at a desired constant level, and the radiator cap allows the system to pressurize. Problems start to crop up when the engine is generating more heat than the radiator can shed. This could be due to an inefficient radiator design or not enough airflow.

The radiator itself is fairly simple. The coolant is forced through a series of small tubes, and the air rushing over these tubes cools them down. One easy way to improve cooling is to

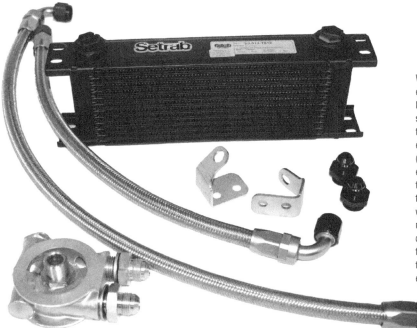

Water isn't the only liquid being pumped through the engine. If your oil gets too hot, it will lose its ability to lubricate your engine properly. Installing an oil cooler such as this one will not only help keep overall engine temperatures down, but it will keep the blood of your engine happy. This particular kit uses an oil thermostat (at the bottom left) to keep oil out of the cooler until the engine is up to operating temperature. Another way to do the same thing is to install a remote oil filter kit and route the lines through the cooler. This isn't a particularly good way to do things, as the remote oil filter setup adds five new points of failure to a critical system, and having the cooler plumbed in all the time will slow warm-up times. A thermostat is strongly recommended. If you can't manage to reach the oil filter in the stock location, have someone else change your oil instead of using a remote filter kit.

The fans on the car can improve cooling as well. A set of stronger aftermarket fans will pull a lot more air across the radiator. They'll work even better if they're mounted to a shroud like this one, pulling air from across the entire surface of the radiator instead of just two big circles. The shroud does need to be spaced back from the radiator core, however. If it's too close, it'll simply prevent any air from flowing. Aim for at least an inch of clearance.

make the radiator bigger, so there are more tubes. This works up to a point, as the radiator starts to get more restrictive as it gets thicker. Mazda used a single-core radiator in all Miatas except for the automatics, which got a double-core. Swapping one of these in to place will provide a good, inexpensive cooling upgrade. The aftermarket will also supply dual-core radiators made out of aluminum, which has better heat transfer characteristics than the factory copper does. Factory radiators also have end tanks made out of plastic, which will eventually crack with age.

Airflow to the radiator is also important. One of the problems with keeping a forced-induction Miata cool is that there's often an intercooler sitting in front of the radiator, blocking airflow and heating up the cooling air. The amount of heat transferred between the radiator and the outside air is directly related to the difference in their temperatures. As the outside air gets warmer, less heat can be dumped by the radiator and the hotter things get. The first modification anyone makes to improve cooling should be to check the ducting in the nose of the car. Air is lazy, and if you give it a way to go around the radiator (and intercooler, and oil cooler, and air conditioning condenser) it will. Spending some time ensuring there are no gaps between the "mouth" of the car and the various heat exchangers will pay off.

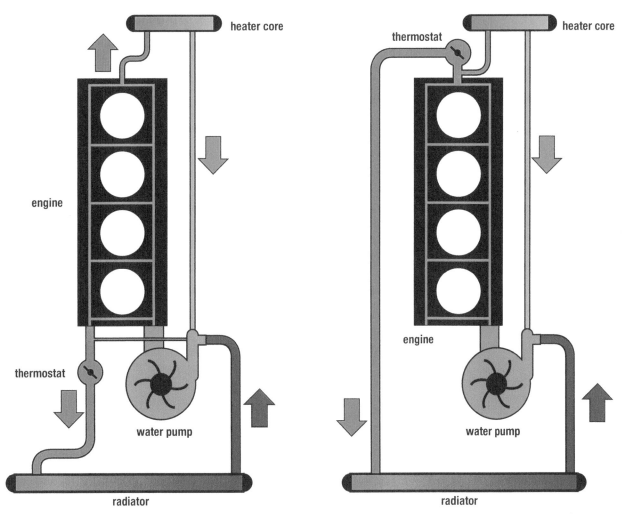

When the B6 and BP engines were first designed, they were used in front-wheel drive cars with the engine mounted transversely. The cooling system was designed so the water pump would pump cold water from the radiator in the front of the block, and it would exit at the back of the head. When the engine was turned 90° to fit in the Miata, Mazda decided to move the coolant outlet from the back of the head to the front for much easier packaging. However, this meant there was a problem—very little coolant got to the back of the head. This works okay in a stock setup, but high horsepower cars can have real problems with both overheating and potential damage to the back couple of cylinders. This is illustrated on the left. The solution is a coolant reroute, as shown on the right. The thermostat housing on the front of the engine is capped off, and one is added to the back. This forces all the coolant to make a complete passage through the engine. A long hose brings the coolant around to the radiator. The aftermarket has stepped up with a number of options to do this as a bolt-on upgrade and it's possible to create your own out of various parts from the other applications of the engine. Keeping the EGR pipe on the BP engines isn't possible with all configurations, but it's required if you're using a stock ECU. Mazda addressed the issue somewhat with a new head gasket design for the 2001-2005 cars.

The coolant you're using can have a big effect as well. Antifreeze not only protects your coolant from freezing, but it also has some anti-corrosion properties and some additives to help prevent spot boiling in tight pockets inside the engine. Unfortunately, it also has a lower heat capacity than water does, so it doesn't cool as well. Most people run a 50-50 mix, which will protect your coolant from freezing in temperatures as low as -30 degrees Fahrenheit (-34 degrees Celsius). Few Miatas have to deal with this sort of weather, and even then it's only for a few months of the year. An inexpensive way to improve your cooling is to run 30 percent antifreeze in the summertime, or use straight water with an additive such as Water Wetter for maximum cooling. In the colder months when cooling isn't a problem (and freezing is!), put the 50 percent mix back in.

Fuel

Chapter 5 will have more information on selecting fuel injectors and tuning them, but let's look at the plumbing. There are two basic types of fuel system, return and returnless. In a return system, the fuel pressure is tied to the manifold pressure in a 1:1 ratio, so if you add 1 psi of boost, you'll get 1 psi more fuel pressure, so the relationship between manifold pressure and fuel pressure is always the same. There are more fuel lines involved, and because the fuel is being pumped around, it can heat up. It's also a bit worse for emissions. It's easy to alter the fuel pressure in a system like this because it's easily accessible.

Most of the NBs and the NC use a returnless system. The fuel stays cooler, and the injectors are designed to work at a fixed, higher pressure. Raising the pressure is more complex because of the location of the fuel pressure regulator inside the fuel tank.

The stock fuel rail has a single inlet at one end or the other. This aftermarket part has a feed at both ends to make sure all four injectors get an equal amount of fuel and lots of it. A stock rail can be modified with an extra fitting at one end and a tee added into the feed line in order to accomplish the same thing, although aftermarket rails tend to also have larger volume to help feed thirsty large injectors.

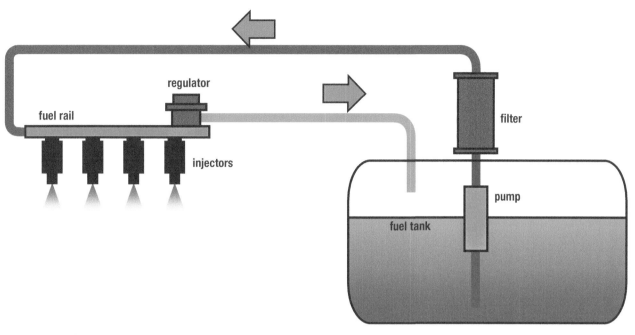

In this diagram of a fuel system with a return line, high-pressure fuel is shown as dark blue. The regulator restricts the return line, and the fuel pressure comes from the fuel pump pushing against the restriction.

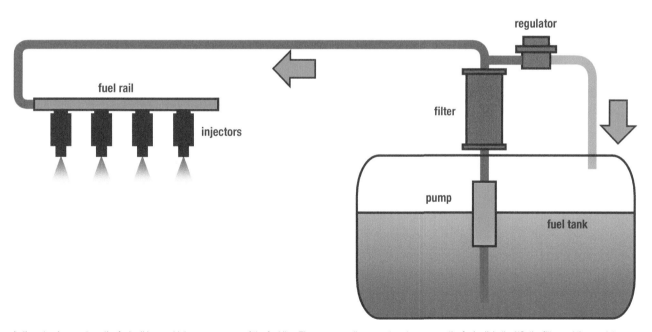

In the returnless system, the fuel rail is on a high-pressure spur of the fuel line. There are usually one or two dampers on the fuel rail. In the NC, the filter and the regulator are all inside the tank.

There's one Miata that's quite a bit different from the others in the engine department, and that's the 2004–2005 Mazdaspeed turbo model, or MSM. From the factory, it produces about 150 horsepower at the rear wheels. With a less restrictive intake, a better downpipe, a nonleaking bypass valve, and a boost controller, this can easily be raised to right around 200 with improved response. In terms of bang for the buck, nothing can touch it.

MORE POWER!

Now that we've been on a tour, how do we make more power? Generally speaking, the goal is to address the weak points first. Of course, fix any worn or broken bits; an engine that's down on compression due to worn rings will never make high power levels.

Unfortunately, the days of simply bolting a new air cleaner on to your motor and gaining 40 horsepower are long gone, and Mazda didn't leave us a lot of easy upgrades. There's no way to pick up 30 horsepower inexpensively. About all you can expect from bolt-ons such as intake and exhaust is 10 to 15 horsepower. You'll learn more about those in the next chapter.

A head shave is a fairly simple procedure that can have a good effect. The flat bottom surface of the head is milled down, which has the effect of lowering the volume of the combustion chamber. This will raise compression slightly. For a rule of thumb, consider approximately one-quarter of a point for every 0.010 inch of shaving, which bumps up

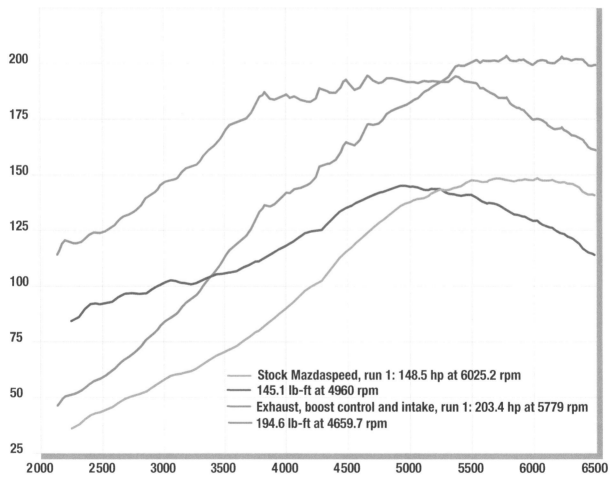

Stock Mazdaspeed, run 1: 148.5 hp at 6025.2 rpm
145.1 lb-ft at 4960 rpm
Exhaust, boost control and intake, run 1: 203.4 hp at 5779 rpm
194.6 lb-ft at 4659.7 rpm

The result of some simple modifications to the MSM. It's not this easy for other Miatas, unfortunately.

both power and torque across the board. I've run as much as a 0.030 inch head shave on my own cars. It's more work than simply bolting new parts on the outside of the engine, but not necessarily very expensive.

Ask your local machine shop for the cost, and don't forget to budget for a new head gasket. It's a good idea to get a valve job done as well when the head is off, because that's where the head wears most quickly.

One modification that can bring some good gains is improved engine management. There's more about this in Chapter 5, but generally speaking a programmable ECU is worth at least 10 horsepower. Expect sharper throttle response as well, and if you go further with high-compression pistons, a higher redline or an aggressive cam, the ECU will allow you to take full advantage of the modifications. Even better, if you add forced induction, you'll already have the engine management figured out. It's an expensive step, but prices are dropping all the time and it's one that really pays off down the line.

Interchange Information

For the NA/NB cars, pretty much any of the engines can be moved from one car to another. You can even mix and match parts.

Because the B6 block has closer bore spacing than the BP, few of the internal parts change over between the two engines. You can use some parts from the B6T turbo engine found in the Mazda 323 GTX, 323 GT, and the Ford Capri XR2 to beef it up a bit. The rods are stronger, the pistons give a very low 7.8:1 compression ratio, and the exhaust cam has a couple more degrees of duration. Unfortunately, the turbo manifold doesn't work in a Miata chassis, so your options are a little limited.

One handy bit of information is that the automatic 1.6 Miata has a throttle position sensor that's a variable unit instead of the on-off switch used in the five-speed cars. This makes for an easy upgrade to accompany a change to programmable engine management that can take advantage (or requires) the more precise unit. The automatic 1.6 also had a 9:1 compression

The first thing to do on NA models is advance the ignition timing to about 14 degrees. It's simple and inexpensive, although it may require premium fuel. You can do the same on the NB if you modify the crank sensor bracket or the timing wheel, although you won't want to advance the base timing much beyond the stock setting. One common area of confusion on the timing is what marks to use on the crank pulley. The basic rule of thumb is that if there's one, use it. If there are two, use the higher one (set to 10 degrees in this picture).

One way to improve power and torque across the board is to simply make the engine bigger. Owners of the 1.6 can substitute the factory "big-block" and install a 1.8. NC owners can use factory bits to build a 2.3, but BP owners don't have a lot of options. One is this stroker kit from Flyin' Miata. Because the stroke comes from the design of the crank, a new crank is supplied. New rods and pistons are also required for the new geometry. It's expensive, but if you're looking for maximum power out of a factory engine block, this is what you have to do.

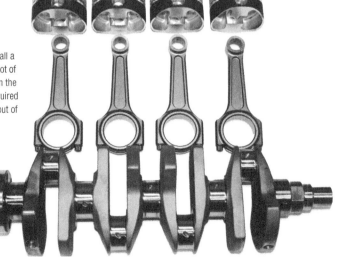

ratio and a lower lift, shorter duration pair of camshafts should you need it. The automatic bottom end is often used for budget turbo cars due to the lower compression.

Among the 1.8s, there's a lot more going on. Any of the BP heads can be matched with any of the BP blocks, although NB heads require NB intake manifolds. Upgrading an earlier car to a 1999–2000 BP-4W head for the improved port design and solid lifters is a popular move, enough of one that these heads are a little hard to find in many junkyards.

The 2001–2005 BP-Z3 head with variable valve timing is a bit more of a challenge to deal with. It uses oil feed locations that exist on the earlier blocks, but to take full advantage of the VVT, it should be controlled by an aftermarket ECU. A few people have tried controlling the VVT with a simple rpm switch, moving the cam from full retard to full advance at a given rpm level. There's some indication that this causes valve damage over the long term, as the immediate and dramatic 34-degree change in cam timing accelerates the valves so hard they float for a moment and then come crashing down on the seats. The same thing has been suspected even with ECU control if the map isn't properly set up.

It's interesting to note that the 2004–2005 Mazdaspeed MX-5 (MSM) uses a BP-4W head for some reason, dropping the VVT. My suspicion is that this was due to the expense of programming the ECU to deal with emissions, but nobody at Mazda is talking.

Because the compression ratios varied over the years, you can pick and choose the bottom end (or the pistons) to get just the ratio you want. Looking for a little more pep for a naturally aspirated motor? Pick up a 10.5:1 BP-Z3. Want low

compression for maximum boost? Slide an 8.8:1 from 1994 or 1995 under the more efficient NB head.

The 2001–2005 engines all used a main bearing support plate (MBSP) to add a little more rigidity to the bottom end. This will bolt up to any BP block, but you'll need the matching oil pan. The MSM engine not only has the MBSP, it also has a couple of oil return fittings for the catch can and the turbo oil drain. Bonus!

The NC engine is part of a family that's been used all over the place. The possibility that gets most people's attention is the 2.3 version. It's a long-stroke unit designed for a lot of torque, but if you want a 15 percent capacity increase in displacement, it's a good option. As long as you avoid the direct-injection "DISI" engines, you can pretty much just drop the 2.3 right in. It's slightly taller, but this doesn't cause any problems. You will have to swap to the 2.0 oil pan and remove the balance shafts from the 2.3 in order to clear the MX-5's subframe. Kits for the balance shaft removal are readily available. The 2.0 head seems to be a slightly higher performance variant, so swapping that on to the 2.3 bottom end is worthwhile. Finally, the 2.3 compression ratio is 9.7:1 instead of 10.8:1, so dropping the 2.0 pistons into a 2.3 block might be the most fun. They have the same bore. With the 2.3 upgrade, most of the gains will be in low-end torque instead of power, as it's only the stroke that increases. Still, it should give a useful wide powerband.

Because the 1.8 and 2.0 MZR engines are externally almost identical, there's the potential for a nice upgrade for European 1.8 owners by simply upgrading their 1.8 to 2.0 specifications.

This is an extremely powerful 1.8 BP built for E production racing, including the carburetors that were required by the rules. Power levels are above 200 horsepower. To get this level of output, both driveability and engine lifespan were compromised.

Chapter 3
Intake and Exhaust

As we discussed in the last chapter, one of the best ways to make some horsepower is to make it easy for air to get in and out of the engine. Coincidentally, the intake and exhaust systems are also fairly easy to access, clearly visible with the hood open, and they make some cool noises. So that's exactly where many people start.

INTAKE SYSTEMS

First, the intake. Like everything else with a car, it's a compromise. It's fairly obvious that we want as little restriction as possible, so it's easy for air to get pulled into the cylinders. Think of sipping a drink through a straw: You have to work harder to suck it through a small straw than a large one. Your engine works the same way, but we also want cold air. Colder air is denser and has more oxygen for a given volume. Factory intake systems add a third requirement: The engine noise has to be kept down to a reasonable level.

Naturally, most enthusiasts will happily discard the last factor to improve the other two. Shiny tubes with big open-element air filters look good under the hood and are relatively inexpensive to make, so there's a big market for them. They make a great growl and, well, just look at them: big filters and shiny tubes, just like a race car.

But most don't take air temperature into account. You'd be surprised at just how hot the air underhood is, and that's not good for performance. Cold air makes the engine less prone to detonation, so you can run more timing and make more power. It's also denser, which means more oxygen and thus more power. There's nothing good about hot intake air. You'll often see marketing references to a cold air intake or the common acronym CAI. When you're evaluating an intake, ask yourself if it really is a cold air setup.

An air intake that pulls air either from the cowl at the base of the windshield or from in front of the radiator will

This high-compression engine is set up to breathe easy with a set of roller barrel throttle bodies and a 4-1 Racing Beat header.

perform better than one that sucks up the hot air from beside the header. One little dyno secret: Most dyno runs are done with the hood open and a large supply of nice cool air blowing over the engine. Perfect conditions for a "hot air" intake. A good cold air intake will perform just as well with the hood closed, which is obviously how most of us choose to drive.

One other thing that needs to be taken into consideration is water inhalation. A filter that's down close to the pavement can suck up water if you drive through a deep enough puddle. That will quite often cause internal engine damage, so it's a good idea to avoid any intakes that put the filter too close to the ground.

Mazda took this into account on the NC. The stock intake is placed in front of the radiator behind the bumper, with access to cool exterior air and a high location to prevent water ingress. It's a fairly easy matter to simply reroute this to the cavernous area in front of the radiator, gulping down air rushing in through the grille. Installation can be a bit of a pain because the nose of the car has to come off, but you only have to do that once. A bigger concern is the potential for sucking up water, so take that into consideration if you decide to install one of these. It shouldn't be a problem in rain, only when fording deep water.

This Racing Beat intake attaches directly to the stock throttle body, and pulls air from a formed duct that is mounted behind the grille. The blue tube at the end includes a fitting for the mass airflow meter. It's a fairly easy installation. Most intakes for the NC try to accomplish the same thing, with variations in filter location and ducting. *Photo courtesy of Racing Beat*

The Randall air intake is simple—a carbon fiber tube attaches to the stock airbox and runs back to the firewall, where it inhales cold air through a hole drilled through the sheetmetal. Because it pulls from outside the engine bay, it's breathing ambient air instead of the hot underhood air. The air at the base of the windshield is also slightly pressurized at speed, giving a slight boost in power. The intake is right in front of the driver, so it's more audible, but the stock airbox does help control noise somewhat. This is an excellent example of trying to solve the problem of hot underhood air without resorting to the usual shiny tubes and big filters. It's not difficult to duplicate this design using flexible hose if you like to build your own parts.

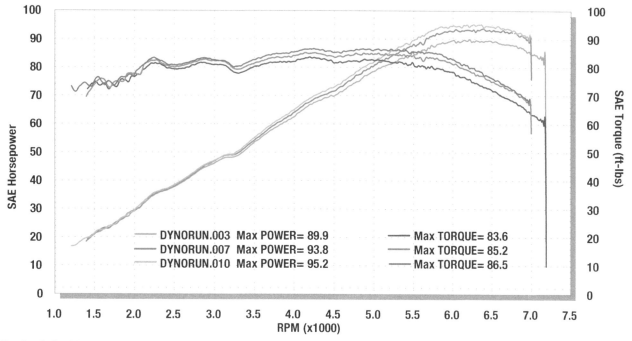

How does the Randall work on the dyno? All three of these runs were done with the hood closed. The blue run is a stock 1990. Red is with the Randall installed. The green run adds a fan blowing over the hood to simulate the airflow of low speed driving. It's possible that the gains would increase as airspeed increases, although this is difficult to quantify without a wind tunnel. Still, that's better than a 5 percent gain simply from pulling the air from a different location.

It's not that straightforward on the NA and NB though. There's no simple way to get air from outside the engine bay. The easiest installation is simply a big filter replacing the airbox, but this sucks hot air from right over the header (probably the worst possible location in the whole car). Better options will isolate the filter from the hot underhood air or find some way to pull from outside the car.

This Racing Beat filter puts a carbon fiber shield around the air filter. There's a factory hole in the bodywork just below the filter, so it can pull cold air from the wheelwell. The filter is well away from any possible water inhalation as well. You can see the rubber pad around the top that seals the airbox against the hood. A baffle made of stiff plastic or aluminum would also work. The trick is to keep the hot air away. Racing Beat claims this box drops the temperature at the filter by 15° F (8° C) on the highway compared to the same intake without the box, and those numbers have been backed up with tests on similar setups. *Photo courtesy of Racing Beat*

The 1990–1993 cars are fitted with a fairly restrictive airflow meter. The air pushes a door open, and the more air the engine is sucking, the more the door opens. Later cars use a hot-wire mass airflow sensor that is much less restrictive. Unfortunately, the electronic signals from the two designs are incompatible, so you can't simply swap the new design in. You can, however, substitute the airflow meter from a 1986–1988 RX-7. It's larger and flows more air, which gives a stock engine around 5 horse power above 6000 rpm. It plugs right in, and you can find more details at solomiata.com. The same basic flow meter was used on other vehicles such as Toyota trucks, so it's possible there are some other options out there as well.

The small box hanging off the bottom of this intake is a resonance chamber. It works with the pressure waves generated at the engine to create a small torque bump at lower rpm. The size of the chamber is related to the size of one cylinder, and it's interesting to note that not every factory Miata intake had one. If possible, it's best to keep this in any home-brewed intake setup.

EXHAUST SYSTEMS

The next upgrade most people consider is the exhaust system. It's not a complicated item. It has to carry the exhaust gases from the engine to the tailpipe. Along the way, they'll pass through a catalytic converter to clean out the worst of the noxious gases and drop emissions. There is also a muffler to drop the sound level, and there may be a resonator or two to fine-tune the sound. All very easy.

So how does it affect performance? By restricting the airflow. Legend has it that back pressure (that is, exhaust restriction) is good for torque. That's not actually true. The lower your exhaust restriction, the better. That's why full-on drag cars run no exhaust system at all after the headers.

The easiest way to drop the restriction is by increasing the diameter of the exhaust tubing and by playing with the internal design of the muffler. There's no real downside to the former other than the packaging difficulties involved in threading a huge pipe under the car, but a muffler usually has a direct relationship between restriction and sound deadening. Is a gain of a few horsepower worth a raucous exhaust noise? That's a decision for you to make, and your local law enforcement community might have an opinion on the matter as well. Of course, the change in exhaust sound goes a long way toward making your Miata sound like a sports car, and many people enjoy an exhaust change for this reason alone.

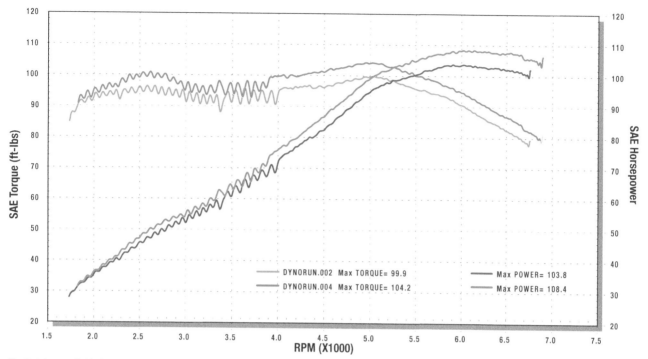

DYNORUN.002 Max TORQUE= 99.9		Max POWER= 103.8
DYNORUN.004 Max TORQUE= 104.2		Max POWER= 108.4

The first dyno run (in blue) was done on a stock 1995, complete with stock exhaust. A large 2.5 inch diameter exhaust system with a free-flowing (and noisy!) muffler designed for turbo use was then bolted on. As you can see, there's no loss in torque anywhere, simply a gain of power and torque across the board. It's a full-on performance increase other than the fact that it's very loud. Don't mistake noise for power, however. It's quite possible for a muffler to be both obnoxious and restrictive.

One thing to watch for is turbo exhaust systems. Because turbos really don't like back pressure and also muffle the exhaust somewhat, a turbo exhaust will have a free-flowing design with minimal muffling. On a naturally aspirated or supercharged car, these exhausts can be earsplitting.

Catalytic Converter

The catalytic converter, or cat, in the exhaust is a restriction as well. The purpose of the cat is to reduce the emissions coming out of the tailpipe, and it is required on street cars in most countries. There are two cats on the 1999–2000 California models and all of the NCs. Internally, they're a ceramic honeycomb design coated with various precious metals to help convert noxious gases into less harmful ones. The honeycomb gives a high surface area so that the reactions take place. It's a tradeoff between surface area and restriction. Aftermarket cats may have a more open design inside or even a stainless-steel base called a metal matrix instead of ceramic for little restriction.

Upgrading to a good free-flowing cat can keep your emissions down whilst lowering your exhaust back pressure. Make sure you get a three-way cat—like the factory one—to ensure you don't start failing your emissions tests. Racers will sometimes replace the cat with a piece of pipe, usually called a test pipe. On a naturally aspirated car, there just isn't enough

benefit to this. Besides, it makes your Miata stinky. Dropping the first cat on the 1999–2000 two-cat models doesn't typically cause a problem with emissions tests, as the first cat is primarily there for cold start purposes. You'll have to move the second oxygen sensor in the exhaust system so that it is after the remaining cat, otherwise the on-board diagnostics system will start to complain. Before removing or replacing any cats on your car, however, check your local laws.

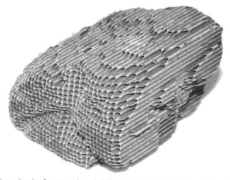

This is a chunk of a ceramic catalytic converter matrix. A free-flow cat will usually just have bigger holes in the matrix, which decreases the efficiency of the converter by dropping the surface area. It can still be possible for it to meet emissions standards though.

Headers

The third of the common and easy bolt-on upgrades is a header, called a manifold in some areas. A header is a surprisingly sophisticated piece of kit, although it looks pretty straightforward on the surface. Most cars are fitted with a simple cast-iron exhaust manifold that gathers up the exhaust from the individual ports and sends it all off down a single pipe. This is cheap to make and packages well. It's what Mazda installed on the 1999–2000 models in North America, but there's a better way. A header consists of longer individual pipes that join at one or more collectors. So?

The exhaust doesn't come out of the exhaust ports in a steady flow. Instead, it comes in a series of puffs as the valves open and close. These pulses act like waves of high and low pressure as they travel down the tube and actually reflect off the collector. Now, as every trumpet and trombone player knows, if you hit the right frequency for a length of tube you'll get harmonics and standing waves. This means the waves going in each direction stack on top of one another. The high pressures get higher and the low pressures get lower. If one of those low-pressure areas is right at the end of the header tube where the port is, it will actually help suck the exhaust out of the cylinder. This scavenging gives a bump in efficiency, which means more power. Not bad for a carefully selected piece of pipe.

There are two main types of header for a four-cylinder engine with four exhaust ports: a 4 into 1, where all four

Almost all Miatas were fitted with a tubular header much like this one. You can see how the four primary tubes come together at a collector at the bottom. It's actually a pretty good piece in stock form.

The 1999-00 Miatas got a cast manifold that doesn't flow as well as the tubular ones. In California and some other US states, it also got this catalytic converter right after the manifold. This is the worst exhaust Mazda ever put on a Miata. Thankfully, they only did it for a couple of years on a limited number of cars!

On the NC, there's a similar tubular header hiding under a heatshield. But right after it is a catalytic converter - not great for flow, but it gets up to operating temperature very quickly because it's so close to the head.

primary tubes come together in a single collector, and a 4 into 2 into 1, where pairs of primaries join together, then the remaining secondaries have their own collector farther down. The latter is sometimes called a "tri-y" because of the three Y-shaped collectors. Generally speaking, the 4 into 1 design has a stronger scavenging effect at a given engine speed, while the tri-y is less efficient but scavenges over a wider range. In reality, there isn't a huge performance difference on the Miata if both are implemented well. Ideally, all four primary tubes need to be the same length, although it's possible to stagger the lengths slightly to spread the peak power around a bit. Usually, though, variations in length are the result of a lack of clever design work.

Other than that moment of weakness in 1999–2000, Mazda actually did a really nice job on the stock parts for the Miata. In North America, they were all fitted with 4 into 1 tubular headers. In some other markets, the NB got a very long tri-y design. So, for the majority of Miatas, a header doesn't offer huge power gains, but if you're looking to get as much as possible out of a naturally aspirated engine, they're part of the formula. The NC can benefit more from a header, but that's in large part because they typically remove the first catalytic converter that's snug right up close to the head. The drop in restriction helps. Similarly, the 1999–2000 California cars also benefit from having that first cat removed.

One thing to keep in mind when looking at headers is your future plans. If you intend to install a supercharger, make sure the header will fit underneath your preferred model. If you're planning to go with a turbo, the header will be removed. You may not want to spend money on one just to install it temporarily.

INTERCHANGE

On the exhaust side, there's not a lot of interchange you'll necessarily want to do, with one exception. The cast BP-4W exhaust manifold and especially the two-cat setup used in California from 1999 to 2000 can be replaced by the manifold from a 2001–2005 model. All you need is the EGR pipe and the manifold. If you have a two-cat car, the O2 sensors will have to be moved to the non-California locations, in front and behind the remaining catalytic converter. This will give a bit of a power boost.

Why use the factory part instead of an aftermarket header? Because it looks completely stock, right down to the tin heat shields. You know, just in case this is important for some reason. Due to the remaining cat, emissions should not be affected other than under cold start conditions.

This NC header from Racing Beat has four equal-length primaries. The shape of each tube has to be quite different in order to make this happen. If they all just took the shortest route to the collector, they'd all be quite different in length.

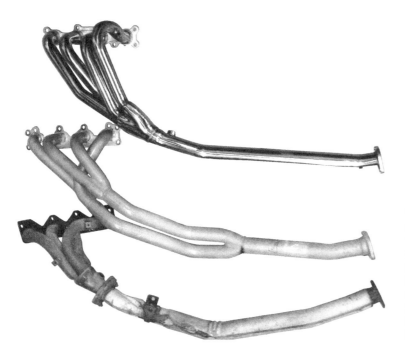

Three different header designs for a 1.6 engine. On top is a 4-1 design from Racing Beat. The middle shows a 4-2-1 or tri-Y design from Jackson Racing, and the bottom is stock. The difference in length of the primary tubes between the top and bottom headers is quite obvious. The Mazda part is intended to be easy to install and tuned for all-around driving, while the top one is a bit more difficult to install and will hopefully make more power. The tri-y is intended to be the best compromise, but the number of tubes involved can make it the most awkward to install.

ANATOMY OF A CUSTOM HEADER

All stock pieces are the result of design compromises. Of course, so are aftermarket parts. Production cost, for example, is less of a priority than with the stock parts, but it's still a consideration. So sometimes you need to go to a custom part if you really want the maximum performance at the expense of just about all other priorities. This header was an example of that.

The engine was a bored-and-stroked 2.0 with high compression. The head was worked over with porting, polishing, and oversize valves. It was intended to be very flexible in nature, as it was used in rallying where you need to be prepared for surprises. There was some suspicion that the existing aftermarket header just wasn't well suited to the engine, so the decision was made to do something different.

After speaking with a number of E Production racers and doing some math, it was decided to go with a primary tube length of 31 inches and a tube diameter of 1.75 inches. The Racing Beat header, by comparison, has a primary length of approximately 16 inches and a tube diameter of 1.675 inches. The longer and fatter tubes would give a boost lower in the rev range, adding to the flexibility of the engine. The decision was made to put the collector up above the steering column so that the large tubes wouldn't have to squeeze past. This meant a real challenge in packaging, as there was more than 10 feet of tubing that needed to be squeezed in.

Once the design was sorted out, mandrel-bent U-bends were cut up to make the primary tubes, and the whole thing was tack-welded together to get the fabrication sorted out. Then came the long and tedious process of welding up all the seams. Adding to the challenge was the oddball shape of the header. It wouldn't have been difficult to get halfway through welding everything together only to discover that a particular seam was no longer accessible. The header was heat-treated in an oven to relieve stresses and bolted on.

On the first dyno run, you could hear the resonances in the tubing. The car sounded different. The result? A gain of 15 foot-pounds at 3,500 rpm and around 10 horsepower at 5,200 rpm when compared to the previous part. It worked. It would never be a commercial product because of the high cost of building it and the difficulty in fitting most intake systems around it, but it shows what is possible when performance becomes the overriding goal.

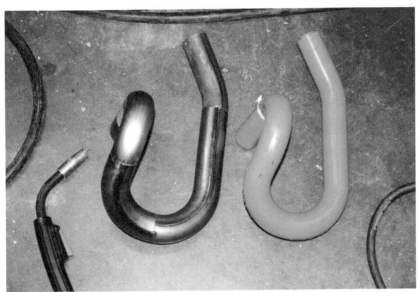

The header was designed with the help of some special tools. The blue tube is made of 1-inch long blocks that snap together, and are made with a variety of radii to match available off-the-shelf mandrel-bent pipes. Lengths of bent pipe were cut to match and welded together. This allows far more complex shapes to be designed easily and quickly than trying to do everything in steel. It takes a certain kind of magician to build a header like this without them.

The header was painstakingly assembled on the car. The collector can be seen just below the tangle of pipes.

The final result! It's an extremely complex design, but the dyno proves the effort was worthwhile. Several years of testing and racing have proven that it's also strong, with no cracking problems at all. There are easily a hundred hours of work in this part, so it's really only feasible as a race component.

INTAKE MANIFOLD

So those are the popular bolt-ons: intake, header, and exhaust. Going further, we can take a look at the intake manifold and throttle body. The volume and internal design of the manifold can make a difference to the engine's output due to resonances similar to those seen in the exhaust. The length of the runners between the plenum (the big chamber in the manifold) and the head is important. Mazda went to some trouble to put fairly long runners on the Miata. This will make the engine more efficient at low and medium engine speeds.

The size of the plenum is also important. If it's approximately equal to the capacity of the engine, then resonances in the intake will improve its efficiency. Obviously, it's not a simple thing to build a new intake manifold, and there aren't many options on the market at the time of writing, but several companies are working hard on changing this. But if you have the ability, a large plenum with short, fat runners will likely give a high-end power boost at the cost of low-end torque. Turbo cars generally appreciate this.

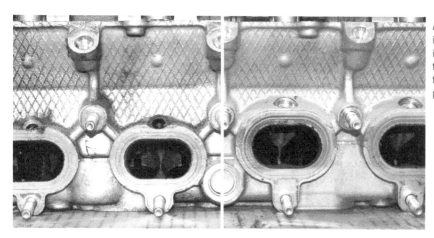

A side-by-side comparison of the NA (left) and NB (right) intake port location. You can see the backside of the valves in both cases, but the NA forces the air to make a sharper turn when it enters the cylinder. The port size is larger on the NB as well, and the shape alterations resulted in a 10 percent increase in velocity according to Mazda.

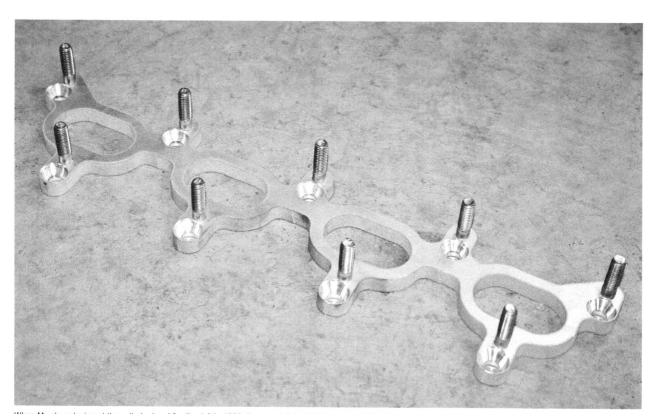

When Mazda redesigned the cylinder head for the 1.8 in 1999, they moved the intake ports up higher to get a better port angle. This means intake manifolds designed for the 1994–1997 engine will not fit the 1999–2005 and vice versa. It's possible to modify the bolt pattern and make it work, but generally speaking, it's not an option unless you can weld aluminum. Fuji Racing came up with a much better solution in the form of this bolt-on adapter.

The VICS manifold found on the 1999–2000 cars is an interesting case. A set of butterflies flip open at approximately 5,200 rpm and change the volume of the manifold. This changes the resonance of the manifold, changing its peak efficiency range. The NC is equipped with a similar system. It's been discovered that hollowing out the 1999–2000 manifold can lead to a power increase on turbocharged and supercharged engines. Naturally aspirated engines don't seem to benefit much at all.

The 2001-05 cars lost the VICS, but gained VTCS. These butterflies are installed right in front of the intake port, and flip closed at cold idle to improve the mixing of air and fuel and thus improve emissions. You can see how much of the port they close off! Even when open, they cause a fair bit of restriction. Removing these is a simple performance upgrade, although the holes for the butterfly shaft will have to be plugged. The stock ECU will notice and complain if the VTCS is disabled and/or removed, however.

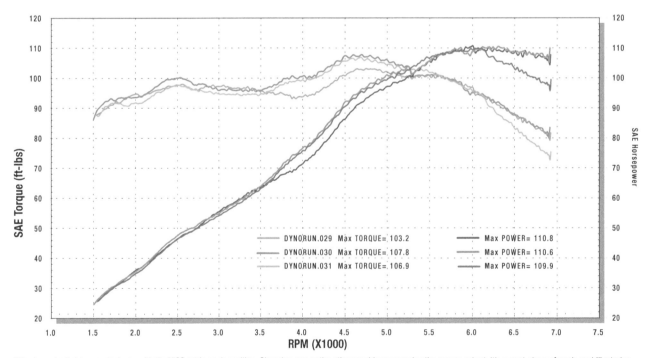

DYNORUN.029 Max TORQUE= 103.2	Max POWER= 110.8
DYNORUN.030 Max TORQUE= 107.8	Max POWER= 110.6
DYNORUN.031 Max TORQUE= 106.9	Max POWER= 109.9

This dyno chart shows a stock car with the VICS set in each position. Choosing one or the other would compromise the power output. It's a neat piece of work, and illustrates the effects of intake manifold volume nicely. The blue line charts the high rpm position, while the green line shows the low rpm position. The appropriate changeover point for the VICS system is right where the two power lines cross, at approximately 5,700 rpm for this car. The red line shows the VICS system operating normally.

A custom intake manifold from Bell Engineering. This design includes a 70mm throttle body taken from a 4.6l Ford Mustang and four fairly short intake runners. It's a worthwhile upgrade to high-horsepower turbo cars.

THROTTLE BODIES

The throttle is what controls the air entering the engine. It's a simple butterfly valve. On most Miatas, the stock unit isn't enough of a restriction to bother with. But on higher-power cars, a larger unit can be effective. This is particularly true on supercharged cars, as they place the throttle before the supercharger. There aren't any easy bolt-on upgrades, but it's possible to get the stock throttle body bored out and fitted with a larger butterfly.

Individual Runner Throttle Bodies

One modification that gets a lot of interest is individual runner throttle bodies, often called IRTBs or ITBs. The single large throttle butterfly is replaced with a set of four smaller ones, each one feeding a single cylinder. This gives maximum airflow. It also usually gets rid of the intake plenum. The throttled volume—the volume between the throttle plate and the port—is extremely small, so the engine reacts quickly to throttle changes. The length of the intake runners can be changed by bolting on new horns or velocity stacks. This allows some tuning of the engine's power range by exploiting the same harmonics used to determine runner length in an intake manifold. This tuning can open up more horsepower or torque if done carefully, but the Miata engine bay is a bit tight to run horns of any significant length.

The fact that many IRTB cars don't have an intake system to speak of means they tend to be very low restriction. Some don't even use filters, which looks super-sexy but is murder on the engine. Literally. The wire mesh screens favored by some tuners combine terrible filtering ability with high restriction, making them a show option only. Foam "sock filters" are an improvement, but the best option of all is an enclosed plenum or airbox where the intake horns can get nice clean airflow. If it's made the correct size, you can take advantage of the Heimholz resonance and stuff a bit more air into the cylinders. You can also feed the air box with a nice fat pipe leading to a filter that's placed to receive cold air.

The small throttled volume can make IRTBs quite fussy to live with. A separate vacuum reservoir is often required in order to provide enough vacuum for the brakes and the engine management. Unless you build an enclosed air box, you cannot use the stock computer as it's simply not able to measure the air entering the four inlet tubes.

There are a couple of ways to add IRTBs to an engine. The first is to buy an off-the-shelf kit. This may be as simple as the physical parts needed to install the throttles, or it may be complete and include any engine management components required to make the car actually run. Watch out for packaging in the case of the MZR. While there are a number of IRTB setups available for that engine in other applications, the position of the firewall in the MX-5 may prevent them from being used. An extra wrinkle is that the throttle on the NC is a "drive-by-wire" setup, where the throttle pedal sends a request to the ECU and the ECU actually opens the throttle electrically. This has some real benefits, but it makes life more difficult when trying to monkey around with different setups.

So IRTBs can be a challenge to install and set up correctly, both from a mechanical and electronic standpoint. It's not unusual for people to actually lose power in their normal driving range with an IRTB setup, although a good implementation will gain power where you need it. Still, the throttle response and the intoxicating sound is often enough reward.

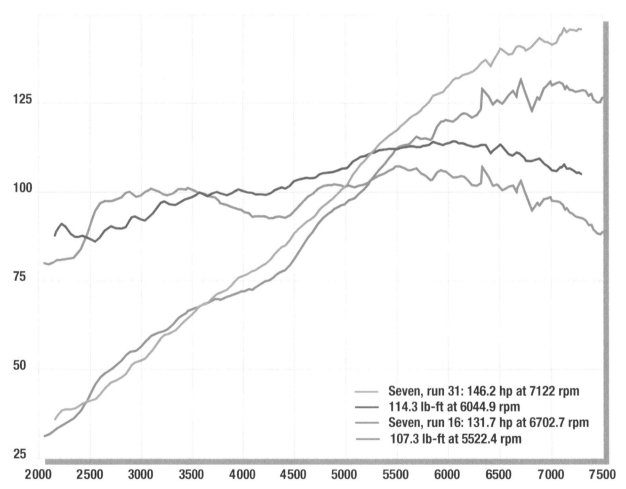

Seven, run 31: 146.2 hp at 7122 rpm
114.3 lb-ft at 6044.9 rpm
Seven, run 16: 131.7 hp at 6702.7 rpm
107.3 lb-ft at 5522.4 rpm

This dyno run is of a fairly heavily modified 1.6, comparing the stock intake manifold to a set of IRTBs. There's a slight loss of torque down low, but a 15 horsepower gain up top. This is a pretty clear win. Several horn lengths were tried, all fairly short. They made a difference of a couple of horsepower here and there, but nothing dramatic thanks to the small space available in the engine bay.

If you want to roll your own IRTBs, it's easiest to start with a manifold like these parts from Mazda Competition. They're fitted with a standard Weber flange, so you can bolt just about anything on to them — bike throttles, specialized car throttles, even carburetors if you want. Making your own is often less expensive, but more work — the usual tradeoff! Since E Production racers were required to run carburetors, they're the best source of Weber adapters like these. All of the IRTB setups pictured in this book are assembled this way, as it gives the most flexibilty to the manufacturer.

Check out the shape of this intake horn. It's called a bellmouth, and it helps guide the air into the tube. This makes the tube more efficient than if it had simply been cut off flat. In fact, any time you have an inlet of some sort, it'll work best with a bellmouth. That includes the transition from a large filter to the intake tube, from an air box to an intake tube and from an intake plenum to a runner. Mazda knew this; you'll find one on the end of every stock intake.

The least restriction of all comes from a roller barrel throttle. In this case, there is absolutely no restriction when the throttle is open. These are available either as a bolt-on option for the MZR engine or as generic units with a standard Weber flange. Light throttle operation can be a little bit abrupt, and they have to be made to extremely fine tolerances to prevent leakage around the throttle cylinder. For this reason, they absolutely cannot be run without a filter. This particular set was made by Titan Motorsports and is sold by Cosworth both as a one-piece unit for MZR applications and with a Weber flange as seen here.

A commercially available throttle body setup from Fuji Racing. There's no denying the aesthetic appeal of these things, and they sound even better than they look! This particular set comes with a reservoir that is attached to each individual runner, to allow for a slightly more stable vacuum signal. It's also designed to have the stock idle speed control valve attached to give the ECU a fighting chance of controlling idle like a modern car.

Chapter 4
Forced Induction

Ah, the lure of big horsepower. The Miata engine, so resistant to making power in naturally aspirated form, loves pressurized air. The B6 and BP take to forced induction better than just about any other engine in production. It's possible to nearly triple the stock horsepower on a B6 or BP without a loss in reliability or drivability. The newer MZR doesn't respond quite as well, but it'll still see some great improvements.

So just what is forced induction? Basically, it means there's some device forcing extra air into the engine. If we go back to our straw analogy from Chapter 3, you're no longer sucking water through a straw. Instead, you have a garden hose in your mouth and someone has turned on the tap. The increased air rammed into the engine means you can burn more fuel, which means more power. Sounds simple, right? Well, on the face of it, it is.

The extra air can be provided by a pump driven off the crankshaft—a supercharger—or a fan spun by exhaust gases. The latter is called a turbo-supercharger or, more commonly, a turbocharger. There's also a hybrid called a centrifugal

The extra air causes higher pressure in the intake manifold, either because it's being compressed by the turbocharger or supercharger, or because air is being pumped into the manifold faster than the engine can take it in. The extra pressure is called boost. If the air pressure in the intake manifold is 5 pounds per square inch (psi) higher than the air pressure outside the car, then the car is running 5 psi of boost. Boost can also be expressed in bar, and 1 bar is 14.5 psi. Some engine management systems will express the manifold pressure in absolute terms, which is the ambient pressure plus the boost pressure. The only time this can get confusing is at high altitude, where the ambient pressure goes down. This means that at the same boost pressure, the absolute pressure is lower or, if a turbo manages to reach the same absolute pressure, it takes more boost to do it. This boost gauge was integrated into the stock instrument cluster by Mark Booth.

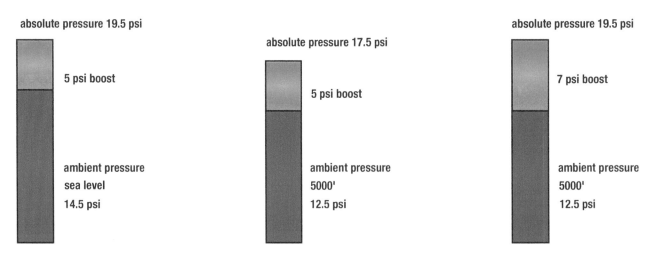

As you drive into the mountains, the air pressure drops and with it so does your horsepower. Naturally aspirated cars will drop approximately 18 percent of their power at 5,000 feet above sea level. Supercharged cars will lose power the same way, possibly even more if the supercharger drops below its efficiency range. Turbochargers, however, can compensate for altitude, as it's the absolute pressure in the manifold that matters. A car with electronic boost control will keep the wastegate closed longer in order to make the same absolute pressure, which means it'll make more boost at altitude and thus won't lose horsepower. It's not a free lunch — because the turbo will have to make 2 psi of boost at 5,000 feet to simply bring the car to a sea level equivalent, spoolup times are longer and the turbo will be operating in a different efficiency range. Outlet air temperatures go up and backpressure rises. In some cases, the turbo may simply not be able to move the extra air and maintain the same absolute pressure. But still, the car won't be as badly affected as the supercharged setups. It's no coincidence that most piston-engined airplanes use turbochargers.

supercharger, which is basically the compressor half of a turbo driven by a belt. Heck, even a leaf blower aimed at the intake can show improvements on the dyno, but that proves awkward on the road.

HOW THEY WORK
Positive Displacement Superchargers

We'll start with superchargers. The most common type seen on Miatas is a positive or fixed displacement supercharger. There are two basic designs of these. The first is the Roots-style or Eaton supercharger, which is basically a pump that moves a certain amount of air every time it turns. It's driven by a belt off the crankshaft, which ties the speed of the supercharger to the speed of the engine. If you double the engine speed (and with it, the airflow needs of the engine), the speed of the pump will double as well, so it will move twice as much

air. This means the boost level remains constant regardless of engine speed. Well, it does in theory. In the real world, internal leakage means a minimum speed is required before it'll come up to full efficiency, but that doesn't take long with a properly sized supercharger.

A twin-screw supercharger, such as an Autorotor or Whipple, has a different internal design that actually compresses the air inside the supercharger before it's forced out into the intake manifold. In practice, it works very much like the Roots blower, but the twin-screw supercharger is much more expensive. Due to the high cost of the components, most aftermarket suppliers go with the Roots type.

One note about terminology. Because the Roots supercharger does not compress the air, it's technically a blower. It creates boost by stuffing more air into the intake manifold. Think of packing a suitcase for a trip: You can keep

A twin-screw supercharger

A peek at the complex lobes of a twin-screw supercharger. There's very little clearance between the two screws to keep air from leaking and dropping efficiency. The two screws also move at different speeds, as can be seen from the different gear sizes. A Roots blower has a different shape to the lobes and they mesh differently. The gears live in an oil bath, and some superchargers do need to have their oil changed on a regular basis. Others are maintenance-free.

The Eaton M45 supercharger. Air enters through the throttle body at left and is pumped out through the triangular exit on top. The butterfly for the bypass is visible — when this opens, air passes directly from the inlet to the outlet manifold without going through the blower. The black actuator at top contains a diaphragm to open and close the bypass.

pushing more clothes in and then sit on the lid to make it all fit inside. The twin-screw is a compressor, as the air exiting the supercharger is compressed. In our suitcase analogy, it's as if the clothes are already folded or rolled up. You can fit the same amount of stuff inside, but the work is done before the clothes go in the suitcase. The end result is the same, though: a very heavy suitcase. I'll use the term "compressor" in both cases to avoid potential confusion.

Because the supercharger is driven off the engine, it does sap some of the engine's power. Quite a bit at higher engine speeds, actually. It takes up to 36 horsepower to spin the MP62 fast enough to generate 10 psi. However, that extra air helps the engine make a bunch more power. To minimize these parasitic losses from the supercharger, these positive displacement setups will have a bypass valve that opens up when the engine isn't in boost. This lets air go around the supercharger instead of through it, dropping the amount of power needed to spin the supercharger fairly dramatically. It still absorbs a little bit of power, but not much.

The throttle is almost always mounted upstream of the supercharger. This means the throttled volume can be affected, especially on a setup that retains the stock intake manifold. Add an intercooler, and you can get to the point where the car has a bit of trouble idling.

Turbochargers

A turbocharger works differently. Instead of being driven off the crankshaft, it's powered by exhaust gases. A special exhaust manifold is used to direct all of the exhaust gas into a turbine, which spins a shaft. Attached to the other end of

A typical turbocharger with a wastegate actuator attached.

the shaft is a compressor, basically a centrifugal pump. This compresses air for the engine to swallow, and that's where the boost comes from. The air exiting the compressor is already compressed, similar to the twin-screw supercharger. The compressor design is very efficient, but it needs to be spinning quickly to move air. This means it could be turning at nearly 200,000 rpm at full boost.

Because the turbo is powered by exhaust gases that were otherwise not going to do anything but exit the exhaust system, it doesn't have any parasitic losses. The turbo can make full boost whenever there's enough exhaust gas available to spin the turbine fast enough. The boost level is controlled by a wastegate, which lets the exhaust gas bypass the turbine once the desired maximum boost level is reached. Turbos make boost in response to load, so it'll only make full boost at full throttle. Partial throttle means lower boost, which makes the car easy to control. A common misperception is that turbo cars are difficult to drive because it's assumed that they're running full boost all the time.

It's not a free lunch. The turbine restricts the exhaust somewhat, leading to back pressure in the exhaust manifold. We already know that will cost some power. But the biggest problem is lag. Because the turbine requires exhaust gases to spin the compressor, it can take a moment for the engine to produce the extra gas to power the turbine when you mash open the throttle. The larger the turbo, the more slowly it will respond. Turbo selection can make all the difference between a successful setup and a poor one.

A peek inside a turbo compressor. You can see the result of some very careful balancing near and on the nut. Tolerances of the rotating components of a turbo are very precise.

A centrifugal supercharger.

51

Centrifugal Superchargers

There's also a hybrid of the two, the centrifugal supercharger. It has the compressor design of a turbo, but it's driven by a belt. An internal gearbox makes sure the compressor spins fast enough. The net effect is a boost level that is directly tied to engine speed. If it's geared to make 3 psi at 3,000 rpm, it will make 6 psi at 6,000 rpm. The result is that most of the power gains are at high engine speeds. It's possible to gear them up to spin faster and then use a valve to vent excess boost in order to achieve a more consistent boost level across the engine's operating range, but this does drop the efficiency a bit as you're spinning the compressor faster than required. That means it will absorb more power from the crankshaft. Generally speaking, centrifugal setups are easy to drive due to their linear nature and relatively low torque levels.

With turbos and centrifugal superchargers, the throttle is kept in the standard location, so throttled volume is unchanged.

Because centrifugal superchargers have to spin at turbo-like speeds, they need an extra gearbox to scale the crank speed up. There are different approaches to this, but the exposed pulleys of this VF Engineering kit make it clear what's going on. The Rotrex supercharger used by Kraftwerks for their Miata kits uses a clever planetary gearset to do the same.

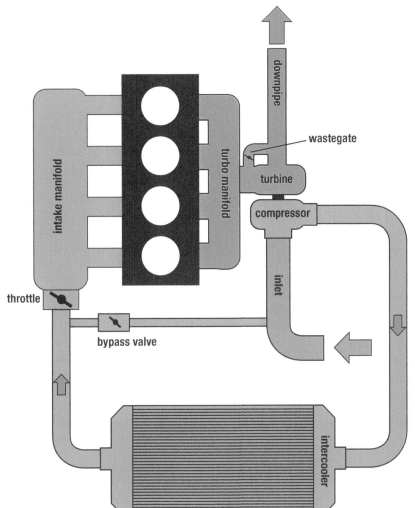

A basic turbocharger layout. Intake air is blue, compressed air is green, and exhaust gases are orange. A centrifugal supercharger is much the same, only the turbine is replaced by a belt.

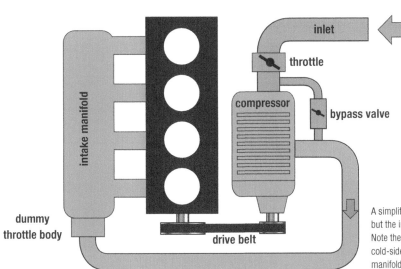

A simplified hot-side supercharger layout. This setup isn't intercooled, but the intercooler would go in the same place as in the turbo diagram. Note the relocated throttle body on the intake of the supercharger. A cold-side supercharger integrates the supercharger into the intake manifold, but is otherwise the same.

HEAT—THE ENEMY

There's an awkward fact about gases that you might remember from high school physics. If you compress a gas, its temperature will go up. The more we compress the air, the more heat we create.

But there's a second aspect. Not all compressors are created equal. There's a certain amount of inefficiency in any design, and this adds to the heat rise. The more efficient the compressor, the less power it takes to run it and the less it'll heat up the air. Turbochargers and centrifugal superchargers share the most efficient compressor design. The twin-screw supercharger is next, especially at higher airflow rates. At low flow rates, however, it's not as good as the Roots design. This means it'll heat the air more than a Roots at idle and cruise, but at full cry, it'll come into its own.

Why are we worried about heat? Because a hot intake charge is more prone to detonation, and that's an excellent way to kill an engine. Heat becomes the limiting factor to how much power we can make. The more boost we ask for, the more heat we create. Add in the temperature rise from the less-than-perfect efficiency of the compressor, and it turns out that heat management becomes a critical factor in forced induction. We want the coolest (and thus the densest) intake air we can get.

INTERCOOLING

So an intercooler—sometimes called a charge cooler or after cooler—is pretty much de rigueur for higher boost levels. The most common type is an air-to-air design, which is also the simplest. The hot compressed air runs through a series of tubes with cooling fins on them, while cool outside air is on the outside of the tubes and fins. This lets heat transfer from the hot air to the cooler air, reducing the intake temperature. Arrange for a constant breeze of cool air over the intercooler, and you can have intake temperatures that are close to ambient. No moving parts, nothing to wear out. It's pretty easy, but you do have to arrange for packaging, moving the air to and from the intercooler. This can range from easy to nearly impossible, depending on how your forced-induction system is set up.

A water-to-air design substitutes water for the cool outside air. Because it doesn't have to be exposed to a flow of air, this can be packaged almost anywhere. It can also be smaller, with less volume. But there's a catch. The water in the cooling system gets hot as it absorbs heat from the intake air, so it needs to go through a small radiator of its own in order to cool down again. There also needs to be a pump in the system to circulate the water. So the total system ends up being heavier and more complex. One neat ability of an air-to-water setup is that, if you chill the water, you can drop the intake temperature down below ambient for a short period of time. This is great for drag racers. If the system can't get rid of heat as quickly as it's absorbing it (such as long periods in boost, as you might get on track), the water will start to heat up and the intercooler will lose effectiveness.

A water-to-air intercooler on a Jackson Racing supercharger. The intercooler is the aluminum box in front of the engine, attached to the supercharger with a black metal pipe. The smaller throttled volume is a benefit in this application.

Two air-to-air intercoolers. The one on top is from a 2004 Mazdaspeed, the lower is an aftermarket upgrade. The smaller unit can get overwhelmed with the heat from sustained boost on a stock MSM, the larger does not have this problem.

WATER INJECTION

An alternative to intercooling is water injection. A high pressure pump and atomizing nozzles are used to squirt a water or water/methanol mist into the intake charge. When the water changes state from liquid to a gas, it pulls energy from the surrounding air and thus drops the temperature. If this is done close to the inlet port, it'll also cool hot spots in the combustion chamber, which decreases the potential for knock. It's a very effective way to increase horsepower — the lower temperature and improved knock protection lets you run more timing and thus make more horsepower. The water is only injected under boost when it's needed. It's a good setup for a low boost system or in combination with an intercooler, almost like running higher octane fuel.

The downside, of course, happens when something goes wrong. If the nozzles plug, the pump shuts down, or the water tank goes dry, you may find yourself running far more timing and boost than is safe without your water injection. High-end systems will monitor water flow and respond if it goes outside normal ranges by illuminating a light, cutting boost, or even altering the fuel and timing maps in the ECU if the ECU has the ability to take this sort of signal. The basic system shown here from Snow Performance can be expanded with a sensor box to monitor fuel flow.

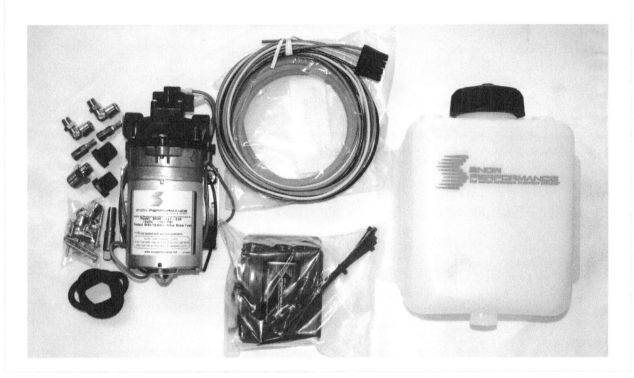

ENGINE MANAGEMENT

Because we're ramming more air into the engine, we need more fuel. And because we're raising the cylinder pressures, detonation becomes more likely. In fact, forced-induction Miatas are usually knock-limited. In other words, their power output is determined by how much ignition advance they can run before detonation kicks in. The higher the boost level and the back pressure, the more the timing needs to be retarded to avoid knock. Some sort of engine management is required with any forced-induction setup. There's more on that in the next chapter, but it's no coincidence that the majority of Miatas with aftermarket engine management also have forced induction.

TURBO VS. SUPERCHARGER

Which is better, turbocharging or supercharging? This is a debate that's never going to be settled. The easy answer is that superchargers are better for low-end power and torque with better throttle response, while turbos make more power but they lag. These are oversimplifications, and not necessarily true in all cases. What matters is how well the whole system is implemented. A well-sized turbo will make more torque than a poorly chosen supercharger, and the right supercharger will make more power than the wrong turbo, both contrary to common belief.

The major manufacturers can't seem to decide. Mercedes used superchargers; currently, the company's moved to turbos. Audi used turbos, now it's using superchargers. Ford put a supercharger on the GT, while Porsche put a turbo on the 911. MINI has used both at various times. VW and Lancia have decided to split the difference and use one of each on the same car. So don't expect an answer here.

Instead of getting bogged down in a debate, let's look at how to implement each well.

BUYING A FORCED INDUCTION MIATA

One of the least expensive ways to get yourself into a boosted Miata is to buy someone else's car. You'll be able to test drive it and get an idea of what you're buying ahead of time. Of course, it's worth asking why it's being sold. Is it a mechanical nightmare, or is the seller reluctantly parting with their prized possession? I've found that it's not unusual for a heavily modified Miata to go through several owners in short order after the original modifier sells it.

Why? Possibly because the new owners aren't ready to deal with the added complexity—real or perceived—of the upgrades. This does often mean the exact details of what was done to the car can get lost as the car moves from owner to owner, so do your best to determine exactly what's installed when you're looking at a car that was built by someone other than the seller. If the manufacturer of the major parts is out of business, take this into consideration.

Once you've found a car and purchased it, assume that it's all wrong. Go through the car from top to bottom. Make sure supercharger belts are aligned, that all hoses are in good shape and routed carefully, that any engine management is set up correctly, all bolts are tight, and so on. If something can be adjusted or programmed, make sure it's adjusted and programmed correctly. Some attention right off the bat will make a big difference to how reliable and fun the car will be in the future.

BUYING A KIT VS. BUILDING YOUR OWN

When most people decide they want more power, they will turn to the aftermarket for a ready-made kit. It's fairly easy to figure out why. Instead of having to design, implement, and troubleshoot a complex system themselves, it's simply a matter of opening up a big box of parts and installing them in a weekend of light labor. At least, that's the theory. If you deal with a good supplier and choose a good kit, that's exactly what will happen. There are a number of excellent kits available that are well designed and complete and come with the sort of helpful support that's so useful when you're sitting in the garage puzzled.

But there's the flip side. Some kits will leave you frustrated, broke from buying a number of essential, but not included, parts and without any reliable source of help. When you find a kit for an unbelievably low price—usually on eBay—there's typically a reason. These tend to be turbo kits, and they'll often consist of a manifold, a turbo of unknown size and manufacture, a pile of random tubes that will have to be cut and welded to shape, and a few other generic or missing parts. Kits like this can be useful if you know what you want to build and you view them as a source of basic parts. If you're looking for a fully engineered solution, you're going to have to pay more.

When looking at your options, do your research. If you don't have any experience with adding forced induction to a car, then support is one of the most important aspects to take into account. Can you look at the instructions beforehand to get an idea of what's involved in the install? The quality of the instructions will give you a hint on how well you'll be supported by the vendor. Can you call up and speak to someone about the kit? Can they answer technical questions, or are they simply reading sales material to you? Depending on the kit you're looking at, it may be possible to actually speak to the person that designed the parts you're considering. You can check up on the reputation of the vendor online as well, of course.

Next, what about the hardware? Is it well designed? Is the kit complete with all the parts you'll need? You should have a pretty good idea of what's required by the time you've read this book. Again, a chat with the vendor should tell you quite a bit here. If you're only looking for a kit to give you the most difficult bits and you'll fill in the blanks, great. If you want a complete kit, make sure that's what you're getting.

More important, is the kit designed to do what you want to do? If you're planning to make your Miata into a real monster, you don't want a system you're going to outgrow quickly. If you don't want more than a moderate power boost, then it doesn't make sense to use a large turbo or top-end engine management. Again, having a long-term plan for the car can save you a bunch of heartache—and money!

If you're not interested in doing the wrenching yourself, there's always the option of having someone else do the installation. Some vendors can do this for you or can offer a nearby shop they recommend.

The California Air Resources Board (CARB) requires any aftermarket part that could affect emissions to underdo special testing. If it passes, it's given an EO number showing that it is legal for use in California in a very specific configuration. That doesn't mean that the kit pollutes any less than one without an EO, though. It simply means it's been through the expensive test procedure. It's also worth noting that CARB approval isn't an indication of the quality of the kit, and that any alteration to the setup will render the EO void. CARB approval also doesn't matter to cars registered outside California — but if you live in California, it's very important and you should definitely find out if any kits you're interested in are covered. Unfortunately, home-brew setups are not CARB approved. Period.

DOING IT YOURSELF

A growing number of enthusiasts are building their own forced-induction systems, particularly using turbochargers. The growth of online forums as support groups and the lower purchase price of the cars are two big factors. Building your own may not save you any money and might cause premature hair loss, but in the end you'll have learned a large amount and will have a complete understanding of just how your car works, as well as a huge amount of satisfaction. When it's all done, most DIY builders are glad they went that way—but not all. Do your research ahead of time and be honest about your abilities and the amount of time you have available. Remember that forums will often gloss over difficult bits.

This chapter will cover the mechanical side of the implementation; the engine management is covered in the next chapter. It's not intended to be an exhaustive treatment of the subject but enough information so you understand what's involved. There are a number of books devoted to the fine details of both turbo and supercharging, if you're looking for more detail.

TURBOCHARGING

The key to a successful turbo system is the turbocharger. You need to pick one that's large enough to provide the power you want, but not so big that it has poor response. For many tuners, there's no such thing as a turbo that's too big. The truth for most people is that this simply isn't true.

There's quite a science to picking out the right turbo, but it all revolves around how much power you want to make. Yes, yes, "as much as possible." But seriously, you need to pick a number. Most people seem to read online and then decide they need 50 horsepower more than is commonly done. This isn't a great way to work.

On the NA and NB, all sorts of things start to reach their limits once you get to around 250 horsepower at the wheels. The transmission and engine internals are two big potential failure points. So that's a good stopping point, unless you want to make a big investment. The limits aren't quite as clear on the NC because there aren't as many high-power versions out there yet, but the limitations seem to be much the same. If you're willing to go further, figure out how much further.

A good view of a turbo system layout.

Now that you know the power goals, it's time to figure out what turbo is best suited to your needs. You can do this by looking at the advertised horsepower levels of various turbos and aiming for around the middle. In other words, if a turbo is advertised to work best from 250 to 360 horsepower, then it's a good choice for a 300-horsepower goal, measured at the crankshaft. Running at the low end of the range will mean the turbo's bigger than it needs to be, and you'll sacrifice response. Aiming for the maximum rated horsepower of a turbo will often mean you're falling off the efficiency range of the turbo, meaning hotter intake air and more back pressure.

This is an approximate technique, of course. You're relying on the turbo manufacturer to match the compressor and turbine well and to give accurate power estimates. If you want to get hard-core about it, you can start digging into compressor maps. That's a bit too much detail to enter into here, but there are a number of excellent books on the market if you want to dive deep into turbo tech.

Garrett turbos are quite popular for aftermarket applications. The GT2560R is the most popular turbo for the NA/NB, with the GT2860RS used on the larger NC motor and on some higher boost applications. For cars aiming over 300 rear-wheel horsepower, the GT3071R seems to be the choice, and 200 rear-wheel horsepower or lower cars will often use the GT2554R.

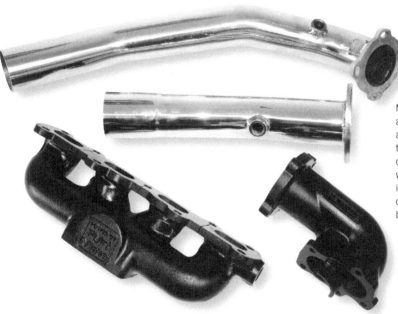

Now that you have your turbo, you'll need a manifold and downpipe to attach it to the engine. They're usually a matched set, as the design of the manifold determines the shape of the downpipe. In this case, the upper portion of the downpipe is a complex casting that keeps the wastegate output separate from the turbine outlet to improve flow. It's possible to make your own manifold and downpipe, but these are generally the parts any DIY turbo builder will buy.

They're dramatically different in size, but each of these two turbos is the right choice depending on the application. The cute little guy is a Garrett GT2554R that gives rapid response but can't produce much more than about 200 horsepower at the wheels. The monster is a GT3582R, designed for cars making up to 600 horsepower. It wouldn't be great on an autocross course, but it would be perfect for drag racing.

A cast manifold. The slots between the ports on the flange are to allow for some thermal expansion. The GReddy turbo kit for the 1.6 Miatas doesn't have these slots, and unless they're added the manifold will crack.

Manifolds

There are two basic types of turbo manifolds: cast and tubular. Generally speaking, cast manifolds are stronger, easier to package, and they're always less expensive. Unless there's a design or manufacturing flaw, cracking simply isn't an issue. A tubular manifold looks more like a header and has the potential for better flow and faster spoolup if well designed. However, due to the high levels of heat and expansion involved in a turbo manifold, it's difficult to keep them from falling apart. This is particularly true with stainless-steel parts. For a turbo bolted to a stock engine, a cast manifold should be sufficient. For a higher-output application, a good tubular can be worthwhile.

This elaborate tubular manifold was part of Matt Andrew's championship winning *Time Attack* car. It helped the car generate high levels of power along with rapid spool, but it did prove to be fragile at first. *Photo by Matt Andrews.*

Lubrication

The turbo's also going to need an oil feed for lubrication. On the 1990–1995 cars (yes, that's a weird break) there's an oil feed on the side of the block below the exhaust manifold, left over from the engine's previous life as a turbo setup and fitted with an M10x1.5 thread. For 1996 and later cars, most people install a tee between the oil pressure sender and the block. The block is threaded with a 1/8 BPT thread, so you'll need a special adapter for this. Most turbo kit suppliers can set you up with one.

As well as the feed, you'll need a drain for that turbo. This has to be a fairly large diameter line as the oil is unpressurized and a bit foamed up. It also has to go down, otherwise the oil will back up and leak into the turbo; the internal seals aren't designed to deal with this. The usual technique is to drill a hole in the oil pan and thread in a fitting. The 2004–2005 Mazdaspeed oil pan has fittings built into it if you can find one.

Some turbos have water-cooled center sections. Because turbos get very hot under operation, this is a good thing for the turbo and the oil inside, but it can put some extra stress on the cooling system. Typically, the water lines are taken from the short hoses on the thermostat neck. These hoses as well as the oil drain should be as heat-resistant as possible and wrapped in insulation. Even then, they'll need monitoring. Using braided stainless-steel or formed-steel lines will remove a potential future failure point.

Wastegates

Boost pressure is regulated by the wastegate, which routes exhaust gas around the turbine when the desired boost pressure is reached. A small hose—the signal line—feeds pressure to the wastegate actuator, which opens up at a certain pressure. This pressure is the mechanical base boost. It's the amount of boost the turbo will make at full throttle. Electronic or manual boost controllers will raise the boost by lowering the pressure in the signal line, essentially acting as controlled leaks and causing the actuator to open up later. It's important to understand that a boost controller can only raise the boost from the mechanical base level; it can't lower it.

This is the turbine exit of a turbo. The round door above the turbine wheel is an internal or integral wastegate. The yellow wastegate actuator—sometimes called a can—has a diaphragm inside that pushes the door open at a certain boost pressure and allows exhaust gas to bypass the turbine.

An external wastegate has the potential to flow more exhaust than an internal gate, which can help prevent boost creep in large turbos and high power levels. The boost level at which it opens can be altered by changing an internal spring. It's more awkward to package than an internal wastegate, but high-end applications demand it.

A simple manual boost control or MBC. Inside, there's a ball with a spring behind it sealing off the outlet. Once the pressure on the inlet gets to a certain point, it pushes the ball off the seat and full pressure is sent to the wastegate actuator which then opens. By increasing the tension on the spring, the point at which the wastegate opens can be increased. But there's a secondary effect as well. The wastegate without a boost controller will start to open gradually, bleeding off boost even before the target pressure is reached. With this ball and spring MBC, no pressure gets to the wastegate actuator before the ball moves and the wastegate doesn't open at all. This improves spoolup. An MBC like this can be assembled out of hardware store parts or purchased inexpensively. Electronic boost controllers (EBC) perform much the same function with an electrically activated solenoid, but can add more sophisticated control strategies to improve spoolup even further and prevent overshoots. Plus they have lights and knobs and can be adjusted from inside the cockpit.

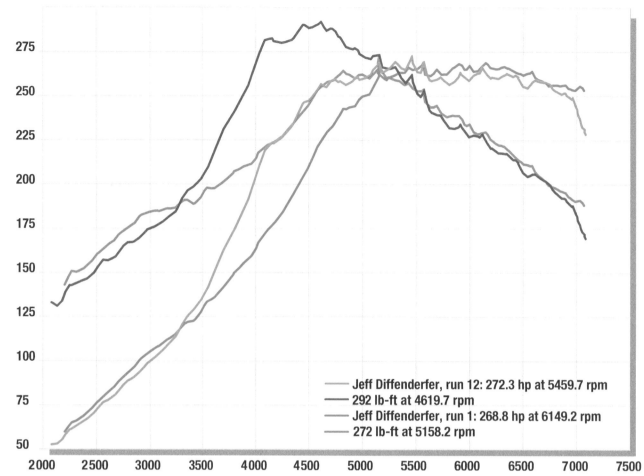

Jeff Diffenderfer, run 12: 272.3 hp at 5459.7 rpm
292 lb-ft at 4619.7 rpm
Jeff Diffenderfer, run 1: 268.8 hp at 6149.2 rpm
272 lb-ft at 5158.2 rpm

An example of what can be done with the right boost control. The turbo in this car was tapped out and couldn't make any more power at the top end. But adding a manual boost control to the standard wastegate allowed the boost to be raised down low, giving a huge torque gain without affecting peak power. This particular car raced in a series that had a power limit, but no torque limit. Turbocharged two-liter WRC cars used the same strategy—they were required to run a restrictor that limited power to 300 horse power, but up to 60 psi of turbo boost gave them 480 feet-pounds of torque over a wide range.

Plumbing

The plumbing for the air is easy enough. The post-turbo hoses need to be strong enough to deal with whatever boost you're planning to run. Most homebrew setups use lengths of steel pipe joined with silicone couplers. A small bead around the end of the pipe will prevent the hoses from blowing apart under pressure at embarrassing moments.

If you're running an intercooler, and most people do, it will be attached to the body of the car. Because the engine moves around under operation, you'll have to provide a bit of flex in your turbo piping to prevent them from being pulled apart. Silicone couplers will be fine.

The turbo and manifold from the MSM can be used on any 1.8. It's a pretty small unit and not the most desirable, but the packaging is nice. You'll need the water pump inlet from the MSM, or you'll have to modify yours. If you find one, the entire MSM turbo package or just about any portion of it can be transplanted into any NA or NB Miata. The exhaust system is unique to that car, so you'll need either a custom exhaust or an MSM exhaust, and the intercooler plumbing relies on some holes in the body that are only accessible on the 2001–2005 cars. But this is fairly easily overcome, and there are a few complete conversions running around out there: early turbo Miatas with what looks like factory packaging.

When you close the throttle on a turbo making boost—say, when you're making a shift—there's a big pressure spike in the intake tubing. This reflects a pressure wave back to the turbo, forcing air backwards through the compressor. This will stall the turbo, dropping the speed of the compressor in a hurry and potentially doing damage to the turbo. A bypass or blowoff valve is designed to open up when you lift off the throttle, dumping the excess pressure and allowing the turbo to keep spinning at full speed. A bypass feeds the air back into the intake system pre-turbo, while a blowoff simply dumps it into the atmosphere. This is the characteristic turbo "pssst!" noise, and some blowoff valves are designed to make this as loud as possible. Most blowoffs can't be used with a stock ECU because they dump metered air and are likely to open up under idle and cruise conditions. A bypass setup is preferable in this case. The picture shows a disassembled blowoff valve—it's nothing more than a piston and a spring. The vented air escapes from the ports around the sides of the red body. The only difference with a bypass valve is that the air would be directed out a fitting in the body where it can be plumbed back into the intake system.

FIXED DISPLACEMENT SUPERCHARGING

Because superchargers tend to be self-contained and are fairly easy to understand, many people think they'll be easy to implement. That's true and false. At their most basic level, they are quite simple. The common Roots blowers have their own sealed oil supply and even built-in bypass valves. All you need is the blower, a way to mount it to the engine, a belt, and a way to get the air to and from the supercharger. Sounds easy enough, right? The difficult part comes in when you start dealing with the amount of fabrication involved. Get the belt alignment off by a little bit and you'll have no end of trouble keeping the belt on the engine. If the supercharger isn't well supported, you can crack whatever it's bolted to. That's usually the head. Generally speaking, homebrew superchargers are far less common than turbochargers although it's hard to say exactly why.

The classic Jackson Racing supercharger. This particular car is running the basic kit, with no intercooler of any sort. The air simply comes out of the supercharger on the exhaust side of the engine and gets fed into the intake manifold, making this a hot-side supercharger. It's a very simple design.

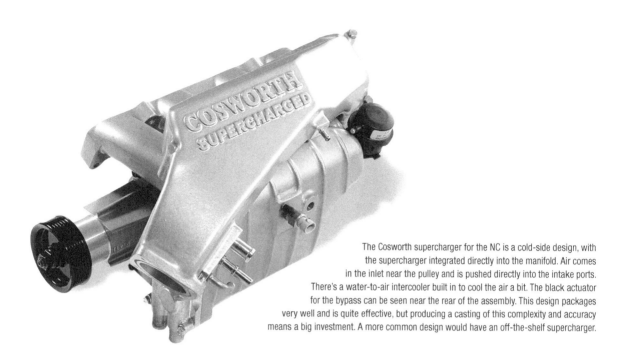

The Cosworth supercharger for the NC is a cold-side design, with the supercharger integrated directly into the manifold. Air comes in the inlet near the pulley and is pushed directly into the intake ports. There's a water-to-air intercooler built in to cool the air a bit. The black actuator for the bypass can be seen near the rear of the assembly. This design packages very well and is quite effective, but producing a casting of this complexity and accuracy means a big investment. A more common design would have an off-the-shelf supercharger.

COLD-SIDE AND HOT-SIDE

There are two basic ways to add a positive displacement supercharger to a Miata engine, depending on where the supercharger itself is placed. The more difficult method is to build a new intake manifold with the supercharger integrated inside, often referred to as a cold-side supercharger. The big advantage is the small throttled volume, which gives the best possible throttle response. There also tends to be the lowest weight gain as well.

The biggest downside, beside the difficulty of fabricating a new intake manifold of course, has to do with intercooling. The small throttled volume leaves little room for any sort of intercooling. The best match is an air and water system packaged inside the new manifold. Naturally, this adds even more complexity to the system. Homebrew cold-side systems are extremely rare, and there are only a couple available through the aftermarket for the NA and NB. The Cosworth supercharger for the NC takes this approach and is so well packaged it looks like a factory installation.

The easier, less expensive, and most popular location for the supercharger is outside the intake manifold. Due to the packaging of the Miata engine, this usually means the compressor is placed above the exhaust manifold. Thus the term "hot-side" supercharger. The throttled volume becomes much larger than stock because the throttle is mounted pre-supercharger, and throttle response will suffer accordingly. Usually, the problems show up in an idle that has a tendency to droop down. Either air-to-water or air-to-air intercoolers can be used in this setup, although any further increase in throttled volume has to be considered. Mounting the supercharger is much easier, however, as all that's required is a few brackets.

The packaging on the NC doesn't leave a lot of extra room, and Cosworth did a great job of packing the new parts in. Luckily, the stock six-rib belt helped out—trying to add an extra belt in that engine bay may have simply been too much!

Why isn't the throttle body left in the stock location? Because of what happens to the pressure in the intake system when you close the throttle. Unlike turbos, airflow simply cannot reverse backward through a fixed displacement supercharger. This means that when you close the throttle under boost, there's a huge pressure spike in the intake and you can actually blow an intercooler apart. A large bypass valve should be able to solve the problem, but nobody's been able to implement it well. Besides, they make an absolutely unholy amount of noise all the time without the throttle in the way, so it's simply not a streetable option.

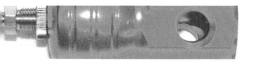

OTHER CONSIDERATIONS

Regardless of supercharger location, there are a few factors that need to be considered. The supercharger needs to be driven by a belt, and you can either hijack one of the factory belts or add a new one. Here's where the biggest challenge of supercharging comes in. The belt has to transfer power to spin the blower. As we saw earlier, it may have to transfer a lot of power at full boost. The size of the belt becomes important. Using the factory NA/NB power steering/AC belt to drive the blower as seen in the evergreen M45 kit currently sold by Moss Motors means you're stuck with a fairly narrow four-rib belt. All else being equal, it requires a lot more tension to ensure the power gets transmitted. More tension equals more drag. Adding a new belt for the supercharger means you can use a wider six-rib belt, which means less power loss in the belt. The factory serpentine belt for the NC is a six-rib, so it's easily used to drive a supercharger.

Of course, every supercharger has an efficiency range. There's a certain amount of internal leakage, so they require a minimum speed to work properly. Similarly, if they're asked to move too much air, the output temperature will get much higher, and if you spin them too fast, the bearings can fail. So just like with a turbo, the right size compressor is important. There aren't as many superchargers available, though, which does make life a bit easier. The small Eaton M45, which moves 45 cubic inches for each revolution, has been available for Miatas since the very early days and will peak out at around 180 rear-wheel horsepower. Recently, the larger and more efficient MP62 (62 cubic inches per revolution) has replaced it as the standard for the 1994–2005 cars and the NC. The two common sizes for twin-screws are 0.9 liter (55 cubic inch) and a 1.2 liter (73 cubic inch).

Because the car is pulling nonpressurized air through the throttle, a supercharged car will often respond well to an oversize throttle body. Several of the aftermarket MP62 kits come with a larger unit, and some owners have even experimented with twin throttles.

CENTRIFUGAL SUPERCHARGING

Because a centrifugal supercharger is basically a turbo compressor driven by a belt, installing one is a hybrid of turbocharger and supercharger concerns. It's driven by a belt, so that needs to be handled. They're never integrated with the intake manifold though. They're typically mounted on the hot side where there's room. Because the compressor has to spin so quickly, the pulley on the supercharger is generally fairly small, so belt wrap and size is important.

Because the compressor is much like that of a turbo, the throttle body can stay in the stock location and a bypass valve is used. The compressor efficiency is high, like a turbo, so intercooling is not needed as badly as other kinds of supercharging. Basically, just treat the drive side of the supercharger like a fixed displacement blower and the compressor side like a turbo.

Belt tension is very important. Too little means the belt will slip, too much means power drain and potential damage to the bearings. Automakers know this, which is why they use automatic belt tensioners like these on new cars such as the NC. They're an excellent solution to getting the correct belt tension, and they make it easy to change belts. If possible, choose a supercharger system with an automatic tensioner to avoid headaches in the future.

The amount of belt in contact with the pulleys is also important. The amount of belt wrap will have an effect on the amount of power the belt can transmit. You can see how the drive belt wraps almost all the way around this supercharger pulley on this Jackson Racing setup. The two pulleys below it are the tensioning system.

Chapter 5
Fuel and Engine Management

Old-school hot rodders are always messing around with distributors and carburetors. They know that the key to making maximum power lies in the fuel and spark. Modern tuners spend a lot of their time poking away at electronic engine management, but it's really no different.

Every aspect of a Miata's engine is under computer control. The engine control unit (ECU, also known as a powertrain control unit, engine control module, or a number of other acronyms) monitors the state of the engine and then decides exactly when to fire the injectors and for how long, when to trigger the spark plugs, when to turn on the cooling fans, and even when the valves should open and close in some cases. This means that the engine runs perfectly at all times. At least, that's the theory.

But what happens when you start to modify the engine? The stock ECU can deal with some small changes in the engine when it's running in closed loop. The bigger the change, however, the less accurate the ECU's programming becomes. On a major modification such as the addition of a turbo, it's not even close. The car needs far more fuel and will probably have to run less ignition timing. In this sort of situation, we need some way to make sure the engine gets what it needs.

Forced induction is the most common reason for engine management changes. After all, we're going to all that trouble to ram extra air into the cylinders so that we can burn more fuel; we need to get that fuel delivered. Also, the higher cylinder pressures mean that forced-induction cars are more prone to detonation, so the timing often needs to be retarded.

Because one of the biggest reasons to go with some sort of engine management is to deliver more fuel, why not simply install larger injectors? That's going to deliver more fuel everywhere, including where you don't need it. You'll find the car will run rich and may start to have trouble idling and starting. The stock ECU is running under the assumption that the injectors are the standard size. It can compensate somewhat for oversize injectors in closed loop, but it will eventually throw a check engine light in protest if you go too far. Generally speaking, you can increase injector size on a stock computer by about 10 percent without causing problems with the programming.

Of course, the stock programming is a compromise. It has to balance emissions with fuel economy and power, and it has to be able to deal with the gradual deterioration of the engine over a decade of use and the potential that someone might fill the tank full of cheap, nasty gas and then give the car to a teenager to drive over a mountain pass with a full load of stuff in the trunk.

CLOSED-LOOP OPERATION

There are two basic control techniques used in engine management: open- and closed-loop. It's important to understand how these work.

Open-loop operation means that the ECU will do something but not bother to check on the results. It's all based on pre-programmed settings. Closed-loop operation means the ECU will do something, then check its sensors to see how it worked out. It'll then make a slight change to its settings and try again. It's incorporating feedback.

Let's look at cruise control as an example. The simplest type of cruise control would simply be a way to hold the throttle at a particular setting, like the hand throttle on a tractor or an old Land Rover. Set it to a certain position and the car will keep going at the same speed. Easy, right? Well, as long as you're driving through Nebraska. As soon as a hill comes into the equation, your car would start to slow down or speed up. Because all you've done is fix the throttle position, nothing happens to prevent this from happening. That's open-loop operation.

If your cruise control system was monitoring your actual road speed, it could alter the throttle position to compensate if the car starts to slow down (uphill) or speed up (downhill). It's taking the feedback from the speed sensor and using that to maintain the target speed. This is a closed-loop operation. The computer adjusts the throttle, checks feedback from the speed sensor, decides what needs to be done, and adjusts the throttle again. It keeps looping around. The stock ECU uses closed loop for all sorts of things, such as idle speed, cooling fan operation, fuel injection, and, yes, cruise control.

Obviously, closed-loop operation is the way to go whenever possible. The only problem arises when the results the ECU is trying to achieve don't match up with what you need.

So there's a big safety margin. By removing some of that or by altering the compromises in the program, we can make more power.

One of the most fundamental aspects of the engine's operation under computer control is the air and fuel ratio. If the engine runs too rich, it'll be down on power, pollute heavily, and get terrible fuel economy. It can even wash the oil off the cylinder walls, leading to rapid ring wear. But if it runs too lean, it's prone to detonation, will run hot, can suffer internal damage, *and* be down on power and dirty. For this reason, the ECU tends to monitor the air and fuel ratio fairly closely via the oxygen sensor in the exhaust system. When it goes into open-loop operation under high load, it'll err on the side of being too rich, as that's safer. The stock ECU will aim for a stoichiometric mixture, as that produces the most complete combustion. With normal gasoline, that's a 14.7:1 air and fuel ratio.

When running under boost, we want a richer air and fuel ratio to help protect against detonation and to keep the exhaust gas temperatures down somewhat. For power, about 12.5:1 at full throttle is best. But to cool down the

	Color	Cubic centimeters per minute
1990–1993	blue top	230
1994–1997	tan top	265
1999–2000	red body	240
2001–2005	purple body	265
2006–2008	orange ring	unknown at time of writing

Stock injector sizes are rated at a standard 43.5 psi. Operating pressures will be different. Miata injectors are high impedance, otherwise known as saturated. Low impedance or peak-and-hold injectors can't be used with the stock ECU.

intake charge a bit and to keep detonation under control, it's common to run closer to 11.5:1 or 11:1. So we have do to something about the stock ECU's targets.

There are four basic techniques of engine management being used. Let's have a look at them.

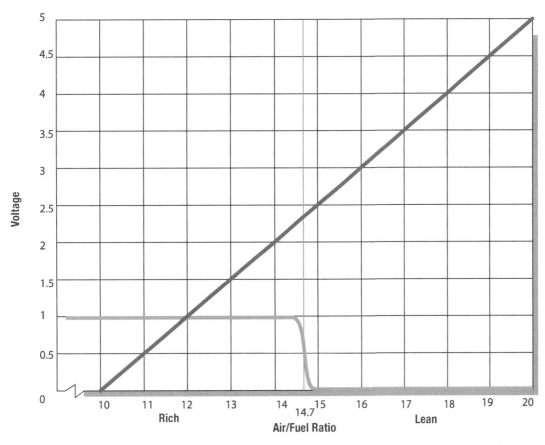

The stock oxygen sensor in a Miata is what's often called a "narrowband" sensor. It returns a signal between 0 and 1 volts, with a richer mixture being higher—shown as a green line in this graph. The signal is fairly crude, though, and it basically only tells the ECU that the car is too rich or too lean. It's more of a digital on-off signal. In closed-loop operation, the stock ECU to dithers or alternate the mixture between lean and rich. Catalytic converters actually respond pretty well to this as well. A wideband oxygen sensor typically returns a signal between 0 and 5 volts that's linear throughout its measurement range. This means that air/fuel levels can be much more accurately measured, even if they're not stoichiometric. The blue line is representative of a wideband, and you can see how it gives easily distinguished readings throughout the sensor's measurement range.

ODB-II (On-Board Diagnostics II) first appeared on the Miata and other cars in 1996. It's a system that monitors the health of the engine and all the emissions devices. If your catalytic converter goes bad (or you remove it!), it'll notice. If your car is running rich or lean, it'll tell you. Even a loose gas cap can trigger a code, as this means the fuel tank isn't sealing correctly. It's very useful for diagnosing problems, but it can be a hassle for those with modified cars. In many areas, an emissions test of an OBD-II vehicle simply involves plugging a scanner like this one into the OBD-II port and checking for error codes. When you're messing around with a highly modified car, the OBD-II system can get in the way. A full replacement ECU won't even communicate with an OBD-II reader, so you'll fail any emissions test that involves checking for codes. It's definitely worth checking the regulations in your area before undertaking engine management changes in order to keep your car street legal.

PIGGYBACK SYSTEMS

This is the simplest and usually the least expensive method. The stock ECU is left in place, and the piggyback works in concert with it. This means that the car should drive just like stock under normal operating conditions and that the emissions controls are happy. It doesn't always work out that way, but there's the idea.

Sometimes the piggyback unit will play with the signals going to the ECU in order to fool the ECU into doing something else. For example, the MSD timing retard alters the signal from the cam angle sensor in order to trick the ECU into retarding the timing when the car is under boost. The crudest example of this is the "power chip" found on eBay, a simple resistor that tells the ECU the engine is cold so that it adds more fuel. This is not something the Miata needs and it won't make more power, but that doesn't cut down on the marketing hype.

Another trick is to alter the signal from the mass airflow sensor, telling the ECU that's there's more or less air entering the engine than is actually the case. Less air means the ECU will deliver less fuel, allowing it to run happily with bigger injectors at idle and cruise, and gives extra headroom for delivering more fuel when it's needed.

Some piggybacks will fool with the signals coming from the ECU. The Powercard from Jackson Racing and the Voodoo Box from Flyin' Miata both add extra fuel by modifying the signal sent to the injectors to keep them open longer under boost, which means more fuel gets delivered. The limitation to this method is that you cannot deliver more fuel than the stock injectors can support.

Other piggybacks are completely separate. An auxiliary injector controller will use one or more extra injectors to add more fuel when required, leaving the stock setup to run without molestation.

This MSD box is simple and effective. It taps into the wires coming from the cam angle sensor. When the car's under at least 4 psi of boost, it delays the signal slightly so that the ECU fires the ignition a little bit late. It offers up to 6 degrees of retard. When the car's not under boost, it doesn't do anything. It only works on the NA due to the way the ignition system works, but it's a good example of a piggyback unit. The downside is that it's not adjustable and there's a limit to how much timing it can pull. It also has no ability to react to knock.

The downside of a piggyback setup is that you can end up fighting the stock ECU. If you're adding fuel and the car's running in closed loop, the ECU will notice the extra fuel and then cut the injector pulse width to compensate for what it sees as a problem. Because stock ECUs can pull out as much as 30 percent of the fuel in a situation like this, it's possible to find yourself much leaner than you expect. Then the car moves into open loop, and all that fuel comes back in a hurry.

You also lose accuracy with a piggyback setup, as you can't always predict exactly what the stock ECU is going to do. Say you want an ignition timing of 16 degrees at a certain point. If the stock ECU usually runs timing of 20 degrees, you know you need to retard it by 4. But if the stock ECU alters the timing in response to intake or coolant temperatures, you may end up with 12 degrees of timing, or, even worse, it might get advanced to 18 and you'll get detonation.

As long as you stay a bit conservative, piggyback systems can work quite well. They're not for people trying to eke ultimate power out of the engine, but for those who want a relatively inexpensive, low-effort solution for a bit more power. One big advantage is that, if done well, the emissions systems of the car are unaffected. Once you start to push the engine's limits and have to add a number of different piggybacks, it's better to look for a more complete solution.

A purely mechanical piggyback device is a rising-rate fuel pressure regulator. This device will raise the fuel pressure in response to boost. You can adjust the rate of gain so that the fuel pressure will jump by, say, 6 psi for every psi of boost pressure. It's a popular inexpensive way to add more fuel, but being mechanical, it can wear. It will also require a fuel pump upgrade, as the stock fuel pump can provide lots of flow but doesn't like higher pressures. Keep in mind that doubling the fuel pressure doesn't double the fuel delivery. Given the amount of work involved in altering the fuel pressure with boost in a returnless system, it's probably a better choice to use one of the electronic options for later cars.

A similar mechanical way of controlling the timing is to simply adjust the base timing. The ECU has to know exactly where the engine is so that it can accurately time ignition. If you purposely mis-adjust the sensor, you can increase or decrease the timing right across the range. It's cheap and easy—a popular way to get a bit more power out of a naturally aspirated NA is to advance the base timing from 10 degrees to around 14. On a turbo or supercharger setup, you can back off the timing. The problem is that you're adjusting all of the timing, so you'll get less advance off boost, raise your exhaust gas temperatures, and make the car less responsive. It's not a sophisticated option, but it's effective for low boost setups. The NB takes its timing signal from a four-prong trigger wheel on the front of the crankshaft. This inexpensive replacement can be rotated, allowing up to 6 degrees of retard—you can see the four slotted holes. A bit of careful drilling and measuring lets you make your own retard wheel at home—or you can set yours to adjust for more advance and more power on a naturally aspirated car. If you do advance the timing, though, listen carefully for knock! You may have to use better fuel.

One way to deal with a stock ECU pulling fuel from a piggyback is to hide it. This O_2 signal modifier tweaks the signal from the O_2 sensor so that the ECU thinks it's running a bit lean when the car goes into boost. This not only prevents the ECU from pulling fuel, it actually helps out a bit. When the car goes into open loop, the modified signal no longer matters. It's a good way to deal with a bit of hesitation when the car goes into boost. Interestingly, one of the cars that benefits the most is the 2004-2005 MSM. Even in stock form, it tries to run a stoichiometric mixture under boost for a moment, and this causes a noticeable hesitation.

REFLASHING

Reflashing (sometimes called "chipping") an ECU means changing its programming. When done well, this is a great way to deal with engine management. Ideally, you'll still get full OBD-II emissions compliance and be able to run any program you want. Depending on the ECU, you can pop in a "power" or "economy" program, depending on your needs. Unfortunately, it's not that easy. None of the NA or NB ECUs can be reflashed without having physical alterations made to the circuit board itself.

The NC, however, has an ECU that can be reprogrammed through the OBD-II port. This approach shows great promise with the newer car, and the ECU has been figured out to the point where new programs can be loaded in.

PARALLEL SYSTEMS

A parallel system takes over some of the control from the stock ECU but not all. For example, the stock ECU might still be in charge of idle, cooling fans, and all the usual housekeeping stuff, while the parallel install runs the fuel and timing. In theory, it's the best of both worlds. The stock ECU still returns emissions codes, and some of the hardest programming is covered for you. The problems lie in keeping the stock ECU happy. Its sensors will not respond as expected, and you could easily end up with a check engine light and a stored error code. This means you'll fail your emissions test. The wiring for a parallel system is often just as complex (or more!) than that for a full replacement, so it's not a common solution.

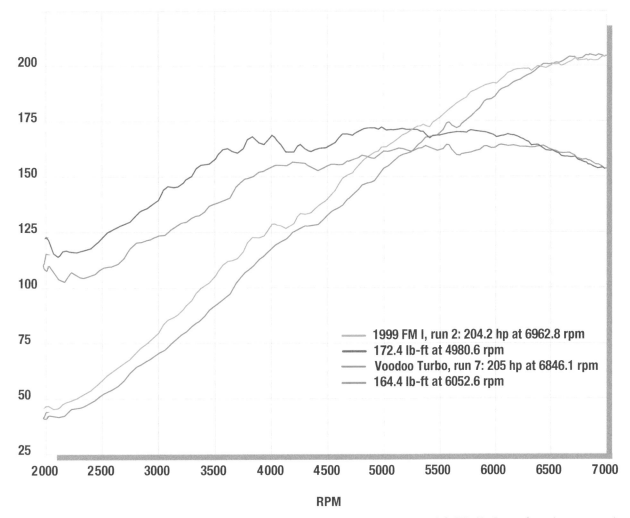

Legend:
- 1999 FM I, run 2: 204.2 hp at 6962.8 rpm
- 172.4 lb-ft at 4980.6 rpm
- Voodoo Turbo, run 7: 205 hp at 6846.1 rpm
- 164.4 lb-ft at 6052.6 rpm

RPM

This is the same car running two different piggyback systems. The red lines are from a Voodoo Box, which only controls fuel. The blue lines are from using a more complex piggyback system that could also control timing, allowing more timing down low. The peak power is practically the same, but with an extra 25 pound-feet at 3500 rpm the blue setup would be faster under almost all circumstances. The tradeoff is more expense and complexity, of course.

This interface box from Sniper Tuning allows you to plug a laptop into your NC and change the factory programming.

FULL REPLACEMENT ECU

The ultimate solution is to replace the stock ECU completely with one that you can program, often called a standalone. This gives the maximum amount of control: Your engine will be optimized under every condition, without interference from the factory parts. You can run larger injectors, program the timing curve to match your own engine, everything. From a performance standpoint, it's the best solution. That's why every fast race Miata on the planet runs a programmable standalone ECU, unless it's not allowed to under the rules. It also tends to be the most expensive option.

However, it also means that you are now responsible for everything. Setting up fuel and timing for a full throttle run is the easy stuff. Making sure the car behaves itself at cold idle when you turn on the A/C, that's the hard stuff that requires a lot of work. A stock ECU program is the result of five man-years of work, most of it on the details. There are also no aftermarket ECUs available that will return OBD-II codes, so emissions can be problematic. A solution for a plug-in ECU is to simply revert to the stock ECU and injectors every year or two if you require the codes to pass an inspection.

Sounds a bit frightening, doesn't it? No worry. ECUs are really just carburetors and distributors turned into electronics, and the concepts are the same. A good ECU should come with a good base map and be able to improve itself by auto-tuning as you drive around.

Because this is the solution that requires the most effort on the part of the tuner, the rest of this chapter is going to focus on standalone ECUs. The concepts still apply to piggybacks and parallel systems.

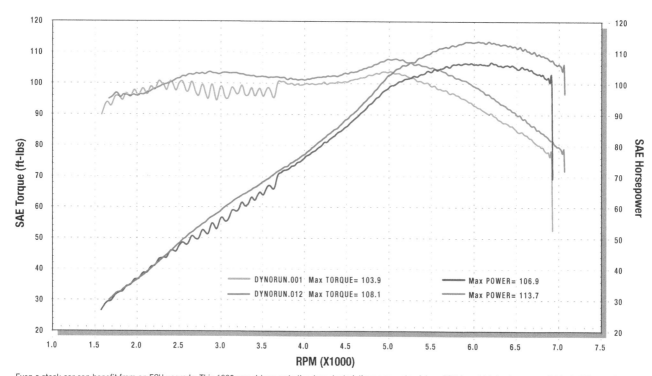

Even a stock car can benefit from an ECU upgrade. This 1995 was driven on to the dyno, tested, then a new standalone ECU from Link (no longer available, but the most popular unit on the market at the time) was plugged in and the car was tested again on the default base programming. The result: an immediate and effective increase. What you can't see on the chart was the increase in responsiveness from the engine. Any standalone ECU should show a similar increase if not more. The wavy signal below 3,700 rpm is characteristic of the 1995 stock ECU on the dyno. Also, note the higher (and programmable) rev limit on the Link.

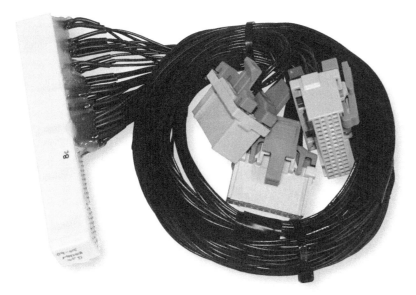

A plug-and-play or plug-in harness means you can install a different ECU without having to alter your stock wiring harness. This makes it easy to return to stock, if need be. It's also a lot easier to install! A wire-in setup will require wiring to fit it to the car. There are several plug-in options available for the Miata, a wire-in system should only be chosen if you have a very good reason to use that particular ECU.

CHOOSING AN ECU

Because ECUs are computers, there's always a fast rate of development. The hot setup today will be old news next year and antique in five years. But ECUs are being asked to take care of one of your most expensive possessions, and new ones on the market may have a few bugs or features you won't appreciate. So how do you choose?

First, and most important, support. As mentioned, you're going to be responsible for everything this ECU does. Who's going to help you out if you have problems? Support can range from "thank you for your money, we'll never speak to you again" to hours on the phone with a tech, troubleshooting and trading datalogs. The best way to find out how well a particular ECU is supported is via word of mouth, but you can get an indication by checking out the instructions and talking to the vendor. Will they let you send in datalogs, or can it only be tuned by a high-dollar "tuner" who has to be flown in and keeps your map a secret from you? Thankfully, the latter is pretty much gone, but it was surprisingly accepted five years ago.

Part of support is also the quality of the base maps. "Map" is a way of referring to the programming of the ECU, and a base map is the one you'll start off with. Can you get a good map that will have you test-driving your car within minutes, or will you be tearing your hair out and changing sensor types trying to figure out why it won't start? Also, how long has the ECU been around? Are there software upgrades, and will the ECU be supported in the future?

Second are the capabilities of the ECU itself. Does it have all the features you need? For example, if your car has VVT, you need an ECU that can control that properly. If you have an NB, you'll need an ECU that can also handle the alternator voltage regulation. An NC ECU has to deal with the

drive-by-wire throttle. On top of that, there are other abilities you may or may not need, such as the ability to control water injection, anti-lag, or to run separate ignition coils for each cylinder. Does it have the ability to run closed loop under all operating conditions, or does it have to change over to open loop in some situations? Can it handle a wideband oxygen sensor? Does it auto-tune? Can you datalog what the ECU is doing so that you can peek into its little silicone head?

Then there are safety questions. How does the ECU handle problems? If it has a knock sensor, what does it do when knock is detected, both mild and severe? Does it have some sort of overboost or overheating protection? You may decide you don't need these, but it's a question you should ask so that you can incorporate that into your decision.

So many questions!

Third is the price. It really should be the last factor. All else being equal, go for the least expensive for sure. But an ECU is a major part of your car and will have a huge effect on how well it drives as well as how much power you make. It's not a good place to go cheap. Saving $500 now might be a great idea, but after you've been chasing a cold start problem for several months, you might not feel the same.

TUNING

Now we're getting into the good stuff. You've just stuck a new standalone computer in your car. It came with a basic map in it, so you can get the car started and running around. Now what? It'll take some tuning. Piggybacks and parallel systems can sometimes be tuned and sometimes cannot, but the principles are the same regardless. The screen shots are from a program called Data Log Lab, tuning an older Link standalone. The Link doesn't have all the abilities of a modern ECU, but this simplicity makes it easier to see what's going on.

73

Most ECUs have the ability to automatically tune. Some computers are better at this than others, and some will have the ability to do rough tuning followed by fine-tuning. This is pretty easy to do. Just set your air and fuel targets and drive. The ECU will add and subtract fuel to get close to the targets. You'll have to go through the entire range of operation of the engine, including light throttle, high rpm and heavy throttle, low rpm as well as everything in between. You'll find that a certain range of operation dials in quickly because those are the areas you use constantly. Most programs will give some feedback as to where you've met your targets. Generally speaking, most naturally aspirated engines like to run about 12.5 to 13:1 and turbo engines between 11 and 12:1 under full boost, depending on octane and boost level.

Timing is more difficult. Forced-induction cars are knock limited on normal pump gas. This means you'll start to get knock before you reach maximum power, so you want to run as much timing as you can for power but not too much. This is where datalogging comes in. A knock sensor is nothing more than a microphone that's tuned to be sensitive in a particular frequency range. From looking at a datalog, you can see the background noise of the engine start to rise with rpm. This is normal and should be discounted, but big spikes are knock. You can often see smaller ones from very light knock. Those are warning signs.

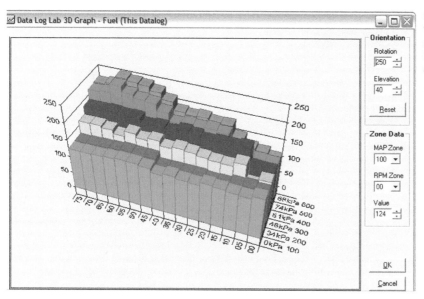

Here's an auto-tuned fuel map. It's pretty good, and the car (a naturally aspirated 1.6) put down some pretty decent numbers on the dyno. But check out the bumpiness in the fuel curves. Auto-tuning isn't perfect, and it'll leave a map like this.

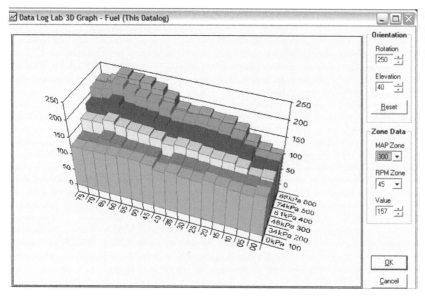

After a bit of manual adjustment, the curves are more gradual. The car will drive more smoothly and the ECU will have an easier time dialing in the air and fuel ratio in closed-loop.

A dyno is often used for ECU tuning because the car's behavior can be precisely controlled, and you can see the results of changes by seeing their effect on power output. It's possible to do some tuning on the road, however, and some analysis programs have dyno simulations built into them. Products like a G-Tech or other accelerometer-based "dynos" aren't necessarily accurate, but they can give consistent and repeatable results. This makes them effective for tuning purposes if you're careful to do each run under the same conditions and on the same stretch of road. Of course, you'll want a passenger (or someone else to drive) if you're trying to monitor a laptop, and you'll definitely want to make sure you're on a road that allows you to do what you have to do. Full

throttle runs from 2,000 to 7,000 rpm can be a bit sketchy on public roads. Due to the wide range of operating conditions experienced on the road, it's often easier to replicate some sort of drivability quirk there and capture it in a datalog.

A safe way to approach tuning is to set the car up to be rich, then dial in the timing. Once that's done, start leaning the car out again while watching the power output and knock sensors. You should gain power as you lean out the car, then the gain in power will stop. Go back to the point where the power leveled off, and you'll be in good shape.

When tuning water or water and methanol injection, use a similar technique. Get the car set up without water first. Now add too much water, about 30 percent of the

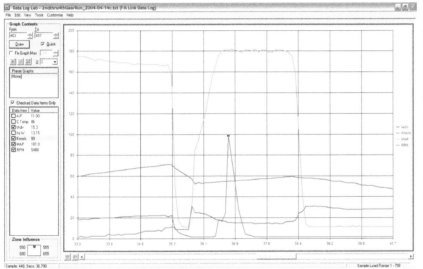

In this graph, the signal from the knock sensor is the red line and runs on a scale of 0 to 100. The big spike in the middle of the graph is a solid knock, one that should have been easily audible to the driver. The actual values are shown at left, 181 KPa absolute manifold pressure, 11:1 air/fuel ratio, 15.3 degrees of ignition advance, and 13.15 milliseconds of injector pulse width. In this case, the air/fuel ratio is good, but the timing's a bit too much advanced. On 91 octane fuel, 10 to 12 degrees would be more appropriate. Even for 93 octane, the 15.3 degrees is a bit aggressive for this particular ECU. You can also see the background noise or noise floor of the engine. As the engine rpm (green line) rises above 6,000 rpm, the knock sensor line starts to climb. But it's a gradual climb and never gets above 10 on the 0 to 100 scale.

Fuel injectors are pretty simple, really. They're just valves that react quickly. When they're open, the fuel is atomized so that it will burn immediately. The ECU will open the injector for a precise amount of time (measured in milliseconds) in order to deliver the perfect amount of fuel. The open time is called the pulse width, and the longer the pulse width the more fuel is delivered. The duty cycle is the amount of time the injector spends open versus closed. If it's open 75 percent of the time, then it has a 75 percent duty cycle. Obviously, it is impossible for an injector to go over 100 percent duty cycle, and you shouldn't exceed 80 percent to avoid the potential of a stuck injector. Injectors are usually rated in cubic centimeters (cc) per minute at a 43.5 psi duty cycle. If you need to deliver more fuel, you can put in a larger injector; however, too big an injector can be difficult to idle due to the very short pulse widths required. The maximum pulse width will be found at the torque peak, and the maximum duty cycle is found at redline.

amount of fuel being injected, and back off the fuel to 12.3 to 12.5:1. Power's going to drop off when you do this. Start cutting the amount of water back and watch the power rise until it plateaus, which should put you roughly back to where it was at the beginning of this exercise. The amount of water should be in the range of 10 to 25 percent of your fuel. Now start adding timing. You should be able to run quite a bit more than before, and this is where the extra power will come from.

To tune the VVT, the best thing to do is to fix it at certain points and do a dyno pull for each one. You'll be able to tell from the power curves what works best through the rpm range. Part throttle behavior is obviously a bit more complex.

It turns out that full-throttle operation, while potentially the most dangerous for the engine, is actually the easiest area to tune. The reason is that it tends to be fairly consistent and easy to measure. Cold start, idle, and rapid transient behavior such as slapping the throttle open or closed is what is really difficult. Lots of time datalogging and driving the car under all conditions is what's needed to really dial this in, although an ECU with good auto-tuning ability will make a big difference.

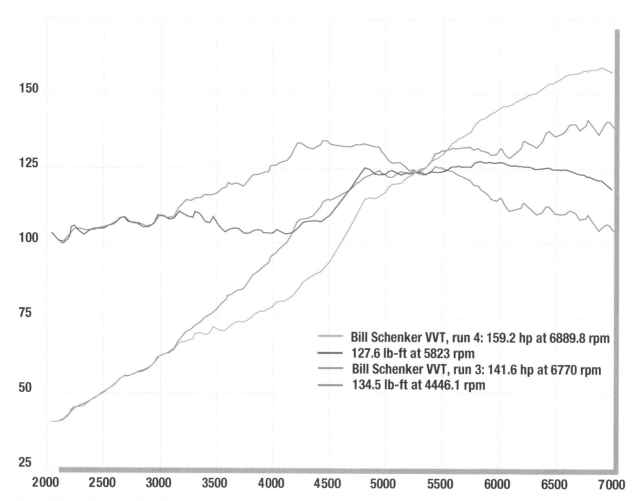

Bill Schenker VVT, run 4: 159.2 hp at 6889.8 rpm
127.6 lb-ft at 5823 rpm
Bill Schenker VVT, run 3: 141.6 hp at 6770 rpm
134.5 lb-ft at 4446.1 rpm

Here's a fairly dramatic picture of the effects of VVT. This is a healthy NB motor built for CSP autocross competition. On the red run, the intake cam was run in the fully retarded position (approximately 34 degrees of retard), providing minimal overlap. On the blue run, it's fixed at the fully advanced position of 15 degrees. It's fairly clear to see how much effect this has at both the top and bottom of the rpm range. The middle of the range needs a cam setting in between the two, which fills in the dip from 4,500 to 6,000 rpm or so. This dyno run only shows full throttle operation, of course. The same sort of testing can be done for part-throttle to improve emissions, turbo spoolup, and throttle response.

Chapter 6
Clutch, Transmission, and Rear Ends

We've been concentrating on making power. Now it's time to start looking at putting that power to good use. The first step, of course, is to get it to the rear wheels. To get there, it passes through the clutch to the transmission, then through the differential to the half shafts. Let's examine these components in that order then.

CLUTCH

The clutch consists of a friction disc and a pressure plate. The disc is sandwiched between the pressure plate and the flywheel. When the clutch is engaged, it's clamped firmly enough that it cannot move—we hope. When the driver steps on the clutch pedal, the pressure plate is disengaged and the disc can spin freely. As the pedal is let up slowly, the pressure clamping the disc builds up slowly, allowing it to slip less and less until it's fully engaged.

So, your clutch has a difficult job. It has to transmit all the torque the car can make to the transmission without slipping. Easy enough. It also has to disengage completely so that you can shift gears. When you're leaving from a start, it has to slip a bit so that you can engage the transmission smoothly, but it can't grab too hard all at once or you'll look

A typical clutch kit from Flyin' Miata. The pressure plate is painted purple. You can see the different materials in the friction disc designed to give both good clamping force and a smooth engagement. Like brake pads, this compound is important to how the clutch behaves. In the boxes are a new pilot bearing and release or throwout bearing. These should be replaced whenever the clutch is replaced. They're the classic $10 part that requires $300 of labor to change if they go bad, so always change them when you have access to them. The black doodad is an alignment tool designed to make it easy to get the clutch properly installed.

like a student driver. It can't require too much pressure to release or it will be tiring to drive and will put a big load on the hydraulics. On top of all this, it's expected to last for a hundred thousand miles. Quite a task.

Handling these requirements with a stock engine is easy enough, and the stock unit does the job well. Once you start ramping up the amount of torque, however, it gets harder. One way to increase the torque-handling capabilities of a clutch is to beef up the springs in the pressure plate, clamping down harder on the disc. The downside here is that it gets harder to depress the clutch pedal, and the driver starts to complain. Another solution is to use a more aggressive friction material on the disc, which keeps the pedal pressure low but tends to make the clutch harder to slip, making the car more difficult to drive. Typically, an upgraded aftermarket clutch will use a combination of the two solutions.

How do you choose? Well, the first step is to figure out how much torque this clutch is going to have to handle. Due to the compromises involved, don't buy more clutch than you need. Not only will it cost more, but it will also make the car a bit harder to drive with no benefit. If you're not planning to make any significant power upgrades, a stock (or stock replacement) clutch will do just fine. These clutches can typically handle a power increase of at least 50 percent over stock without problems. One nice upgrade for NAs and NBs is the factory clutch from the 2004–2005 Mazdaspeed MX-5 turbo model. It's proven itself to handle 250 horsepower at the wheels without almost any effect on drivability. Mazda did a good job there.

The 1990–1993 models used a smaller clutch than the 1994–2005 cars did. You can see the difference in diameter in the shiny friction surfaces in this comparison of the flywheels. The 1.6 is on the right. The overall diameter of the flywheel is the same, so you can install the larger "1.8" flywheel on a 1.6 engine without any other modifications. The larger clutch can handle more torque without any other changes to the system. For this reason, many aftermarket clutches and flywheels are only produced in the larger size. However, the 1.6 clutch and flywheel are lighter, so some people—particularly autocrossers—will run the smaller unit if torque capacity is not important.

A puck clutch increases the torque-handling capabilities by cutting down the surface area of the friction disc. This means the clamping force is spread over a smaller area; however, they are notoriously difficult to drive as they basically will not allow any slip at all. This can be a good solution for an extremely high-horsepower drag car, but they're not something you'd want to drive on the street.

One other way to handle more torque is to simply add another friction disc, as seen on this dual plate clutch from 949 Racing. This doubles the torque-handling capability without the need for stiffer springs or grabby friction materials. You can also make the discs smaller, which means less rotational inertia. This lets the transmission internals change speed more rapidly, helping the synchros do their job and making shifts faster. From an engineering standpoint, it's an excellent solution, and you'll find them on just about every motorcycle. In this case, the clutch is also mounted to a flywheel that has as little mass as possible for maximum engine response. The downside? Cost, and lots of it. One other potential downside is that they don't handle heat quite as well. Once they get too hot, they'll start slipping fairly badly. This means they're not the ideal choice for a car that spends a lot of time stuck in traffic, but if you need a fast shift action and a high torque capability, they're the ultimate answer. *Photo courtesy of 449 Racing*

If you install a clutch with a stronger pressure plate, you're going to put more strain on your clutch hydraulics. The victim on an NA or NB is usually the clutch slave cylinder, on the right side of the transmission and seen here through the wheelwell. If the clutch is not fully releasing, pull back the boot on the slave and check for fluid. If it's leaking, then it's time for a new or rebuilt slave. Details on how to change it can be found in *Mazda MX-5 Miata Performance Projects*.

FLYWHEEL

The clutch is mounted to the flywheel. The purpose of the flywheel is to add a bit of rotational inertia to the engine, allowing it to idle smoothly and make it less likely to stall when leaving from a stop sign. However, this extra inertia also means the engine won't change speed as quickly. A lighter flywheel will make the engine respond more quickly when you blip the throttle to shift to a lower gear, or let the revs drop faster when shifting into a higher gear. Basically, the car feels more like a sports car. There's also a bit of a gain in acceleration in the lower gears, as the engine no longer has to spin the extra weight of the original flywheel.

Miatas can usually handle a flywheel of 10 pounds or so without suffering at idle or at launch. That's about half of the original weight.

It's possible to remove weight from a flywheel by machining it down. This has to be done well, though, as the flywheel is under a fair bit of stress from having to transfer all the engine's torque. It also has to be able to spin quite quickly, and if it comes apart, it can do some serious damage to your legs and feet as it'll rip through the transmission and body of the car without much difficulty. For this reason, it's probably a safer bet to stick with an aftermarket flywheel than to have anyone but a very experienced machinist cut down a stock one.

This is an aluminum flywheel made by Fidanza. It weighs about the same as the steel one. Since soft aluminum wouldn't survive long under the assault of the clutch disc, the friction surface is a separate piece that's attached by bolts. The advantage to this is that if the flywheel ever wears down below the minimum thickness, a new friction surface can be bolted on. A steel flywheel would have to be replaced in this situation. The ring gear is also steel and bolted on. Both of the bolt-on parts can potentially come free, which doesn't end well, but this is extremely rare. It doesn't really matter if your flywheel is steel or aluminum. One important thing to know is that aluminum flywheels often use a coarser thread on the bolts that hold the pressure plate in place. That's what's in the bag beside the flywheel. Before installing, make sure you have the correct fasteners.

This is a lightened steel flywheel from Flyin' Miata. The teeth around the outside form the ring gear, used by the starter to spin the engine. The posts around the outside (not found on the 1.6 design) are what the pressure plate bolts to, and the shiny area is the friction surface where all the work is done.

Because the flywheel spins at the same speed of the engine, it's important that it be well balanced. While most flywheels are pretty close right out of the box, spending the money to have any flywheel balanced can make for a smoother-running engine. These holes are where material has been removed to balance this factory part. You'll find these balancing holes on the crankshaft as well.

TRANSMISSION

The vast majority of NA and NB models came with a five-speed manual transmission, and it's a good one. Originally introduced with the 1990 model, it has a tight, accurate shift action and has proven to be fairly strong. You need to make at least 250 horsepower at the rear wheels and drive fairly aggressively before it will start to show signs of weakness. When it does fail, typically it's by simply ripping the teeth off the gears. The cheapest solution is to simply stick another transmission in, as they're fairly inexpensive at junkyards. Of course, you don't win races by destroying gearboxes. It's unlikely to happen at a convenient time, but I did say it was the cheapest. Quaife makes a set of internals that are designed to be stronger and have a different set of ratios, but they're not cheap.

In 1999, Mazda redesigned the five-speed transmission slightly. The overhaul consisted of an extra internal synchro or two, a redesigned shifter turret, and a slightly modified shift pattern, so it was nothing spectacular. The big news that year was the introduction of six-speed. Everyone expects it to basically be a five-speed with an extra gear for highway cruising. It's not. In fact, the top gear in the six-speed box is lower than top in the five-speed. The shift action tends to vary a bit more between transmissions than with the five-speed, and it can be tougher to find the right gear on the racetrack. However, it's stronger than the five-speed, so some racers will use it instead, despite the shift quality.

Luckily, the six-speed is almost a direct replacement for the five-speed, making it an easy swap. On an NB, all you need is the transmission and the shifter. It doesn't get any easier.

The guts of the excellent five-speed manual transmission: All the torque your engine makes has to be passed through these gears.

An upgraded aftermarket transmission (right) compared to stock. The aftermarket unit has much beefier gears to take a heavier load. The angle of the teeth on the gears is also less to decrease the side loads. It's a bit noisier, but much stronger.

This five-speed transmission came out of a car that was making more than 390 horsepower at the rear wheels. That's just too much for a stock five-speed. The teeth simply ripped off fourth gear. The other gears are also at risk; it's just a matter of which one will fail first in a case like this. The owner of this car is quick to change transmissions.

One unusual thing about the Miata's design, and one that's been a fundamental part of the car all along, is the Power Plant Frame (PPF). It's an aluminum girder that ties the differential to the transmission and makes the entire drivetrain into a single, rigid unit. This makes the car much more responsive to the throttle and keeps the differential well located without transmitting noise or vibration to the body. According to Mazda, it also makes the car easier to manufacture as the entire drivetrain can be assembled and the body dropped on top. In fact, it works so well that it's a bit of a mystery why it's not used in every front-engine, rear-wheel-drive car.

The five-speed used in the NC is basically the same unit internally as the classic NA/NB unit, and that's good. It will take the same Quaife internals with some slight modifications. The case is a different design, and it hasn't proven to be quite as robust, unfortunately. The MX5 Cup racers had problems with third and fourth gear shearing.

The NC six-speed is a new unit with an excellent shift feel. It also has a one-piece case that's very stiff, and the gears are nice and hefty. In racing, one of the shift forks has shown itself to be vulnerable to abuse. When it breaks, you're limited to third and fourth gear. The racers have come up with an improved unit. It's quite possible that Mazda has put this into production at some point. This doesn't seem to affect anyone other than the racers, though, and it's a nice unit to drive.

The three- to four-shift throw can be adjusted to improve the feel a bit.

With the introduction of the NC came a six-speed automatic with a paddle-shift gearbox. It's very popular with buyers. Just how strong is it? Hard to say, but so far it's been stronger than any of the engines it's been asked to deal with.

One option for a stronger transmission is to use one from the RX-7 Turbo II. It's not a straight bolt-on and requires an adapter plate as well as some sort of substitute for the power plant frame. This means a transmission mount as well as something to restrain the differential.

Unfortunately, none of the NC transmissions will bolt up to an NA or NB. A six-speed swap into a five-speed NC or vice versa should not be complex, however.

Swapping an NB transmission into the NA is slightly more complicated because the starter is a bit different. The NB starter shares two of the three bellhousing mounting holes with the earlier design. The arrow shows which one is different. If you get the steel plate that goes between the bellhousing and engine, you can simply install an NB starter along with the transmission. As a bonus, the newer starter is lighter. For the easy option, just leave one of the three bolts out. It's been done a bunch of times without any ill effects so far.

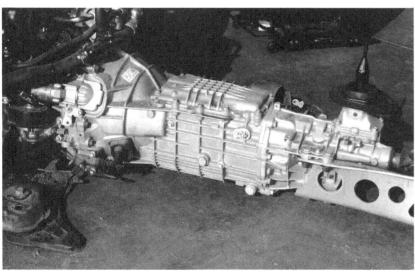

The NC's six-speed transmission. Because a twisting case can lead to transmission failure, Mazda went to a one-piece design for this part. The ribs add stiffness to the case as well. The NB six-speed is also ribbed, and many believe this is the reason it is stronger than the original five-speed design.

FACTORY TRANSMISSION GEAR RATIOS

	NA/NB/NC 5-speed	NB 6-speed	NA/NB automatic	NC (U.S./Canada) 6-speed	NC (Europe) 6-speed	NC automatic
1st	3.136	3.760	2.450	3.815	3.709	3.538
2nd	1.888	2.269	1.450	2.260	2.190	2.060
3rd	1.330	1.645	1.00	1.640	1.536	1.404
4th	1.000	1.257	0.730	1.177	1.177	1.000
5th	0.814	1.000	N/A	1.000	1.000	0.713
6th	N/A	0.843	N/A	0.832	0.832	0.582
Reverse	3.758	3.56	2.22	3.603	3.603	3.168

RING-AND-PINION

The ring-and-pinion takes the power from the transmission (via the driveshaft), turns it 90 degrees, and sends it out to the rear wheels. It has a gear ratio of its own, known as the final drive ratio. There were two different sizes of ring-and-pinion that were used over the years. The 1990–1993 cars got a 6-inch diameter ring gear that is a bit of a weak point. With enough abuse, you can break one with a stock Miata. High-power Miatas can shatter them quite dramatically. When one of these breaks, you are stranded.

The 1994–2005 cars run a much stronger 7-inch gear that is generally stronger than the transmission. As an added bonus, there is also a decent selection of different ratios available. Because it can easily be swapped into the earlier cars, this is a popular option.

The 7-inch NC rear also came with a number of different ratios, depending on the transmission used and the country of sale. The ring-and-pinion sets from the NB can be fitted, opening up a wide range of options.

The rear-end ratio affects the gearing of every gear in the transmission. It's also relatively easy to change, especially if you change the differential at the same time. So if you're looking for more relaxed cruising on the highway, or you can't use first gear because you simply don't have enough traction, you may find a taller (numerically lower) rear end will work for you. Go too far that way and you'll find that the car is more difficult to launch from a standstill and doesn't have much acceleration available on the highway without a downshift. Personally, I quite like the five-speed with a 4.10. Someday, somebody will make a 3.33 gear set and all the NB six-speed owners will be overjoyed with the nice tall top gear and a good spread in the lower set.

The downside to the NA/NB six-speed swap is the gearing. The gears are closer together than the five-speed, so you need a taller rear end to make this work. Mazda used a 3.909 in most of the cars in North America and a 3.636 in other parts of the world. If you have a 1990–1993 and want a six-speed, that means it's time for a rear end conversion to the bigger design from the later cars.

DIFFERENTIALS

When you go around a corner, the outside wheel has to travel farther than the inside wheel. It's a simple matter of geometry. If both wheels are forced to turn at the same speed, one of the tires will slip the whole time. Because it would be easiest for both tires to turn the same speed, they'll try to force the car to go straight, and it will understeer and refuse to turn. So all cars are fitted with a differential that allows the wheels to spin at different speeds.

The cheapest and easiest mechanism for doing this is called an open differential. The problem is that it sends the

FACTORY REAR-END RATIOS

1990–1993 (all) 4.30
1994–1997 (all) 4.10
1999–2003 (5-speed) 4.30
1999–2003 (6-speed) 3.909
1999–2003 (automatic) 4.10
2004–2005 (all) 4.10
2006–2009 (all, North America) 4.10

Some NB six-speed cars in Europe came with a 3.636 rear end, and these can sometimes be sourced in North America. Various other ratios were available in cars that used the same rear-end design, including the Honda S2000, but they tend to be shorter and not much use in a Miata.

The NC came with a 3.909, 4.10, or 3.73, depending on the engine and transmission combination, varying by country.

same amount of torque to each wheel. If one wheel is on a low-traction surface such as ice or sand, it can't take much torque before it starts to spin. The wheel with traction will get the same torque, and you won't go anywhere. Also, coming out of a corner, you'll discover that you can only apply as much torque as the inside wheel can handle. Once that low-traction wheel starts to spin, it can handle even less torque, and you basically have none going to the wheel with traction that can actually accelerate the car. This is not fast.

A limited slip differential (LSD) will limit the difference in speed between the two wheels. This means that even if one wheel starts to spin, you'll still get some drive from the other one. Obviously, this is much better for performance driving. Differentials are rated by their bias ratio: A 3:1 (or 75 percent) bias ratio can deliver up to three times as much power to the high-traction wheel as it can to the low-traction one. A lower bias ratio

UNDERSTANDING GEAR RATIOS

Gear ratios are expressed as numbers, such as 2.35 or 0.843. That's the ratio of the input speed to the output speed. A gear with a 2.35 ratio has an output that turns once for every 2.35 turns of the input. In other words, it will slow down the speed. An 0.843 ratio will only require 0.843 turns to turn the output by one turn. Because the output is turning faster than the input, that's called an overdrive. A 1.00 ratio means there's no change in speed between the input and output.

A ratio that's high numerically is a "low" or "short" gear. In other words, the car won't travel as fast for a given engine speed, but it will have faster acceleration.

Both the transmission and the rear end have gear ratios. If you want to know the effective ratio, you need to multiply them together. A top gear of 0.843 with a rear-end ratio of 3.9 will have an effective ratio of 3.29.

How do we turn this into road speed? Here's the formula.

$$\text{road speed (mph)} = \frac{\text{engine speed} \times 60}{\text{effective gear ratio} \times \text{wheel revs per mile}}$$

To convert this to kilometers per hour, divide the result by 1.6. A normal tire size in an NA or NB will turn around 890 revolutions per mile, while an NC will turn around 860.

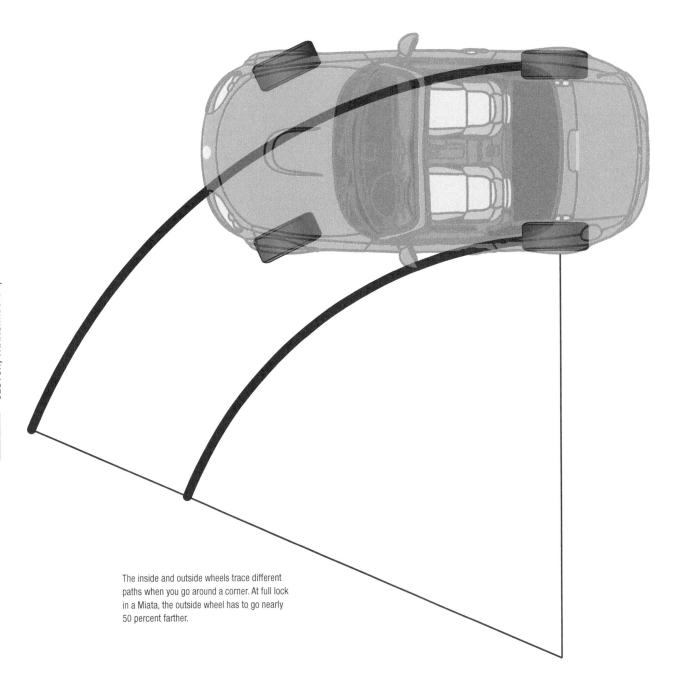

The inside and outside wheels trace different paths when you go around a corner. At full lock in a Miata, the outside wheel has to go nearly 50 percent farther.

will drive like an open differential but won't be as effective at dealing with putting power down. A locking differential will allow 100 percent of the power to go to the wheel with the most traction, which gives it an infinite bias ratio. An open differential has a bias ratio of 1:1.

A clutch-pack limited slip has several clutches inside. In order for the wheels to turn at different speeds, it takes some torque to overcome the clutches. This torque is added to the amount being sent to a low-traction wheel, so there's more drive available for the wheel with traction. In other words, it'll act somewhere between an open differential and a locking

differential. The amount of extra torque (felt by the driver as extra traction) depends on the clutches and the springs that press them together. It's a fairly effective design if set up well, but it requires special differential fluid and the clutches can wear. Depending on the setup, it can lead to turn-in understeer. They also have an effect under braking, which can make the car a bit less stable. Mazda never used this type of differential in the Miata from the factory, but aftermarket versions are available with a wide variety of bias ratios. The 1984–1988 RX-7 had a clutch-pack LSD that can be installed with the 7-inch ring gear in 1994–2005 rear ends.

A peek inside an open differential. The four beveled gears allow the half shafts to turn at different speeds. It's a simple device.

A common question is how to identify a Torsen differential. There aren't any hints on the outside of the case, and only Mazda can check the VIN against its database. The classic test of lifting the rear of the car off the ground and turning one wheel won't work, as a Torsen acts like an open differential in this case. Many Torsens have been declared open as a result. You can use the spotter's guide in *Mazda MX-5 Miata: Find It. Fix It. Trick It.* to identify if the car was equipped with one from the factory, but this means research, and there's no guarantee nothing's been changed in the meantime. The easiest way to identify any LSD is also the most fun. Put the wheels on surfaces with different traction levels (say, drop a wheel off the side of the road) and accelerate hard. Does the low-traction wheel simply spin, or does the car accelerate? An LSD will accelerate the car. A mechanical inspection is a bit more complex. With the differential in the car, the easiest thing to do is to pull the fill plug out of the differential and peer inside with a flashlight. You may have to rotate the it to get a good look. If you see worm gears with a spiral pattern, you're looking at a Torsen. If you see spider gears with a 45-degree bevel, as seen above, that's an open. A visible spring means you have a Tochigi-Fuji. In case you're wondering, that's a Type 2 Torsen in the picture. It's not easy to see the worm gears; you can only spot them through that small porthole. The 1.6 VLSD uses different flanges on the half shafts, so a quick visual inspection comparing both sides will help identify this one. It can be tested by turning one wheel as well.

A helical gear limited slip uses worm gears to shuffle the power around. You pretty much have to be a rocket scientist to understand them, but they work quite nicely regardless. The best known versions of these are the Torsen (for torque sensing) or Quaife differentials. They last forever, are nice and strong, and don't require any special maintenance. They also don't have any effect under braking, making the car more stable overall. The downside is that if one wheel lifts up in the air, the limited slip will lose its ability to transfer torque, and the wheel will start to spin. This is because a helical gear limited slip can deliver, say, twice as much torque to the wheel with traction. If the amount of torque being transmitted to one wheel is zero, then the other wheel also gets zero.

Miatas from 1994 to 2002 used either an open differential or a Torsen. The Type 1 Torsen was used in 1994 and a few 1995 models, then the factory switched to the superior and stronger Type 2. The 2003 and later cars use a Tochigi-Fuji, which is basically a helical gear differential with a clutch to help out and transfer a bit of torque regardless of the traction level of one wheel. The factory Torsens had a bias ratio of around 2.5:1. The Tochigi-Fiji is closer to 2.

A viscous limited slip (VLSD) has a series of plates inside, surrounded by a special fluid. The plates are driven by the two wheels. When one wheel starts turning much faster than the other, the fluid heats up and thickens. This forces the other wheel to spin at the same speed, delivering more torque to the non-spinning side. Unfortunately, you have to have some slip before it will come into play. Mazda offered this type of LSD as an option on the 1990–1993 models. The low 40 percent bias ratio, the age of the differentials, and the fact that they only work with the fragile 6-inch ring gear means they're not held in high esteem in the Miata world. Still, they're better than an open differential.

There are a number of other hybrid options, combining aspects of all of the above—sometimes, with great success.

This is almost everything you need to retrofit the larger 1.8 differential into a 1990 to 1993 model. You'll also need the driveshaft and the bolts that fasten it to the differential.

A good look at the worm gears of a Type 1 Torsen. On a Type 2, the gears are placed parallel to the half shafts.
Photo courtesy of Lance Schall

Fitting the larger rear end from the 1994–2005 cars—often referred to as a 1.8 rear end, which can be confusing since the differential itself isn't rated by displacement—into an early car is simple. The details are explained in *Mazda MX-5 Miata Performance Projects*, but basically you'll take the complete differential assembly, including the aluminum housing, the half shafts, and the driveshaft from the later car and replace the originals.

To swap a Torsen into a 1994–2005 model that has an open differential, all you really need is the differential itself. The least expensive way to do it is to find one that's still complete with a ring-and-pinion and mounted in the cast-iron third member. Then it's simply a matter of dropping the old one out, removing it from the aluminum housing, and replacing it with the new one. There's no need to set up lash or perform any difficult work. Make sure you know what ring-and-pinion is in the new unit so you don't accidentally change your gearing, of course.

Naturally, none of the NC parts will bolt directly into the NA or NB. For other sources for upgrades, there are a couple of options. The RX-7 Turbo II rear can be bolted into the Miata's aluminum rear housing, but it's a bit longer and will need a modified power plant frame (PPF) and a custom driveshaft.

Since the companies building kits for V-8 conversions also need upgraded differentials, there are some bolt-on options available that may include stronger half shafts and hubs. One of the most popular is the Ford 8.8. It's widely available, strong, and comes with a wide variety of gearing options. The 2006–2008 Cadillac CTS-V is also used in some situations due to lighter weight and smaller size. Because both of these are already being used in commercial kits, it should be possible to buy everything you need other than a driveshaft. You will also need to sort out a rear transmission mount because the PPF is not accommodated.

This rear end was originally intended for a Cadillac and was installed in a Miata as part of a V-8 conversion. It's a high-strength option for Miata-powered Miatas as well, though. The differential is a clutch type that's proven to be effective at laying down the power. It comes in some nice tall gear ratios such as 3.42 and 3.23, which work well with the NB 6-speed gearing. At the time of writing, you could buy a brand-new one for about the same price as a used factory Torsen.

Chapter 7
Handling Theory

This chapter is an overview of what handling is and some of the factors affecting it. This should help you understand why various changes will affect your Miata the way they do. It's not meant to be an all-encompassing treatise on the subject. If you want to dig deep into handling, there are a number of excellent volumes on the market. Disclaimer aside, let's dive in.

Before you can talk about handling, you have to define it. Just what is handling? To many people, it's simply the amount of grip a car can generate. That's easy to understand, but it's only part of the equation. All aspects of a car's dynamics fall under "handling," whether it's straight-line stability or the amount of steering feel when you first turn the wheel. To me, the most critical aspect is how the car behaves at the limit of grip. It needs to be communicative, responsive, and forgiving. Luckily, the Miata handles nicely from the factory, but that doesn't mean it can't be improved.

OVERSTEER VS. UNDERSTEER

Two of the basic terms to understand when talking about handling are *oversteer* and *understeer*. The fun way to explain it is that oversteer is when you go off the road tail first; understeer is when you go off the road nose first. On a more mundane level, oversteer is when the back end is sliding, and understeer is when the front is sliding.

Here's the more technical definition. It's when you're in a corner and your tires are slipping slightly, even if you're not actually sliding. Why? Because tires are flexible, and the movement of the sidewall and the rubber at the surface of the road allows them to move sideways slightly as they deal with cornering forces. The difference between where the tires are pointing and where they're going is called the slip angle. Obviously, when the car is sliding sideways, it has a large slip angle; but there's always some slip present due to tire deformation, even at very slow cornering speeds.

Understeer is when the front of the car has a bigger slip angle than the rear. In other words, the car's not turning as fast as it should. Oversteer is the opposite, with the larger slip angle at the back. Oversteer is a big favorite of Hollywood and the *Dukes of Hazzard* because it looks dramatic, but it's not really the fast way around a corner when delivered in large quantities. Understeer is the default setup for most production cars because it's safer and easier for most drivers to control. Lots of understeer isn't the fast (or fun) way either. Big slip angles scrub off speed as the tire is dragged across the surface.

When a car is well balanced and both ends slip at about the same angle, it's referred to as being "neutral." And that's a pretty good description of the Miata, most of the time. It's one reason why it's such an easy car to drive quickly, because it doesn't have a lot of bad habits. The car will oversteer or understeer depending on what the driver does, of course.

Let's walk through some of the factors involved.

Here's an extreme example of understeer. The front wheels are turned all the way, but the car's simply sliding forward. It's a pretty helpless feeling for a driver, and this car did end up sliding off the road. Against the driver's instincts, the best thing to do would have been to apply less steering angle so the wheels would have a chance to grip.

The exact same corner, but this time there's lots of oversteer. The rear of the car is sliding more than the front. It's the Hollywood way around a corner and a lot of fun, but it's actually quite slow. At least the car stayed on the road in this case.

A neutral handling balance. The slip angle of all four wheels is about the same. The driver can adjust the direction of the car with the throttle.

TIRES

Let's start with tires. Tires grip the road. The amount of grip available from a certain tire varies, depending on the slip angle, the tire temperature, the inflation pressure, the amount of vertical load on it, and the road surface. When you take away all the variables, it comes down to the tire's coefficient of friction, also known as μ. If a tire has a μ of 1.00 under a given set of conditions, then it can deliver 500 pounds of cornering, braking, or acceleration force when it has a load of 500 pounds on it. If μ is 0.80, then it can only deliver 500 x 0.80 or 400 pounds of force with that same 500-pound load. This is easy enough to understand, and it tells us two things. First, the more weight on a tire, the more cornering force it can generate. Second, the higher μ is the better.

Tires are interesting things in that they can actually have a coefficient of friction greater than 1.00. This may contradict what your physics teacher told you in school, but it's true. The reason is that the tire can deform and actually interlock itself with the rough pavement surface. If you're cornering hard enough, you're actually tearing the rubber off the tire. That's why you can leave black marks in a corner without sliding.

As you may remember from physics class, the coefficient of static friction is greater than the coefficient of sliding friction. In other words, once a tire is doing more sliding than gripping, its ability to generate traction drops off dramatically. Despite what you see in movies, you don't get maximum braking, acceleration, or cornering traction by generating lots of tire smoke. But a tire doesn't immediately change from gripping to sliding, it's a gradual change as the slip angle increases.

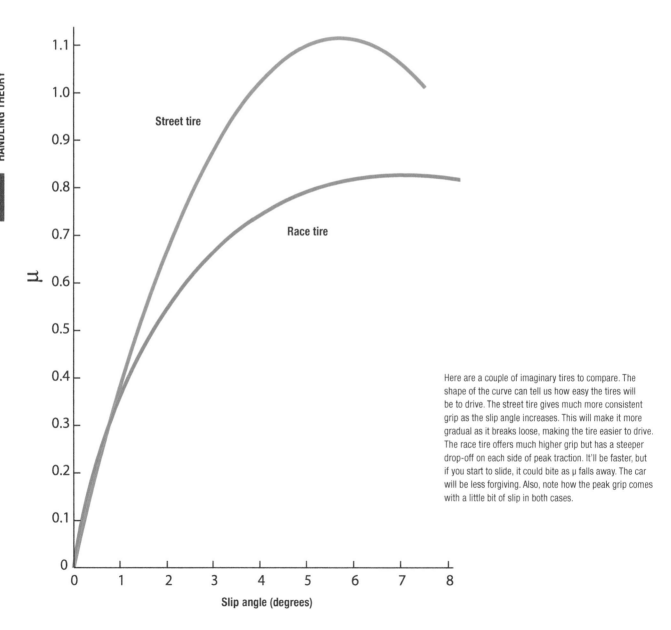

HANDLING THEORY

Here are a couple of imaginary tires to compare. The shape of the curve can tell us how easy the tires will be to drive. The street tire gives much more consistent grip as the slip angle increases. This will make it more gradual as it breaks loose, making the tire easier to drive. The race tire offers much higher grip but has a steeper drop-off on each side of peak traction. It'll be faster, but if you start to slide, it could bite as μ falls away. The car will be less forgiving. Also, note how the peak grip comes with a little bit of slip in both cases.

WEIGHT TRANSFER

One of the most important concepts to understand in vehicle dynamics is weight transfer. Every time you ask your car to do something—whether it's go around a corner, slow down, accelerate, or some combination of the three—it will shift its weight around. This is called weight transfer, and it's key to understanding how your Miata's dynamics work. Chances are you already know some of this subconsciously, the same way you can figure out how a ball is flying and catch it without knowing calculus. There's going to be some math in here, but it's fairly simple. We're dealing with high school physics.

Whenever you ask your car to change its direction or speed, the change comes from the tires. They're exerting a force on the car, and they're doing all of their work at ground level. But the car has inertia and wants to keep doing what it's doing. In a corner, you feel this as centrifugal force. The inertia applies a force through the center of gravity (CoG), which is the center of mass of the car. The tires are exerting their force either at ground level (braking and acceleration) or through the roll center (in cornering), which is fairly close to ground level. Because the CoG is above ground level, these unbalanced forces create a torque that shifts some of the weight around between the four tires.

Time for some numbers: First, let's talk about g and cornering speeds. The symbol g is the acceleration due to gravity (32 feet per second per second, or 9.8 meters per second per second), and weight is defined as mass x g. Because we're not leaving the surface of the earth, most people will treat weight and mass as the same thing. When we're talking about car acceleration, whether it's forward, backward (i.e., braking), or sideways, we like to use the same unit of g. A car that's cornering at 1 g is accelerating sideways at 32 feet per second per second. This requires a cornering force equal to the weight of the car. A car that's accelerating in a straight line at 1 g is accelerating just as fast as if it had driven off a cliff. Happily, the theoretical maximum acceleration in any direction is the same as the μ of the tires, assuming all four are being used equally. Street cars that can corner at 1 g are pretty unusual, but well modified Miatas can manage to hit that mark. The higher the level of lateral acceleration, the faster we're going around a corner.

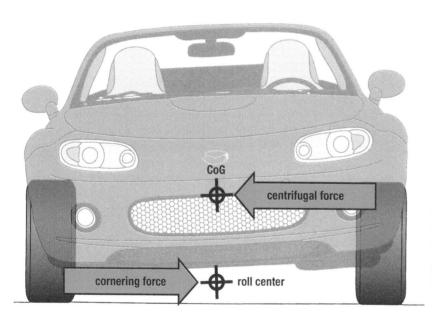

The tires are trying to drag the car around the corner, and their grip is the cornering force. The centrifugal force is the car trying to keep doing what it's doing. You can see how the two forces affect the car at different places. You can think of the distance between the two points as a lever. Physicists refer to this as a "torque."

Take braking, for example. When you apply the brakes, the tires apply a force toward the back of the car. The car's inertia provides a force toward the front of the car, applied through the CoG. This shifts weight forward, putting more downward force on the front wheels and unloading the rears. Any kid who's ever left big skid marks on the ground with a bicycle understands this.

In order to figure out how much weight is transferred in our braking example, we need to know the rate of acceleration, the weight of the car, the height of the CoG, and the wheelbase of the car. A Miata's CoG is approximately 17 inches above the ground. This will change with lowered cars, but it's a good rule of thumb for now. Let's use a car that weighs 2,500 pounds with the weight evenly distributed over all four wheels. This would be a fairly normal 2006 MX-5. The wheelbase of the NC is 91.2 inches. If the driver brakes hard enough to decelerate at 0.5g (a moderately hard stop on the street), we get the following:

$$\text{Inertia force} = \frac{(\text{weight x acceleration})}{g}$$

$$\text{Weight transfer} = \frac{(\text{inertia force x cg height})}{\text{wheelbase}}$$

Plugging in the numbers, we get an inertia force of (2,500 x 0.5 g ÷ 1 g), or 1,250 pounds. The weight transfer is (1,250 x 17 ÷ 91.7), or 232 pounds. This weight is being shifted from the rear wheels to the front. This means that instead of having 1,250 pounds pressing the front into the ground and 1,250 pounds on the rear tires, we have 1,482 pounds on the front wheels and 1,018 on the rear.

Looking at this, a few things become apparent. First, the only way to affect the amount of weight transfer at a given acceleration is to lengthen the wheelbase, lower the CoG, or make the car lighter. That's it. If the center of gravity was 6 inches higher, then we'd get 314 pounds of weight transfer instead of 232. You already understand how this works. Get a friend and have them try to push you over sideways. If they push you down low—say, at your knees—it's easy to resist because you still have your weight fairly evenly distributed. Not so easy if they push you higher up. Similarly, if you spread your feet apart and widen your track, you'll have an easier time staying up than if you have your feet close together.

Second, there's no mention of spring rates. That's because body movement—roll, squat, and dive—is a result of weight transfer, not a cause. In our 0.5-g stop above, the nose of the car will drop because the front springs are having to support an extra 232 pounds, while the back rises because there's 232 pounds less compressing them. A car with solid suspension will still get the same amount of total weight transfer, but it will sit flat.

Actually, when the sprung weight of the car moves under weight transfer, the CoG will move slightly as well and this will affect the weight distribution. But this movement is minimal and the resulting weight shift is so small that we can ignore it.

The same sort of transfer happens in a corner. The physics of the weight transfer are more complex and can be separated in several components based on the location of the roll center, but the total lateral weight transfer is calculated the same way, based on the height of the CoG and the track width.

Now, let's look at what happens in a corner. The basics are the same, only this time it's the track that affects our weight transfer. Our NC has a track of 58.7 inches. In a 0.75-g turn, this means we'll have 543 pounds being transferred from side to side. Our two outside wheels will be pressed into the ground with 1,793 pounds of force while the insides have only 707 between them.

Now here's where it becomes important. The more weight forcing a tire into the pavement, the more grip it generates. But the relationship between grip and load is not a straight line. As the load increases, the coefficient of friction falls off. A street tire with a cf of 0.75 when loaded with 625 pounds might only have a cf of 0.72 when it's loaded up with 900 pounds and .78 when it's only seeing 350. This is important. Really, really important.

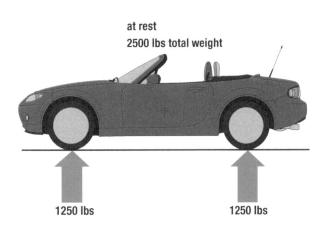

at rest
2500 lbs total weight

1250 lbs   1250 lbs

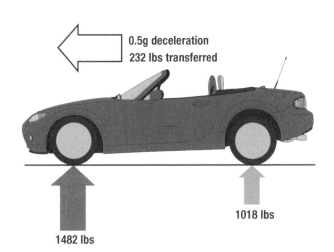

0.5g deceleration
232 lbs transferred

1018 lbs

1482 lbs

Here's a diagram of what's going on under braking.

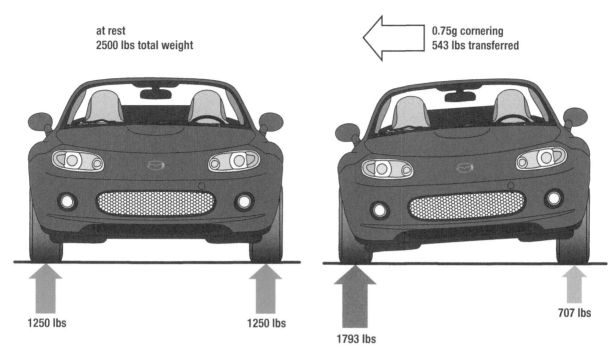

at rest
2500 lbs total weight

0.75g cornering
543 lbs transferred

1250 lbs

1250 lbs

1793 lbs

707 lbs

The same sort of transfer happens in a corner. The physics of the weight transfer are more complex and can be separated in several components based on the location of the roll center, but the total lateral weight transfer is calculated the same way, based on the height of the CoG and the track width.

What does this mean to our hypothetical Miata? With 625 pounds on each corner and a cornering force of 0.75, each imaginary tire can generate 469 pounds of cornering force for a total of 1,875 pounds and theoretically corner at 0.75 g. But when we plug in our weight transfer, here's what happens:

Outside tires 1,793 lbs total x 0.72 = 1,291 lbs
Inside tires 707 lbs x 0.78 = 551 lbs

Our total maximum cornering force has dropped from 1,875 pounds to 1,842. Uh-oh. The outside tires are providing more grip than before, but not enough to make up for the grip lost by the inside. There's not enough grip to support this

cornering speed, so the car is going to slide sideways until it slows down enough to regain grip or it falls off the road.

And that's the big lesson. **Weight transfer will cost us total grip.** That's bad for braking and cornering. The amount of weight transfer is going to determine the ultimate limits of the car, and by managing this transfer we can set up the car for maximum performance.

If you run the same numbers with an NA or NB, you'll discover that the shorter 89.2-inch wheelbase and narrower 56-inch track mean more weight transfer. It's a good thing they're a bit lighter to start with. A 2,300-pound NA will transfer 219 pounds forward under our 0.5-g stop and 523 pounds sideways under a 0.75-g cornering load. It's a smaller amount but a larger percentage.

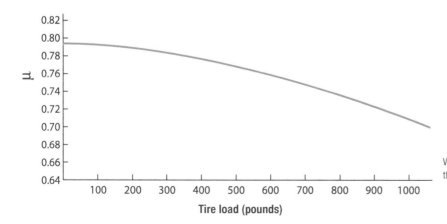

Vertical tire load versus coefficient of friction in our theoretical tire.

REAL-WORLD TIRE NUMBERS

The imaginary tires used in this chapter have idealized μ curves, so they provide better examples. What do the graphs look like with real tires? This information is actually quite hard to find, but Toyo Tires has provided a couple of graphs that compare one of their high-performance street tires with a Toyo race tire. A big thanks to Toyo for this!

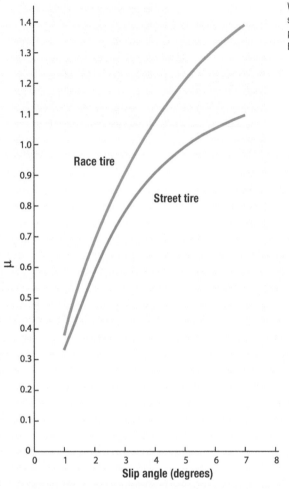

When we compare slip versus μ, we see that both tires keep gaining grip as the slip angle increases. The street tire is starting to taper off here and will probably plateau somewhere around 9 degrees, but the race tire just keeps gaining. Eventually it will peak, but where?

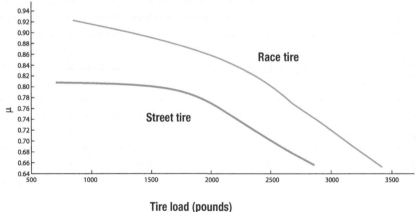

Here are the tires compared with different loads. This is at a constant 5-degree slip angle. It's interesting to see the different behavior between the two tires. The street tire is much more tolerant of increased load but falls off suddenly when it gets too high. The race tire provides more traction overall but punishes weight transfer much more severely. This matches up well with their intended uses, as a street car has a wider range of operating weights depending on passenger and cargo load and generally has more weight transfer due to a higher center of gravity.

TUNING WITH WEIGHT TRANSFER

We can do some interesting things with weight transfer in a cornering car. While we can't affect the total amount of weight transferred without altering the geometry of the car, we can move it between the front and rear wheels, and thus, the relative traction at each end.

Roll stiffness is the car's resistance to roll. You can adjust the roll stiffness at each end of the car by playing with spring rates or anti-roll bars. And here's the trick: The end with the higher roll stiffness will get a higher percentage of the total weight transfer. If you increase the roll stiffness at the front, you'll get more weight transfer at the front and less at the rear. This means the front will lose traction and the rear will gain it, leading to more understeer or less oversteer. It's important to remember the total weight transfer doesn't change, though. Increasing the roll stiffness at both ends, but keeping the proportion the same, will result in the same handling balance. This is important. It's the key to tuning your Miata's handling, especially because it's a lot easier to adjust the roll stiffness than it is to start playing around with your center of gravity or your suspension geometry. We'll get into how to tune with weight transfer later.

FRC

The amount of weight transfer at each end of the car is directly proportional to the roll stiffness. So a good way to express the roll stiffness distribution is to look at how much of the total roll stiffness is on each set of wheels. Usually this is simply expressed as a percentage, such as a front roll couple (FRC) of 58 percent. The higher the percentage for the front, the more weight transfer will take place on the front wheels, and the more the car will be biased toward understeer. Lower FRCs mean more oversteer. Stock front roll couples tend to be around 55 to 58 percent.

Is there a situation where weight transfer is good? There sure is: in acceleration. Since the Miata is rear-wheel-drive, the front tires aren't involved in trying to accelerate the car. We want as much of the weight transferred to the rear wheels as possible. Luckily, physics is on our side here, as that's where the weight goes. The harder the car can accelerate, the more transfer there is and the more grip we get out of our rear tires. Drag racers know this, it's why you see them jacked up to get a higher CG and thus higher weight transfer. When a dragster has the front wheels off the ground, it's reached 100 percent weight transfer.

TRANSIENT BEHAVIOR

If all we had to do was get the car balanced in a long sweeper after it's had time to settle down, chassis tuning would be pretty easy. Unfortunately, there's a whole lot more to it than that. We also have to get the car working well in transitions. Basically, when it's changing what it's doing. Entering a corner, exiting a corner, changing from a right to a left turn, a good handling car has to be able to cope with them all quickly without getting out of shape. In this sort of behavior, the weight isn't just being shifted front to back or side to side, it's moving diagonally. When exiting a corner, you're accelerating both laterally and forward, and weight is being transferred from the inside front wheel to the outside rear.

The speed at which the weight is transferred comes into play as well. The higher your roll stiffness, the faster your weight transfer. Quick weight transfer will make the car more responsive but can also make it twitchy and a bit harder to control. Slow weight transfer is easier to manage, but the car won't be able to react as quickly.

The NB in the background is in the middle of a corner and is fairly settled. The NA in front is in the middle of transitioning from turning left to turning right. This particular corner is a good place to spin a car if it's not set up well because of the rapid transition required.

Autocrossing is a fantastic test of transient behavior. The car never really has a chance to settle down. *Alan Branch*

THE EFFECTS OF BODY ROLL

Now, we know that body roll isn't going to affect our weight transfer, but it does have other effects. First, it takes time. This affects our transient behavior, as the car is not settled while the body is still moving around.

Second, it affects the suspension geometry. Our tires want to be flat and square on the pavement or even leaning into the turn somewhat. But as the body of the car rolls, the tires will be tilted outward into positive camber. This will drop the amount of grip the tire is generating, and we don't

want that. The Miata's suspension is designed to lose little camber in roll, but it still happens. We'll discuss camber more in Chapter 9.

So body roll is evil then. Well, not quite. Many drivers will use the body roll as an input on how hard the car is cornering, so we don't want to eradicate it completely. That's pretty much impossible though. As long as the suspension is allowed to move to absorb bumps, a Miata will always roll somewhat.

So, there's the theory. Now, what about the practice?

Body roll in a stock NC and lots of it! Despite the NC's well-designed suspension, you can see that the tires are starting to move into positive camber as the car leans, and that costs us grip.

Chapter 8
Suspension

This chapter is a guided tour of what's in the suspension and what each component does. We'll get into how to adjust it all in the next chapter.

The basic purpose of the suspension is to allow the wheels to follow the surface of the road. Seems simple enough. When a wheel hits a bump, it has be able to move without transmitting too much shock to the chassis of the car. Once the bump is past, the wheel needs to be able to get back to the surface without spending any time in the air. All four wheels have to be able to do this independently.

When the wheel moves up—say, when it's going over a bump—that's referred to as "compression." Sometimes this is also called "bump," for obvious reasons. When it's moving down (returning after hitting a bump, or dropping into a pothole), it's called "extension" or, more commonly, "rebound" or "droop."

Suspension tuning, like every other aspect of performance, is a set of compromises. The springs need to be soft enough to let the wheels move without upsetting the chassis but stiff enough to keep the body from moving around excessively. The shocks need to damp any extra movement of the body, but not so much that the suspension is no longer free to move when it has to. The sway bars have to be stiff enough to keep the car from rolling too much, but soft enough that the suspension remains independent and a bump on one side of the car doesn't upset the other. It's quite a juggling act, and one that will never be perfect for everyone. Let's look at the interaction of the components in detail.

SPRINGS

The springs support the weight of the car. They're rated by the amount of weight it takes to compress them by a certain amount. A spring referred to as a "300-pound" spring will compress by 1 inch when it's got a 300-pound load on it. With a 600-pound load, it'll compress 2 inches, and so on. A 600-pound spring will compress 1/2 inch with the 300-pound load and 1 inch with the 600-pound load. Simple enough.

There are progressive rate springs available, where the rate goes up as they compress. The first inch might be 300 inch-pounds, the second 350 in-pounds, the third 425 in-pounds, and so on. The theory is they will give a softer ride on small bumps, but they can have odd behavior as the rate changes during cornering. These are fairly rare for the Miata.

The units most often used in the United States are inch-pounds, although most people will simply refer to pounds. In metric countries, you'll sometimes come across kilograms per millimeter, usually referred to as "kg." To convert between the two, multiply the metric rate by 56 or divide the U.S. rate by the same. In other words, a 6 kilogram spring is (6 x 56) or 336 pounds. Just to keep things interesting, you'll sometimes see race springs rated in kilograms per centimeter. Divide that by 10 to get kilograms per millimeter.

One thing that's important to remember is that the spring rate isn't as important as the wheel rate. Due to the geometry of the suspension, the wheel moves farther than the spring does. This means the effect of the spring rate is lowered. Changing to longer control arms or even using a wheel with a different offset will affect your wheel rate without a spring change. The ratio of spring movement to wheel movement is called the motion ratio, and you can convert spring rates to wheel rates by multiplying them by the square of the motion ratio.

For example, a 300-pound spring on the rear of an NA will have a wheel rate of $300 \times (0.88)^2$ or 232 inch-pounds. Put that same spring on the rear of an NB, and it'll have a wheel rate of 202 inch-pounds.

The length of a spring when unloaded is called the free length. A 7-inch spring will be 7 inches long when it's sitting on the workbench. Simple enough. Spring lengths from 5.5 to 10 inches have been used on various Miatas, although typical lengths are 6 to 8 inches. You can also see the differences in the thickness of the wire used in these springs. That's part of what determines the spring rate, and a small change in thickness has a big effect. The yellow spring in the middle has a rate that is double that of the red spring.

When a spring is compressed so far that the coils come in contact, that's called coil bind. At this point, the spring is a solid tube and the suspension can no longer move. The marks around the top and bottom of these coils are characteristic of coil bind. The typical result is a spring perch torn off the shock and a collapsed suspension. Obviously something to be avoided. The difference between the free length and the coil bind length is the amount of travel available in the spring.

MOTION RATIOS FOR MIATAS		
	Front	Rear
NA	0.72	0.88
NB	0.72	0.82
NC	0.79	0.84

SHOCKS

The shocks are also called shock absorbers or dampers. From a technical viewpoint, the latter is correct. I'll keep using the term *shock* because that's what many people are used to seeing. The shocks' primary job is to damp the vibrations of the springs. When you hit a bump and compress the spring, the spring stores up energy. Once the compression of the bump is gone, the spring will extend and release that energy. And it's enough to push the suspension beyond its normal position, lifting the car up. Gravity pulls the car back down again, and it's just like hitting a bump. The car will bounce down the road like this until the friction in the suspension manages to dissipate all of the extra energy from that bump.

The shock's job is to absorb this excess energy stored by the spring, so when the wheel returns after hitting a bump, it goes right back to its normal position. That's their basic job, to keep the car from bouncing around. They're valved to deal with a particular spring rate. If the spring is too stiff for the shock, it won't be able to damp the movement properly and you'll end up with a bouncy ride. But there's more than that. They can be tuned to offer different levels of damping based on the speed of the shock shaft. Shaft speed has to do with how fast the wheel is moving up or down. A sharp bump will have a fairly high shaft speed because the wheel moves quickly, so high-speed damping comes into play here. Suspension movement caused by body roll is a fairly low shaft speed, so that's the low speed damping at work. It's important to remember that we're talking about the shaft speed, not road speed.

The shock will also have different damping behavior on compression and rebound. In other words, while the spring is a fairly simple device that can have a big effect on how the car rides and handles, the shock is a fairly complex and finely tuned device that will also have a big effect on the car's handling and ride. Due to their nature, they're also the component that is most prone to wear and naturally most expensive.

An adjustable coil-over setup is installed.

Miatas are fitted with "coil-over shock" assemblies. This means that the shock runs up through the middle of the coil of the spring. It's great for packaging in a small car. This is also seen in the common strut-type suspension, and so you'll often see the shocks referred to as "struts." This mistake in terminology will get some people all wound up, but it's an honest mistake.

SUSPENSION

MONOTUBE VS. TWIN-TUBE SHOCKS

There are two basic types of shocks: monotube and twin-tube. This refers to the internal design and construction of the shock. All shocks have to deal with the fact that when they compress, the shaft enters the body of the shock and takes up space. Because most of the shock is filled with incompressible oil, there has to be something that can compress and deal with this change in volume. This is dealt with by a gas chamber inside the shock.

A twin-tube—as the name implies—has two tubes, one inside the other. The inside tube contains the shock piston, and the outer tube has room for the gas.

A monotube has just a single tube, with the gas either emulsified into the shock oil or separated by a floating piston. This gas needs to be pressurized in order for the shock to function.

Because the twin-tube needs room for both tubes inside the body of the shock, there's not as much room for the piston. The larger piston area of a monotube is an advantage, making it more sensitive on small movements. But a twin-tube can separate the compression and rebound damping by putting what is called a foot valve or base valve between the inner and outer tubes to take care of compression, allowing the valves built into the piston to only have to deal with rebound damping. This overcomes the smaller piston size and allows for separate adjustment of the two damping curves.

Meanwhile, due to the high pressures inside a monotube, the seal where the shaft enters the body of the shock and on the floating piston need to be able to deal with high pressure and this introduces a potential problem with increased friction. The internal compression also adds a bit of stiffness to the suspension on bump, which can steal a bit of sensitivity away. But the single-wall design of the monotube shock means it sheds heat better, and that means it can deal better with sustained abuse such as off-road racing. Meanwhile, the dual-wall design of the twin tube makes it more resistant to external damage from flying rocks, such as found in off-road racing.

Which is better? Whichever is implemented better. The fundamental design is not as important as the details. Not just the shock valving, although that's critical. The designs of the pistons and valves, the location of the valves, the type of adjustments, the quality of the material—that's what makes the difference. Koni uses twin-tube designs. Bilstein uses monotubes. Mazda used both twin-tubes and monotubes on the NA and NB, and (at the time of writing) monotubes on the NC. Both work. There can be quite a bit of enthusiasm in the marketing of a particular shock based on the number of tubes, but what really matters is how well the shock works.

A cutaway view of twin-tube (top) and monotube shocks. The shock oil is orange and the gas is green. Sometimes a twin-tube shock will be fitted with a gas bag to keep the oil and gas separate and avoid any chance of cavitation or foaming.

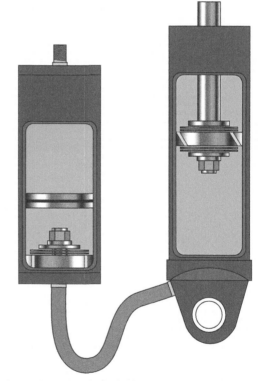

A monotube shock can be fitted with an external reservoir, which adds a number of capabilities. A lower pressure can be used as well as a larger volume of both gas and oil. The separate compression valve in the reservoir allows this to be adjusted separately from the rebound. The reservoir has to be fitted somewhere, which makes packaging a concern, however. It's also an expensive solution, so it's generally only seen on dedicated racing parts. Diagrams based on some provided by Mark Bush and his Racewise school, as well as AFCO.

SUSPENSION

COIL-OVERS

While the Miata does have a "coil-over shock" design, you'll often see reference to "coil-overs" as an upgrade. In the case of the Miata, this is usually reserved for shocks that have an adjustable perch for the spring. They can be simple sleeves that convert a normal shock to a coil-over setup, or they can be complete systems with shocks that have fully threaded bodies and come with matched springs and upper mounts. By moving the perch up and down, the ride height of the car can be changed—and this is the real power of coil-overs. As a secondary benefit, they typically use a race spring in a standard size. These springs come in a wide variety of rates and lengths, so you can change them to tune your car's handling.

UPPER SHOCK MOUNT

At the top of the spring and shock assembly is the upper shock mount. This isn't an exotic piece, but it's interesting because it helps determine both the ride height and the range of suspension travel. The higher the perch on the mount, the lower the car will sit, all else being equal. Because the shock changes angle slightly as the suspension moves, there needs to be some way for the shaft to rotate in the upper mount. The higher the shock mounting point, the more compression travel you will have. However, you'll lose droop travel, as the mount design can't affect your total available travel.

The NA upper mount is on the right; the NB mount with the associated bushings is on the left. You can easily see how much thinner the NB design is, moving the top of the spring up higher relative to the large flat mounting surface. If you don't change anything else, the NB mount will lower the car relative to the NA version. The rubber bushings allow the shaft to move in the NB, while the NA mount is actually two pieces bonded together with rubber. The NC design is similar to the NB, but with an exceptionally deep mount in the rear to allow the use of a long shock.

On the left is a coil-over shock assembly. On the right is a coil-over sleeve designed to add an adjustable perch to a standard shock.

Some upper shock mounts use rubber bushings; others will use a spherical bearing like these. Sometimes called pillowballs, the spherical setup offers a little more precision in the damping at the expense of extra noise and vibration. In the real world, however, there's little discernible difference.

BUMPSTOPS

When you do run out of compression travel, the shock butts up against a bumpstop. The purpose of the bumpstop is to provide a cushion so the suspension doesn't instantly stop moving, leading to a terrible ride and abrupt handling changes. You can think of a bumpstop as a short, stiff spring that comes into play at the end of travel. The NA used a rubber bumpstop that was quite stiff, but the car spent a lot of time on it. When cornering, it was essentially running on a rubber suspension like a classic Mini. The NB went to a polyurethane stop that was longer and softer, giving more suspension travel, a much smoother transition onto the stop and a better ride.

The NC continued with a similar design. A bit of attention to the bumpstops can make a big difference in the way the car works and can also increase overall suspension travel. Of course, the best bumpstops are the ones you never hit, but every car will hit them sometimes. The NA in particular can be improved with a good urethane bumpstop.

An exploded shock setup from an NB. The spring and shock are easy enough to figure out. The array of parts are also laid out in order. There are rubber isolators for the top and bottom of the spring, the bumpstop and dust boot, a support washer for the bumpstop, the upper shock mount and the bushings that allow the shock shaft to move. The NC has a similar stack of parts while the NA is simpler, without any of the isolators, a one-piece dust boot and bumpstop, and no bushings on the upper mount.

A coil-over setup for the same NB. The red threaded sleeve converts the shock into one with an adjustable perch and allows the use of a standard size spring. There's a black isolator at the top of the spring that also makes sure the smaller diameter spring stays centered in the upper mount. The tan bumpstop is slipped over the shaft, and a red cap is above it to support the bumpstop. On top of that is the first of the bushings for the upper mount, then the upper mount and the second bushing and washer. There's no rubber isolator for the lower part of the spring.

SWAY BARS

The sway bars, or anti-sway bars, are best described by the term *anti-roll bars*, sometimes abbreviated as ARB. I'll use the term *sway bar* here. A sway bar is a piece of spring steel that connects the left and right suspension at one end of the car and can be used to adjust the roll stiffness. When both wheels hit a bump, the bar simply rotates in its bushings and has no effect. When the wheels try to move independently (such as when the car rolls, and one side compresses while the other droops), the bar is forced to twist. Its resistance to twist will transfer some of the load from one side of the car to the other. This will prevent a car from rolling as much in a corner. It'll also make a car rock side to side on a bumpy road, as the sway bars try to keep the body parallel with the road surface. Miatas come from the factory with a sway bar at each end of the car.

One important thing to know is that the stiffness of a sway bar is tied to the change in diameter to the fourth power. This means that if you double the diameter of the bar, it'll be 16 times stiffer. A 19 percent change in diameter will double the stiffness. So even if an aftermarket bar doesn't seem all that much larger, it can have a big effect.

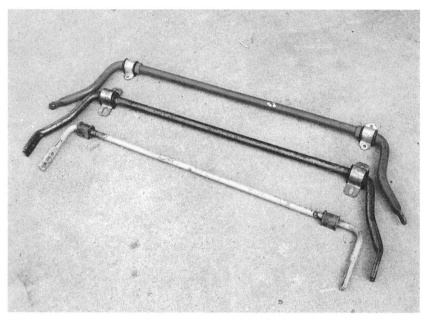

The red bar is the 23-millimeter (0.9-inch) stock front sway from a 2004 Mazdaspeed. Dark gray is an aftermarket 7/8-inch front bar for a 1990–1993 model, and the light gray is an aftermarket 5/8-inch rear unit for a 1990–2005.

Aftermarket bars are not only stiffer than the factory ones, they're often adjustable. At the end of the arm on the bar are multiple holes that allow you to adjust the leverage over the bar. Holes close to the end of the arm will make the sway bar softer. It's a simple and foolproof way to adjust the bar's stiffness. The red bar is stock, with no adjustment available.

The sway bars are attached to the suspension with short links called end links. On the NA, they're fitted with rubber bushings to allow the angle between the links and the bar to change as the suspension moves. On the NB and NC, they're a ball joint. The goal of these links is to transfer the forces to and from the bar without any slop or resistance. The rubber bushings from the NA weren't a great choice, as they resist deflection and they don't age well. This resistance can make it difficult to line up the end link with some of the holes in adjustable bars.

The ball joints are a better design, but under high loads they can actually come apart. The aftermarket is full of end links that use spherical bearings at the ends or are adjustable for length. The spherical bearings provide a solid connection between the end links and the bar but are more prone to wear over time as the precision surfaces get worn down by the large amounts of dirt and grit thrown onto the end links. The length adjustment allows you to set up the car so that there is no twist or preload in the bar when the car is at rest. If the bar is preloaded, the car will act differently depending on if it's turning right or left.

From left, a stock NA end link, an NB or NC end link, an adjustable end link with urethane bushings, and one made out of rod ends.

A slick little trick from a competition car. Pull the pin out, and the end link can be disconnected in seconds without tools. This allows for rapid adjustments of the handling. This is a non-adjustable bar, but it works just as well for changing from one hole to another.

BUSHINGS

Any place you have two parts that have to be able to move relative to one another, you have either a bushing or a bearing. In the suspension, it's usually the former. Most stock bushings are a steel tube with rubber bonded to it, pressed into a part like the control arm. The steel tube is bolted in to place. When the control arm rotates up or down, the steel tube stays fixed to the body while the rubber stays fixed to the arm. Flex in the rubber is what allows the movement. It also absorbs vibration, taking some of the harshness out of the ride. Because the rubber has to flex to let the arm move, it acts like a spring and tries to return to its resting position.

To make the handling more responsive, these rubber bushings can be replaced with stiffer rubber, polyurethane, or some other stiff material like Delrin. Most nonrubber bushings work a bit differently. The steel tube in the center isn't bonded to the bushing material, but it is lubricated. When the control arm moves, the bushing material rotates around the steel tube. This means you lose the springing effect of the rubber. The stiffer material also allows less deflection, keeping the suspension geometry consistent even under high cornering loads, so the car feels more precise. However, you also get more harshness through the suspension. They also have to be kept lubricated.

That's a short tour of all the components of the suspension. Now, what do we do with them?

A polyurethane bushing set for a Miata from Energy Suspension. Each stock bushing is replaced by two of the black inserts and a gold tube. The required lubricant isn't shown.

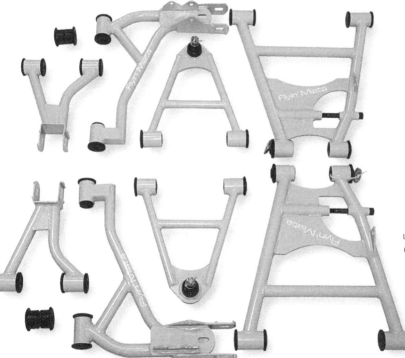

These tubular control arms are a set from V8 Roadsters that replace the factory arms. They remove about 3 pounds of unsprung weight from each corner of the car as well as provide extra strength. They add some extra adjustability to the camber through a slotted mount for the lower ball joint. They're not cheap, but they're part of the ultimate race Miata.

Chapter 9
Suspension Tuning

The suspension is the area of the car where small changes can have the biggest effects. In other words, the bang-for-the-buck factor is pretty good. An inexpensive set of springs, a sway bar change, or even a different alignment can make a difference in how the car rides, corners, or behaves in a straight line. This difference can be an improvement, or it can be a step backward.

Now that we've covered the theory, how do you begin to set everything up? There are a huge number of adjustments and alterations you can make. Let's start with the most common upgrades and work from there. Keep in mind that most of these factors are interrelated, so there are a number of ways of reaching a particular handling goal. Because they are all related, it's likely that a change in one area will send you back to something you've already adjusted. I'll try to separate them out for you.

An important thing to keep in mind is that your intended use is going to have a big effect on the perfect setup. Transitional behavior is important in autocross, as the car is almost never settled down. Because you're in a lower gear, you'll have more trouble putting down power than the same car on a high-speed circuit. Autocross courses tend to be fairly smooth as well, and if there are any bumps, they'll be sharp ones that test high-speed damping. Track driving requires more high-speed stability, more throttle steering and more time (generally speaking) in a stable condition as opposed to a transient one. Street driving tends to be more similar to track driving, but with a much greater emphasis on the ability of the suspension to absorb bumps of all kinds. A car that's intended to do everything will need a setup that's either adjustable or a compromise of attributes.

SPRING RATE

The spring rate determines a lot about how the car rides and handles. The quality of the ride is fairly easy to understand: a stiffer spring means the wheel will deflect less for a given bump, transmitting more shock to the body. Also, the mass of the body will be better controlled when the car turns, brakes, or accelerates, leading to faster reflexes and less body movement. But there's more to it than that.

Remember the effects of roll stiffness? Roll stiffness comes from the spring rate and the sway bars, and we can use it to tune the handling of the car. The stiffer the springs, the higher the roll stiffness. By playing with the ratio of roll stiffness front and rear, we can shuffle our weight transfer between the front and rear of the car. Remember that when weight is transferred between a pair of wheels, there is an overall loss of traction over that pair. So more weight transfer at one end of the car means less grip at that end.

Also, let's look at the speed at which the weight transfer is affected by the roll stiffness. The more the car resists roll, the faster the weight is transferred. Quick weight transfer makes a car more agile, but too fast can make it twitchy.

Because the sway bars also affect the roll stiffness (in fact, that's exactly what they're designed to do), they also have to be taken into consideration. And here we get into one of the big questions: How much of the roll stiffness should come from the springs and how much should come from the sway bars?

Good question, and there's no simple answer. There's almost a philosophical divide between the "big bars, soft springs" and "soft bars, stiff spring" camps. Naturally, the ideal comes in the middle. You need enough spring rate to keep the car off the bumpstops as much as possible but enough compliance to let the car absorb pavement imperfections.

The intended use of the car comes into play as well. A track-only car will run much stiffer springs than one intended to be used on the street, as it doesn't have to deal with pavement that's as badly battered. Controlling the dive and squat under braking and acceleration becomes more important, as does the speed of the weight transfer. Generally, it's easier to choose your spring rates first and then get sway bars to suit. Most aftermarket sway bars can be adjusted, so it's easy to fine-tune the balance of the car quickly and easily with the sways.

Again, it's important to keep in mind that we can't really affect the total amount of weight transfer by messing with roll stiffness. We can only move it around. If we decrease the weight transfer on the rear wheels, we'll increase it by the same amount on the front. In other words, if we install stiff springs at the front and relatively soft ones at the rear, we'll make the car more prone to understeer (or less prone to oversteer, as it's the same thing). So we can use the spring rates to not only affect the ride, but also the fundamental handling balance of the car.

Generally speaking, NA and NB Miatas seem to prefer springs in approximately a 3:2 ratio. In other words, the rear spring rate should be about two-thirds of the front. A popular high-performance streetable track setup for an NA or NB would be 450 inch-pounds front and 300 inch-pounds rear. A more street-biased setup would be 300 and 200. The NC wants a ratio closer to 4:3. Sway bars can be used to fine-tune the balance from there. Remember that too stiff doesn't just mean a poor ride, it can also mean the wheels can't keep in contact with the ground.

Because this is all fairly straightforward physics, it is possible to calculate what effect the spring and roll bar rates will have on the car's balance if you know the geometry of the suspension. Various online calculators allow you to do this, such as the one found at Fat Cat Motorsport's website. It's important to remember that the springs and roll bars are not the only factors in the car's handling balance. Alignment, ride height, tire pressures, and tire types will all play a part. The shocks will also have a huge effect on what spring rates can be used effectively. Still, you can get a good idea of what specific changes will do if nothing else is altered.

FREQUENCY

One way to get an idea of how stiff your springs should be is to play with the bounce or natural frequency. This refers to how quickly the suspension would bounce up and down without a shock installed to damp the movement. It turns out that we can use this frequency to get in the ballpark of spring rates. Performance street Miatas generally go for a frequency around 1.5 to 2.0 Hertz (Hz, or cycles per second), while track Miatas will run from 2.0 to 2.5 Hertz. Stock Miatas are in the 1.1- to 1.3-Hertz range. The bounce frequency is not affected by sway bars, so it's possible to use springs to obtain the frequency you want and then use sway bars to adjust the roll stiffness.

In order to get the bounce frequency, you're going to need to know your corner weights and your unsprung weight. This means you'll have to pull off your wheels, tires, brakes, and control arms to weigh them. Once you have all your weights, plug them into this formula:

$$3.13 \times \sqrt{\frac{\text{Wheel Rate}}{\text{Corner Weight} - \text{Unspring Weight}}}$$

SHOCKS

Just as important as the spring rates are the shocks. A good set of shocks can make a stiff spring useable on the street, and poor shocks will let down the whole car. The most popular way to select shocks is by recommendation or experience. Ask other owners or try as many cars as you can. One word of warning, though, you can't really take experience from one type of car and apply it to another. One brand might work well on a Toyota, but the valving on the Miata version could be all wrong. Even across different generations of Miata, you'll find some shocks work well on some platforms and poorly on others. Selecting an adjustable shock improves the odds that you'll end up with something that works well, but it's no guarantee.

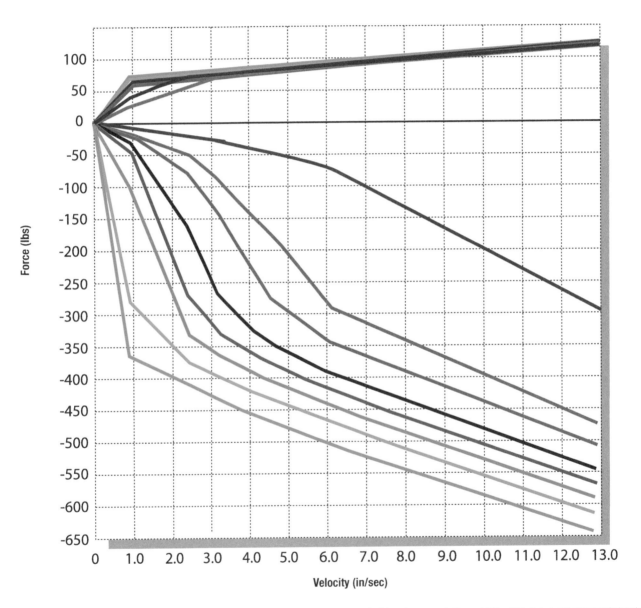

A more scientific method is to use a shock dyno such as this one from AFCO. These generate a graph of damping versus shaft speed. This will illustrate exactly how much damping the shock has through the full range of shaft speeds. Remember, low-speed damping is going to affect roll, while high-speed damping is involved with bumps. The higher the force for a given velocity, the "stiffer" the shock will be and the more it will resist movement. The curve above the 0 line is compression. In this case, the adjustments only affect the low-speed damping, so it's good for adjusting handling. The lines below 0 are rebound, and they vary both the high-speed and low-speed damping because spring control is primarily done with rebound. These particular shocks have an usually wide adjustment range and can handle a wide range of spring rates, up to around 750 inch-pounds.

SETUP

Once you've installed adjustable shocks, how do you set them up? The most important thing is that they need to be set stiff enough to control your springs. I prefer to start with the shocks too soft and then stiffen them until the body is well controlled. If you have the ability to adjust compression and rebound damping separately, then concentrate on the rebound for spring control. If you go too stiff, the ride will suffer and the wheels will have trouble keeping contact with the pavement. Too soft, and it will float around.

Shock damping has no effect by the time the car has settled into a turn, but it can have a big effect on transient behavior. The shock damping can control the speed of the weight transfer. Contrary to what you might think, a softer shock will speed up weight transfer, and a stiffer one will slow it down. You can almost treat them as temporary sway bars. If your car is understeering on corner entry, then stiffening the front and softening the rear will cause the weight transfer to happen faster at the rear of the car, decreasing the tendency to understeer. It will also have the same effect on corner exit, of course.

With most commercially available consumer grade shocks—the Konis, KYBs, Tokicos, and Bilsteins that make up the bulk of the market—you don't have the ability to adjust compression and rebound separately. If you do, you can play with those to adjust the balance, using the rebound damping to adjust the speed of weight transfer when that wheel is unloading and compression to affect the speed when that corner of the car is getting loaded up.

SWAY BAR SETUP

Because sway bars are relatively inexpensive, easy to install, and don't have a lot of downsides, they're often the best place to start for suspension alteration. The correct size bar will depend on a number of factors: your spring rates, your desired handling balance, how you want to use the car, and so on. The springs and sways in particular are intertwined, as they're the two contributors to roll stiffness and thus your handling balance. Some people prefer to set up the car with a much larger front bar than stock and little or no rear bar, adding some more roll stiffness to the rear with spring rates. The idea here is that the more independent movement of the rear wheels leads itself to better traction out of a corner, which is particularly important to autocrossers and drivers with high-powered cars. However, too much front stiffness relative to the rear (the FRC percentage mentioned in Chapter 7) will make the car less likely to turn in and dead-feeling, never mind prone to understeer. You can compensate for this by

SPRING PRELOAD

Spring preload refers to how much the spring is compressed when the shock is fully extended. On a stock Miata, there's a fair bit of preload, which means you need a spring compressor to remove and install the spring. On some coil-over kits, the spring will be loose at full droop, allowing it to rattle around. This is something to avoid if at all possible, because once the spring is unloaded there's nothing to extend the shock other than the weight of the wheel. This basically means that there's no more suspension travel once the spring has unloaded.

When adjusting the ride height using a coil-over setup with adjustable perches, you're essentially adjusting the amount of spring preload. When the car is at rest, it is compressing the spring. To pick some numbers, let's say that we have a Miata that puts a load of 400 pounds on each front spring when it's sitting still, and we're using 7-inch long springs with a 400 inch-pound spring rate. The springs are adjusted so that they're not loose at full droop, but they're not preloaded. At full extension, there is exactly 7 inches between the upper and lower spring perches. It's fairly easy to see that the spring will compress 1 inch from full droop, with a loaded length of 6 inches.

Now, we preload the spring by moving the spring perch up 1/4 inch, compressing the spring from 7 to 6 3/4 inches. That's a 100-pound preload. In other words, the spring is pushing against the suspension with 100 pounds of force. You'll have to put 101 pounds of weight on the spring before it will compress any more. But when the car's weight is added, the 400 pounds of weight on the spring will still compress the spring down to 6 inches at ride height. *The spring's length at ride height will not change, despite the amount of preload.* Because the spring was already compressed by 1/4 inch, that means the spring and shock assembly will only get 3/4 inch shorter and the car will sit higher than it did before we moved that spring perch up. The only thing our preload has done is lift the car.

There is an exception, of course. If we move that spring perch up by another 1 inch, our spring is now only 5 3/4 inches long at full droop and has 500 pounds of preload. It will take 500 pounds on the spring before it's ready to start moving any farther. But the car's only putting 400 pounds on the spring, so it's not going to compress at ride height. We'd have to hit a bump that put 101 pounds of force into the spring before the suspension can move at all, and because the suspension is fully extended at ride height, the wheel can't drop down at all if there's a hole in the road. This is obviously not good. The only time I've seen this happen was with a racing suspension design that was far too low for any other use, and the owner was trying to get the car up high enough to drive it on the road.

Some coil-over setups allow the length of the shock body to be adjusted. That separates the spring preload from the ride height adjustment. If you read the marketing for these coil-overs, you'll be led to believe that this means a better ride and more adjustment to the handling, but that's not true unless you've put a ridiculous amount of preload into your springs. The main reason the shock body lengths are adjustable is because this kind of construction allows a universal shock body to be used with Miata-specific end pieces screwed on. That's good because it keeps costs down, but it's not going to give you a handling or ride advantage.

running stiffer rear springs, but if you go too far that way, you'll start to have trouble putting the power down as well.

Other drivers prefer a matched set of bars, closer to the factory's ratio but stiffer overall. This keeps the balance the same without going to stiffer rear springs. Because sway bars are easier to change, less expensive, and more adjustable than springs, this is often where the tuning is done.

Once you have a set of sway bars chosen and installed, they can often be adjusted to fine-tune the balance of the car. It's easy to do and free, so I strongly recommend experimenting with it. The holes near the end of the bar are the softest settings, and the holes nearest the bend in the bar are the stiffest. This bar is on the stiffer of two settings.

Large sway bars and high cornering forces can put some high loads through the sway bar mounting points, particularly in the front. This can rip the mounts right off the car. The front mounts of the NB in particular are at risk. If you're running a front bar larger than 1 inch in the front, some sort of reinforced mount like this one from Mazda Motorsports is a good idea.

The primary purpose of adjustable end links like these is to avoid preload in the sway bar. In fact, you can get away with a single adjustable link per bar in most cases. Put the car on the ground, attach one link, and adjust the length of the other so that the bolts slip easily into the end of the bar without any tension.

ORDER OF OPERATIONS

If you're starting from scratch, what's the best way to go? The first thing to do is to fix any problems. If you have a set of worn-out shocks or mismatched no-name tires, deal with them first. If everything is healthy, start with the items that have the biggest effect and smallest downsides: the setup of the components you have. A good alignment and well-chosen tire pressures will benefit any car. Once that's done and you want to move past the limitations of your current hardware, I'd recommend starting with a set of sway bars. They're inexpensive, easy to install and adjust, and have little effect on the ride.

Next depends on what your goal is: more fun or more fast? If simple speed is critical, put on some good tires. This could arguably come before sway bars, but you'll mostly get more grip and better response out of this. If the car is understeering or flopping around on the suspension, they won't help. If your goal is more fun as well as improved speed, look at springs and shocks. Running different springs on stock shocks isn't a good plan, as they'll usually be too stiff for the shock's valving.

As mentioned in Chapter 8, coil-overs give you the ability to choose a spring rate and to adjust ride height and corner-weight the car. If you're interested in taking advantage of these capabilities, then definitely step up to a coil-over setup. If not, the extra money could be spent elsewhere. It's important to evaluate the shock and spring combination carefully independently of the fact that they're coil-overs. There are some fully threaded coil-over setups that aren't as effective as a set of slip-on sleeves over a standard adjustable shock due to poorly chosen valving.

The stiffer your spring rates are, the more important chassis rigidity becomes. There's more on that in Chapter 12. As a nice side benefit, a stiff structure actually makes the car ride better.

The Sport suspension on the 2006–08 NC is not very effective. A tall ride height and poorly valved Bilstein shocks make it prone to massive body movement and sloppy handling. A new set of shocks should be first on the list for these cars.

INTERCHANGE

All of the suspension improvements that Mazda added to the NB can be retrofitted to the NA. The most popular and simplest is to replace the front and rear upper shock mount from the NA with those from the NB. This lowers the car by approximately 1/2 inch and allows for some extra compression travel. Along with the new mounts—available straight from Mazda—you'll need bushings of some sort along with washers. A good DIY option is to use sway bar end link bushings such as the Energy Suspension 9.8105 set or purpose-built ones such as those from Fat Cat Motorsports. If you use the sway bar bushings or Mazda factory bushings, you'll need to cut them in half in order to make them thin enough. Otherwise you won't have any threads left on the shock shaft.

Remember that because this drops your ride height, you may end up too low if you already have aftermarket springs on the car.

You can also swap the complete spring/shock/upper mount assembly. Just use all NB parts, including the bushings. This won't lower the car. Due to the different motion ratio of the NA, it may sit slightly higher than an NB would with the same suspension. If you're buying new springs and shocks, this is an excellent and easy option. You can't mix and match NB and NA springs and shocks though. The NA spring has a closed coil at the end while an NB has an open coil, and the perches on the shocks are designed to match.

If you really want to go to town, the complete subframes can be swapped out. The NB units bolt right in place of the NA. In the front, this will get you a stronger steering rack mount and improved geometry. The control arms are built to the same dimensions, but the mounting points for the lowers are moved forward slightly. The steering arms on the uprights are also slightly higher for improved bump steer. If you change the front subframe, you will also have to use an NB steering rack.

The subframe and mounting points are the same in the rear, so there's no real reason to change it. However, the uprights in the rear give another 5-millimeter of track on each side if you want a slightly wider stance. It's not a dramatic change, but every little bit can help. Or hurt, if you're trying to stuff fat tires under the fenders.

At the time of writing, there wasn't much information available about exactly what changes had been made to the 2009 NC. The press releases talk about improvements, but details are not yet available. Sorry.

ADJUSTING IT ALL
Ride Height

What effect does ride height have on the handling? First, the CG height is directly related to ride height. You may remember that one of the factors affecting total weight transfer is CG height, and that weight transfer costs us overall grip. So lowering the car can cut down on our weight transfer and thus improve grip.

But also related to ride height is suspension travel. All else being kept equal, lowering a car will decrease the amount of travel in compression and increase it in droop. Droop travel is important, but not as important as compression when it comes to keeping the car composed over rough roads. So when you lower a car, you need to either increase the suspension travel or increase the spring rate to keep the car off the bumpstops as much as possible.

Lowering the car at one end can also affect its handling balance. The lower end will have less weight transfer and thus a higher amount of grip. So if you've got a car that oversteers, dropping the back down a bit can help bring the tail in line,

Mazda and many enthusiasts measure ride height from the center of the wheel to the bottom of the fender lip. It seems like a bit of an odd dimension, but it does have the advantage of not being affected by tire diameter or inflation. That makes it easy to compare from car to car. A good ride height for a street-driven performance NA or NB is around 12.5 inches in the front and 13 inches in the rear, while the NC works well at around 14 inches front and rear. Much lower than that, and there won't be much suspension travel left to deal with bumps. The longer measurement in the rear is simply a result of the shape of the body, the car does end up level.

as long as it's oversteering because of weight transfer. If it's oversteering because the outside rear corner is sitting on the bumpstop, leading to a high spring rate, then the lower ride height might hurt as much as it helps.

Ride height is also tied in to spring rate. The lower you run your car, the more spring rate you need to have in order to keep the car off the bumpstops most of the time. A spring that's too soft, dropping the car on to the stops frequently, will perform badly and ride badly. It might seem counter-intuitive, but going to a stiffer spring will help the ride quality in this case.

A note about "lowering springs." It's common for companies to state how much their springs will lower the car. The problem is that they can't actually know this without knowing how high the car sits beforehand. The final ride height will depend on the spring, assuming everything else is left stock. But the ride height of the Miata varied dramatically over the years. A 1990 could sit quite a bit lower than a 1997, and in the factory manual Mazda gives a 2-inch range of acceptable heights even over a given model year. Add to that the fact that a couple of decades could have passed since the car left the factory, and you'll understand how it's impossible to say how much a given spring will drop the car if all you know is the final ride height. Ask the spring manufacturer what the final ride height will be, then go measure your car to compare.

ALIGNMENT

The alignment of your tires can have a big effect on handling. Your Miata's tires are the only contact it has with the ground, so having them all pointed in different directions is obviously going to have an effect on how the car works. The Miata's

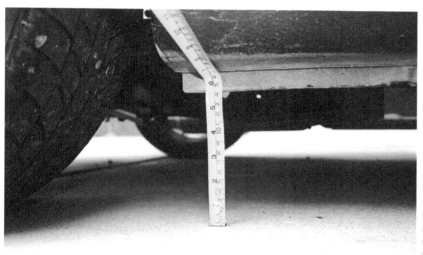

Spec Miata racers tend to measure ride height from the seam along the base of the car. It's much easier to measure accurately than the one to the fender, but it's also affected by the tires. Because all Spec Miata racers run the same tires and within a couple of pounds of the same tire pressure, that's not a problem for them. The recommended ride height for them tends to be around 4 5/8 inches front and rear at lowest. If you want to convert from one to the other, add approximately 7 1/8 inches to the front measurement and 7 5/8 inches to the rear to get the wheel-to-fender distance. Keep in mind that an over- or under-sized wheel/tire combination will change this number. Due to their high spring rates and track-only use, they sit lower than the street car in the picture. This car is sitting right at 5 1/2 inches by this measurement. It's running on 205/40-17 tires that are just a bit taller than the 205/50-15 ones used by Spec racers, so the measurement to the seam will be a bit higher even with the exact same suspension setup.

The Miata, unlike a lot of other production cars, has a large amount of alignment adjustment built in. Cams like this one are used to adjust the position of the wheels, and they need to be torqued down tight afterward to prevent slipping.

suspension design is very adjustable for alignment, which is great news for us. But how to adjust it properly? First, let's look at what's involved.

Camber is the most obvious one. You can see it. It refers to the angle of the tire relative to the ground. If you squat down and look at the rear of your Miata, you'll see the rear tires are leaning inward. They're closer together at the top than at the bottom. That's negative camber. If they were leaning outward, that would be positive camber. It's measured in degrees. Generally speaking, more negative camber means more cornering grip, especially with R compound tires. But as the tires move away from 0 camber (straight up and down), you start to lose traction under braking and acceleration, so

going too far can cause problems particularly in very high-power cars.

It's important to remember if you're discussing camber relative to the road or to the chassis. When the car's sitting level, it's the same thing. But as soon as the car starts to roll in a corner, this will make the camber of the outside tire more positive and the inside tire more negative relative to the ground, and it's the ground the tires are interested in. Suspension geometry design takes this into account by increasing negative camber as the suspension compresses.

Next is toe. Viewed from above, if the front of the tires are closer together than the rear, the car has positive toe or toe-in. If they're farther apart at the front, that's negative

Negative camber.

A stock 2006 on the track. There's quite a bit going on here (lots of roll for one), but check out the angle of the wheels against the ground. They have positive camber, and the car's not gripping well at all.

A stark contrast from the NC, this NB is cornering happily. It's not just the ride height and the lack of roll, note the camber in the wheels. The tires are much better planted, and the car was generating enough grip to strain the driver's neck.

toe or toe-out. Toe can be measured in fractions of an inch, millimeters, or degrees. A tire with any significant amount of toe is literally being dragged across the pavement as you drive, leading to extremely rapid tire wear. Generally speaking, toe-out will make the car more eager to change direction while toe-in will make it more stable. Toe-out in the rear of the car leads to a lot of oversteer.

Caster is a little more complex to visualize. With positive caster, the steering axis leans back. The fact that the pivot point (where the steering axis meets the ground) is ahead of the contact patch means that the wheel self-centers and tries to go straight. Shopping carts work the same way, their pivot point is well ahead of the wheelwell. That's the theory, although we

all know that this isn't always true when it comes to shopping carts. The more positive caster you have, the more the car will want to go straight. Great for stability, not so good for nimble handling. As an added bonus, a car with positive caster will also gain some camber as the wheel is turned. The more caster you have, the more camber you gain. Still, of all the alignment settings, your Miata is least sensitive to caster settings.

So what's the perfect alignment? That depends on what you're doing. Street cars tend to run a slightly different setup than track cars do. For years, Miata owners ran a setup that used about 0.5 degrees more negative camber in the rear than in the front. The Miata's suspension adjustment range works well for this, and it does give a good balance.

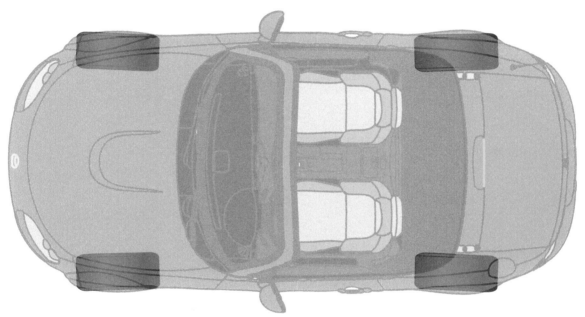

This car has toe-out in the front and toe-in on the rear wheels. With this much toe, the tires would probably only last a few hundred miles at best.

Front toe can have a big effect on the car's responsiveness. It's also the easiest of all alignment settings to adjust, as it doesn't affect any of the others. You adjust it by screwing the tie rods in and out. Just be sure to adjust both sides equally or you'll find your steering wheel will be off-center. It's not unknown for autocrossers to increase the amount of front toe out on the weekend for competition, then set it back again for weekday driving. If you keep track of the number of turns you make on the tie rod, this is a fairly quick and easy adjustment to make.

An easy way to measure toe is with a set of toe plates. They're nothing more than a pair of flat sheets of wood or metal with slots cut in them. Put one plate against each front wheel. Hook tape measures to the slots in one plate, and then compare the measurement on the other one. Depending on the location of the slots, the numbers might not match those from other alignment techniques, but they'll be in the ballpark. More important, they'll be consistent, so you can experiment with what works.

Spec Miatas, which are required by the rules to run stiff front springs and can have low ride heights, tend to run more front camber than rear in order to get the handling sorted out. A number of other high-power track Miatas are using a similar setup to help put the power down. Because the rear tires are flatter against the track, they'll be able to transfer more torque. Stability is also less of a concern, so they'll run less toe. Autocrossers and track cars running on race tires tend to run as much camber as is physically possible, especially in the front. Race tires like lots of camber, and it helps the car turn in aggressively around the cones.

COMMON ALIGNMENT SETTINGS

	Front camber	Front caster	Front toe	Rear camber	Rear toe
Street	-1.0	+4.5	1/16 in	-1.5	1/16 in
Spec Miata	0.-3.0	+4	0	-2.5	0

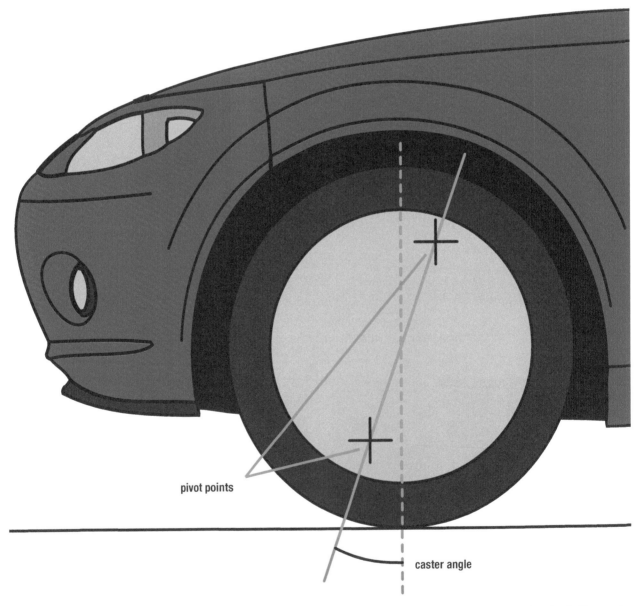

pivot points

caster angle

If you draw a line between both of the pivot points of the front wheel, that's your steering axis. The difference between the angle of your steering axis and vertical is your caster angle, and in this case it's positive caster. You can adjust it by moving one or both of the pivot points forward or back.

CORNER WEIGHTING

Corner weighting or corner balancing refers to adjusting the suspension so that the car is well balanced across all four wheels. By adjusting the perch height or shock length on each corner, the weight distribution can be changed. It's similar to adjusting the length of legs on a four-legged table so that it sits flat instead of rocking back and forth. Some sort of coil-over suspension is required.

It's important to note that you can't change the front/rear or left/right weight distribution with corner weighting. Remember our four-legged table? When one leg is too short, it rocks diagonally. Our weight transfers the same way. If we raise one corner of the car (making the table leg longer), it will support more of the weight of the car, and so will its counterpart diagonally opposite. The other two corners will then have less weight to split between them. The only way to move weight front to back or side to side is to physically move stuff inside the car.

In order to corner-weight a car, you'll need a set of scales. If you can find bathroom scales that can handle 600 pounds, great. If not, you'll need a set of corner-weight scales. They need to be on a flat and level surface. Check this: You might have to shim them. Once you've got those, you need to prepare the car for its weighing session. Start by setting your tire pressures and filling or draining the fuel tank to your preferred level. Install the driver and (if required) passenger. Basically, set the car up in your ideal condition. Disconnect your sway bars and set your shocks to full soft.

Now, get the car's stance set the way you want it by setting the ride height. Make sure it's level side-to-side with the occupant(s) on board. It's time to roll onto the scales.

The scales will give you the weights of each corner. The front and rear and left or right numbers are interesting, but you can't do anything about them by simply adjusting the shocks. If you want to play with moving things around, now's the time to do it.

The numbers we're really interested in are the sums of the diagonals. We want them to be as close as possible. The corners that make up the heavy diagonal need to be lowered while the other two need to be raised. Again, think of your table legs. The long ones are the ones that are going to carry the weight. If you adjust all four corners by the same amount, the car will continue to sit flat and level. If you adjust one or two, the weight will still move around the same way, but the car will end up crooked. This is important. After you adjust all four corners, bounce the car or roll it back and forth to make sure there's no binding in the suspension.

Keep notes of what you're doing, as it's easy to get mixed up and forget which corner is supposed to be going up and which is going down. I'll usually write a +1 and -1 on my notes for the various corners to remind me which corners are going up by a turn and which are going down. As you get close to a perfectly balanced car, you'll be dealing with fractions of a turn.

664	620
624	653

total: 2561 lbs
LR+RF: 1244 lbs
RR+LF: 1317 lbs

cross % (LR+RF): 48.5%
front: 50.1%
right: 49.7%

	-1	+1
	+1	-1

638	646
647	630

total: 2561 lbs
LR+RF: 1293 lbs
RR+LF: 1268 lbs

cross: 50.5%
front: 50.1%
right: 49.8%

A nice corner-weight rig. All four wheels are sitting on scales that have been perfectly leveled. The ramps allow the car to be driven on easily.

Here's an example of a corner-weight session. The cross is a great way to lay out the weights; the arrow points to the front of the car, and it's easy to sketch and understand. The right front corner is referred to as RF, the left front as LF, the right rear as RR, and I'll let you figure out what the left rear is. The RF weight goes in the upper right corner, LF in the upper left, and so on. If I'm going to make a change, I'll make a note on a similar cross showing what I plan to do: +1/3 means move the perch on that corner up by one third of a turn; -1 means I lower it by a full turn. You can see the result of the first adjustment. The car's now within 0.5 percent of a perfect corner-weight. It's not always this quick of course, and you can expect some back and forth as you zero in on the correct setting. This car is a rally car being weighed full of tools and with two people on board, thus the fairly even side-to-side weights. You'll almost always find the RR to be light in a left-hand-drive Miata. It's no coincidence this is where Mazda put the battery and the spare tire in the NA.

Because the wheels move slightly sideways as the suspension moves through its travel, using a jack to lift up the car so that you can adjust the suspension means you can end up with a side load on the wheels when you drop it back down. You can roll the car back and forth to settle the wheels. A simple way to let the wheels slide is to put a bit of oil inside a garbage bag to create a liquid bearing of sorts.

Once you're done with the balancing, adjust the sway bar end links, lock your adjusters on the shocks into place, stiffen up their adjustments to your desired settings and you're done.

TESTING TECHNIQUES

Skid pad testing will tell you a lot about a car's behavior and is a nice driver-training aid to boot. All you need is a large piece of pavement. It will help if you set up four or more cones to mark out your circle. Get the largest diameter you can with enough room to run off if the car spins or understeers. It's a good idea to have permission from the owner of the pavement. Keep in mind that the car will handle differently with a full versus empty tank of fuel and with one versus two people on board. Do your testing with the car in the condition in which you want it to be ideal. If that means just the driver and a gallon of gas, do your testing that way.

Start off by circling the pad and increasing your speed until the car's at the limit of grip. Try to keep the throttle steady. This should put the car into a steady-state condition, which takes the shock absorbers out of the handling equation. Does the car oversteer or understeer? The driver can have a big effect on the car's balance, as this is a great way to learn how to throttle steer and to play with weight transfer. But that's not what we're trying to do here. Based on the behavior of the car, adjust it to get the balance you want. Feel free to make big adjustments first and to do things that are wrong. It's how you learn and why you're testing in a controlled environment.

You can also do this sort of testing on a track if you have a big sweeper to play with. The important thing is that the car is settled into the corner, so you can get the steady-state cornering balance sorted out before you start to chase the transient behavior.

One thing to remember when adjusting handling is to try to improve traction on the end that's loose instead of cutting down traction on the end that isn't. For example, if the car

Steady-state cornering such as this large-radius 180-degree corner on an autocross course is useful for setting up the basic handling balance of the car.

is understeering, work on getting the front to stick better instead of making the rear stick less. This is unavoidable with some suspension changes, of course, but keep this in mind when playing with settings that only affect one end of the car such as tire pressures or camber. Also keep in mind that driving style will have some effect. By working on a skid pad, we're trying to isolate that somewhat.

Grab a helper and something with which to measure tire temperatures. Best is a proper tire pyrometer that actually sticks into the rubber and measures the temperature of the carcass, but an inexpensive handheld infrared thermometer is better than nothing. After doing several laps of your skid pad to get the tires up to full temperature, come to a stop and have your helper immediately check the tire temperatures at the middle of the tire and the two edges. You'd be amazed at how fast the tires cool off. We're primarily interested in the two outside tires. What we'd prefer to see would be an even temperature across the tread.

If the car has too much negative camber, you'll see a hot inside edge and a temperature that tapers off as you move to the outside. Too little negative camber will heat up the outside edge. Too much tire pressure will cause the tire to swell in the middle, heating it up and leaving the edges cool. Too little, and your edges will be hot with a cooler center. This isn't a foolproof way to set up handling, but it's a good way to get in the ballpark.

QUICK FIXES

	Understeer	Oversteer
Corner entry (transition)	Increase front shock compression	Decrease front shock compression
	Decrease rear shock rebound	Increase rear shock rebound
Mid-corner (stable)	Stiffen rear sway bar	Soften rear sway bar
	Soften front sway bar	Stiffen front sway bar
	Increase rear spring rate	Decrease rear spring rate
	Decrease front spring rate	Increase front spring rate
	Raise rear ride height	Lower rear ride height
	Lower front ride height	Raise rear ride height
	Increase front camber	Increase rear camber
	Decrease front toe-in	Increase front toe-in
	Increase rear toe-in (careful with this one)	Decrease rear toe-in
Corner exit (transition)	Increase front shock rebound	Decrease front shock rebound
	Increase rear shock compression	Decrease rear shock compression

TABLE OF TIRE TEMPERATURES

	Inside	Middle	Outside
Needs more negative camber	180	190	200
Needs less negative camber	200	190	180
Needs more air pressure	210	190	210
Needs less air pressure	190	210	190
Perfect (and almost unattainable)	200	200	200

Here are some imaginary numbers and what they mean.

Okay, we have our steady-state behavior set up. Now what about transitions? They're a lot more difficult to test consistently, but there are a few tricks you can use. Back to the skid pad. Take note of what your speed is for the steady-state testing. Now approach the skid pad in a straight line going that speed and turn in to join the pad with a steady throttle. Again, the driver can have quite an effect here, so try to be smooth and consistent. How does the car behave?

You will probably find that you'll need to adjust the car for maximum performance on a given track or autocross course, and the ultimate guide should be the stopwatch in that case. However, once you've learned just how your car reacts to various changes—and more important, what needs to be done to achieve various changes—you'll be able to zero in on your perfect setup quickly.

Chapter 10
The Braking System

Brakes are important. After all, they're what you resort to when something else has gone wrong. One of the best ways to make a car faster is to make it go slow faster. The faster you can make your car go slow, the longer you can spend going fast before you have to start to make it go slow. Got it? Read it again, it did make sense.

First, how can you tell if you need to upgrade your brakes? Well, there are two aspects to braking performance: resistance to fade and the maximum stopping power. Brake fade is when your brakes start to lose their effectiveness due to heat. The pedal can go soft, so you can't apply enough pressure to slow the car, or the pads will overheat (and get smelly!) and the car won't stop no matter how much pressure you put on the pedal. Obviously, both of these are a bad thing. Unless you are coming down a long mountain pass, they really shouldn't be a problem on the street unless something is wrong with your braking system. The track is a different matter, of course.

The maximum stopping power is easy to understand. How well do your brakes work in a single stop? Even on the street, you can benefit from a shorter stopping distance.

Now, the theory. Books have been written about how brake systems work, but this will be an overview to give you the basics. First off, your maximum braking is determined by the traction of your tires. It's that simple. No matter what

you do to the braking system, you cannot break through the limits created by the tires. But a brake system can fail to take full advantage of the tires, either by how the braking forces are distributed or by not being able to apply enough braking torque to reach the tires' limits.

When you apply the brakes in a Miata, you're squeezing two pads onto an iron rotor at each wheel. The friction of the pads against the rotor is what provides the force to slow down the car, and the harder you press those pads into the iron, the more friction they provide. So far, this is pretty easy to understand. It's the same basic concept as a set of brakes on most bicycles.

Even on a light car like a Miata, brakes can make a big difference to performance. A big brake kit like this might be a bit of overkill for street driving for many people, but if you need the extra heat capacity and brake torque, it may be the only solution.

A peek at the brake pads with the caliper removed. The shiny black is the rotor, and the two dark gray pieces are the pads. The big U-shaped springs are there to pull the pads away from the rotor slightly when you're not using the brakes but mostly to keep them from rattling around.

But we know that the energy being absorbed by the braking system has to show up somewhere. The brakes get hot. In physics terms, you're converting kinetic energy into thermal energy. Actually, you can simplify the job of the brakes right down to this explanation. It's all about converting kinetic energy and generating (and absorbing and shedding) heat. The amount of kinetic energy involved determines just how quickly a car can decelerate. If the brakes get too hot, they'll "fade" or lose the ability to slow the car down.

Kinetic energy is a function of the mass of the car times the square of the speed. That's important. Doubling the mass of the car will double the amount of kinetic energy, and thus the amount of distance it takes to stop the car. That's easy enough to understand. But as your speeds go up, your stopping distances go up much faster. Doubling the speed means four times the kinetic energy, and thus you need four times as much room to stop. It takes twice as much distance to stop from 71 miles per hour as it does from 50, due to the increase in kinetic energy involved.

This illustrates why good brakes become even more important as you modify your Miata for greater performance. An increase in horsepower, and thus speed, means a much bigger job for the brakes.

BRAKE TORQUE

Brake torque refers to how much the braking system resists the rotation of the wheel. The higher the amount of brake torque, the more braking force will be generated by that wheel. Once the brake torque is higher than the available traction, the wheel locks up. Brake torque is related to the pressure forcing the pads onto the rotor, the friction coefficient of the pads, and the diameter of the rotor.

COMPONENTS

To discuss the braking system, we need to identify all of the parts involved. Let's start where it all begins, at the pedal. The driver presses on the pedal with a certain amount of force, indicating he or she needs the car to slow down. The pedal acts as a lever that multiplies the force and applies it to the master cylinder via the brake booster. The booster multiplies this force fairly dramatically. The master cylinder uses a piston to pressurize hydraulic fluid that is distributed to all four wheels.

At the wheels, the pressurized fluid pushes on pistons in the calipers. Due to the relative sizes of the pistons in the master cylinder and the calipers, the pressure is increased again. The pistons, in turn, press the pads against the rotors, and the friction slows the spinning rotor. There are a number of variables in the system that can be juggled to affect how it works, but that's the fundamental system. We'll look at what components make the biggest difference to braking performance later.

ABS

In order to stop the car as quickly as possible, all four wheels need to be right on the edge of locking up. As we discussed in Chapter 7, a tire provides far more grip when it's rolling or slipping very slightly than it does when it's sliding. An expert driver can modulate the amount of pressure on the brake pedal to maintain the wheels right at that point. On a consistent surface in a straight line, this is challenging, but not impossible. However, throw some uneven traction (such as sand on the road or a puddle), a curve, or a bump into the mix, and you'll find that one wheel will want to lock before the others. The driver is forced to let off the pedal pressure to keep that one wheel from locking. The total braking capability is only as good as the wheel with the worst traction.

ABS adds an extra bit of complication into the brake system to address this. All of the brake lines go through an ABS unit, which is a collection of high-speed valves controlled by a computer. Sensors on each wheel monitor how fast they're spinning. If one of them starts moving much slower than the others, the ABS computer assumes that this wheel is starting to lock and will release some of the pressure to that wheel while maintaining pressure on the others. This means that every wheel will get as much braking torque as it can handle, allowing wheels with lots of traction to provide lots of braking power while the wheels with low traction are prevented from locking up. You can feel the pulsing of the valves through the brake pedal if you've managed to activate the ABS. All the driver has to do is stomp on the brake pedal and steer.

Whoops! Locked wheels don't steer, and they don't stop the car as quickly as rolling wheels do on the racetrack. This might look dramatic, but the driver would go faster and keep more control if he was able to keep the wheels from locking.

The ABS pump is found on the passenger's side of the engine bay, near the firewall. Because this is a three-channel system on a 1995 Miata, there are two lines coming in from the master cylinder (at the back) and three going out: one for each front wheel and one for both rears. The best way to tell if a car has ABS is to simply look for the pump.

Locking brakes isn't just bad for braking performance, it's hard on tires too.

The ABS system in the NC has the ability to control braking at each wheel independently. This is called a "four-channel" system. The NA and NB Miata's ABS shares a set of valves for the rear wheels and treats the front wheels individually, making it a "three-channel" system. Because ABS relies on comparing wheel speeds to tell if a wheel is locking, fitting different diameter tires front and rear can confuse it and cause it to kick in early, resulting in longer stopping distances.

Some drivers don't appreciate having this power taken away from them, but until cars are fitted with three or more brake pedals, the driver simply can't modulate the wheels individually. In race classes where ABS is allowed, the cars are faster with it than without it. In the real world with an average driver who has to make a surprise emergency stop, the ABS takes care of the hardest part of braking.

HEAT MANAGEMENT

Now, because the brakes have to turn all this kinetic energy into heat, what they do with it is important. First, the heat is absorbed by the brake components: the caliper, rotors, and pads. The more mass these parts have, the more energy they will absorb for a given temperature rise. That's one reason you see huge brakes on supercars, but there's only so much energy they can absorb before temperatures get too high and problems start to appear. The brake pads can start to lose their friction as they overheat and melt on the surface. The result of this "pad fade" is a brake pedal that feels the same but don't seem to do anything and the classic smell of hot brakes. The fluid can boil, ridding you of pesky hydraulic pressure and thus sending the brake pedal to the floor. The rotors can crack and, in extreme cases, come apart with predictable results.

Overheating brakes are one situation where brakes can fail to produce the maximum deceleration offered by the tires.

So the braking system not only has to temporarily absorb heat, it also has to get rid of it before things get too hot. The rotor takes care of most of this by simply radiating the heat. To make this job easier, the front rotors (which do most of the work, more on that later) are ducted. In other words, they have air passages running from the center of the rotor to the outside edge. This increases the surface area of the rotor, allowing it to radiate heat faster. The air passages are also designed to pull air from the center of the rotor to the outside, improving the cooling by supplying fresh, cool air constantly. The rear brakes don't work anywhere near as hard, so they're a solid disc.

For racers, keeping the brakes cool is a constant battle. So they'll install ducting to supply lots of cold air to the rotor.

Done properly, this will direct high-pressure cool air at the center of the rotor, allowing the vented design to pull air through the rotor and cool it at an even rate. This is a fairly easy thing to do and doesn't really have any downsides, so it's a good, inexpensive project to play with.

WHEN TO UPGRADE YOUR BRAKES

Now that we know how everything works, how do we know what to upgrade on the brakes? Again, it all comes down to making full use of the traction provided by the tires. If you're not able to take full advantage of the traction available due to proportioning, difficulty in modulation, or overheating problems, then it's time to figure out the problem and address it. For example, if you're not having a problem with fade and you keep locking up the front wheels, you should look at adjusting your brake bias instead of installing bigger brakes.

The front rotor on the right is vented, while the one on the left is a solid rear unit. These aftermarket units are also slotted and given a high-temperature coating to prevent rust everywhere but where the pad wipes the rotor. The latter doesn't matter for performance, but it does look good.

The first step in building brake ducting is to find a source of air. It needs to come from the front of the car for as much pressure as possible. If you have factory fog lights, removing them will give you an excellent source of air. Otherwise, you can use the ducts in the optional factory front air dam, install some aftermarket inlets, or simply take air from the "mouth" of the car.

The next step is to get all this cool, fresh air to the brakes. You can buy brake ducting hose from race shops. The hose needs to be able to handle high temperatures, be flexible, and not kink. The thin white plastic hose used for dryer ducting can't handle the heat, but otherwise that's the idea. Race shops sell specific hose for the job. The bigger the better, but it has to be small enough to fit. Three inches is probably about the limit. At the caliper end, aim the hose at the center of the rotor. The internal venting will pull this cool air out through the rotor. If you simply aim it at the inner rotor face, it won't cool the outer half of the rotor at all. This car uses a custom-made fitting to hold the hose in place.

Too much heat can lead to a cracked rotor. The next step is when the rotor comes apart and the driver gets quite excited.

One way to measure the temperature of brakes is to use special paint from Tempilac. It comes in several colors. Each color burns off at a certain temperature, and it's a quick way to see what the maximum temperature of the rotors (or any other part) was since the paint was applied.

An extreme brake setup from an autocross car. Since autocross runs are so short (often under a minute), there's not a lot of problem with heat; but weight is critical. This racer took a stock 1.6 rotor, cut out the middle, and added an aluminum hat. Then the rotor itself was drilled full of holes for a minimum weight. The caliper is one more often seen on motorcycles, and it had to be widened with a custom insert to fit it over the vented rotor. It's definitely not something you'd want to test on the track with too much heat, but in this case, it does what it's supposed to.

PROPORTIONING/BIAS

The role of brake proportioning is critical when it comes to maximizing a car's stopping capability, and it's not well understood by many people. As with so much else in handling, it comes down to weight transfer. Due to this weight transfer and the resulting shift in traction, the front brakes are able to provide much more braking force than the rears. In other words, we can apply more braking torque to those wheels without locking them up. The proportion of braking provided by the front and rear brakes is often referred to as the brake bias or brake proportioning. If the front wheels are doing more braking than the rears, the car is said to have front bias.

As discussed in Chapter 7, lateral weight transfer is a function of the car's track, its mass, the CG height, and the rate of acceleration. The same concept applies to braking, but the car's wheelbase is used instead of the track. Note that spring rates aren't a factor here.

This last bit can be hard to wrap your brain around, actually. Brake dive is a result of weight transfer, not a cause. Installing stiffer springs in the front to keep the nose of the car from dropping while braking will not change the weight transfer by any significant amount. However, it will mean that you have more suspension travel available to deal with bumps while the front of the car is fully loaded. Once you're on the bumpstops, the car will become less stable if you have to deal with pavement imperfections.

We can't adjust the wheelbase of the car, and the CG height is set by the ride height of the car. But one thing that changes dramatically is the rate of deceleration. The harder you brake, the more weight is transferred, and thus the available traction in the front increases while the available traction in

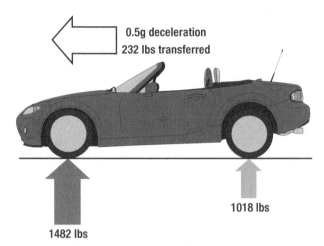

0.5g deceleration
232 lbs transferred

1018 lbs

1482 lbs

Remember our weight transfer calculations from Chapter 7? We were concerned with the loss in overall grip, but here we're also looking at how much braking force we can get out of each wheel before it locks up. The rear wheels have gone from having 50 percent of the weight—and thus half the traction—to 41 percent, with a resulting drop of traction. So it's fairly obvious that the front brakes are going to have to do most of the work here, because the rears are going on vacation as we start braking harder.

Brake dive lets you see the result of weight transfer. The good pads and race tires on this car let it brake pretty hard, and you can see how much less weight there is on the rear tires from the nose-down attitude.

the rear decreases. If the brakes supplied equal braking torque at the front and rear wheels, the car would have far too much rear bias and the rear wheels would lock up long before the fronts started taking full advantage of the traction available. This not only means the car will take much longer to stop, but locked rear wheels make the car unstable and it will try to spin. So too much rear bias is a definite problem.

In order to make full use of the traction available, the front and rear brakes are designed differently. The fronts have bigger pistons in the calipers to provide more pressure on the pads. The front rotors are vented to deal with greater heat, and in many cars—not the Miata—they are larger in diameter for more brake torque. But that's still not enough. So cars are fitted with something to make sure the front brakes get more hydraulic pressure than the rears.

In the case of race cars, that might be two separate master cylinders, one for the front and one for the rear. The two masters are often sized differently and the linkage that attaches them to the pedal is usually adjustable to apply more pedal force to one than the other. However, the proportioning offered by this sort of setup is fixed, and it is usually tuned to work best at maximum braking. It's not a good solution for a street car.

In the Miata, Mazda used two techniques. The most common is a proportioning valve. This little piece allows the front and rear brakes to get the same hydraulic pressure up to a certain point. Beyond that, the rears get a lower percentage of the pressure than the fronts do, shifting the bias forward.

It's a simple, reliable, and clever way to take care of the brake proportioning problem. However, because locked rear wheels are so dangerous, they're set up to be on the safe side and run more front bias than is necessary. After all, in different road conditions, the ideal bias will change as the rate of deceleration changes. So the rear tires don't get fully utilized, and the car takes longer to stop than it potentially could.

In cars with ABS, the rear wheels are unable to lock up because the electronics won't let them. So Mazda installed proportioning valves with a bit more rear bias. In fact, starting with the 2001 "Sport" brakes and continuing through the NC, there was no proportioning valve in the system at all. The ABS system takes care of the brake bias. It's not as simple as the mechanical system, but it lets the car take more advantage of the tires leading to shorter stopping distances.

One way to dramatically improve the effectiveness of a braking system is to change the brake bias so that all four wheels are supplying a braking force as close as possible to the maximum allowed by the tires. A lower ride height means a lower CG, which means less weight transfer. This means the rear wheels have more traction, so the car needs more rear bias for maximum braking. But stickier tires mean a greater rate of deceleration, which means more weight is transferred, and so the car needs more front bias. Even putting the top up has an effect, although it's mostly theoretical. So the factory's conservative, front-biased setup may not be a good reflection of the ideal, but it's safe.

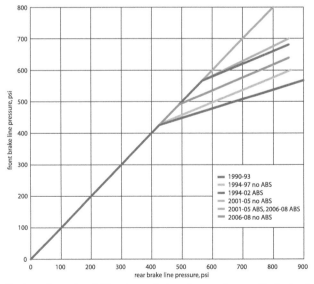

Mazda used a number of different proportioning valves over the years. The front and rear brake pressures are the same until the knee point. After that, the rear brake pressure rises more slowly than the front. In the chart, you can see the relationship of the front and rear pressures after the knee point. The slope in the chart gives the rate of rise: The steeper the slope, the more rear bias the car has. The graph shows the same information, so you can spot the differences easily. Because all the NA/NB valves interchange, it's possible to adjust the factory proportioning by swapping around factory parts.

FACTORY BRAKE PROPORTIONING VALVES

Year	Knee Point (psi)	Front (psi)	Rear (psi)	Slope (post-knee)
1990–1993	427	995	597	29.9%
1994–1997, no ABS	427	850	597	40.2%
1994–1997, ABS	569	850	683	40.6%
2002, no ABS	569	853	702	46.8%
2002, ABS	No proportioning valve			
2006, no ABS	497	852	639	40.0%
2006, ABS	No proportioning valve			

131

The easiest way to change the brake bias is to change the proportioning valve. An adjustable aftermarket unit will let you dial in the perfect balance for your car at any given time. However, a change in conditions might turn your perfect balance into a dangerous one. A street tire setup will be prone to rear wheel lockup when sticky race tires are installed due to the greater weight transfer. A rainy day with less traction will mean less braking force and thus less weight transfer, so you'll want more rear bias to take full advantage of those rear brakes. The ideal brake bias means all four wheels will reach the locking point simultaneously, but if the rears go first then it's an exciting ride. It's easy to install an adjustable valve in an NA or NB, but the separate rear lines of the non-ABS NC means you'd have to install two valves and (with any luck) adjust them to the same setting.

You'll need a valve with metric fittings, more specifically, M10 x 1 flare fittings. Most of the options on the market use an NPT thread with an adapter. NPT to metric flare adaptors are difficult to find for some reason, but are available through Flyin' Miata. Tilton also sells a valve that includes the adaptors. The brake union is easy to source at any auto parts store.

For tuning your brake proportioning, set it to use as little rear brake as possible. Find a deserted area where you can test safely, and start dialing in more rear brake until the rears start locking earlier than the fronts. Now go back so that the fronts lock first. Remember, the ideal bias will change depending on the road surface, tire selection, and even the weather, so be prepared to change it if you're right on the edge.

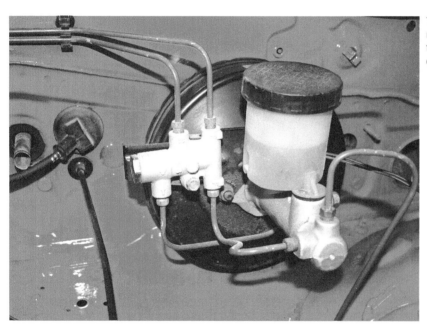

The factory brake proportioning valve is found by the master cylinder on NA and NB models. That's it with the four brake lines going in and out. On the non-ABS NC, it's on the other side of the engine bay.

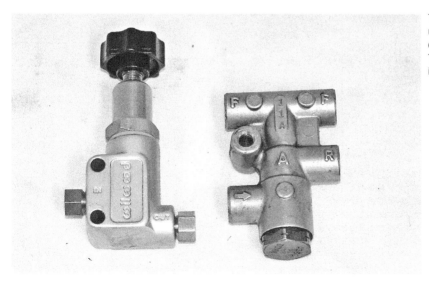

That's a knob-style adjustable valve on the left, a stock unit on the right. You can clearly see the R and F markings on the stock part as well as the arrow to indicate the inlet. This Wilwood valve has adapters installed already to allow it to be fitted to the metric brake lines in the Miata.

A Wilwood valve is in place, with the rear lines passing through it and the front lines joined together with a union. It's bolted to the bracket for the stock valve. This bracket can be bent 90 degrees to put the knob in a more accessible place and to give more clearance for turbos. Note the line from the master cylinder attached to the IN port and the line to the calipers attached to the OUT.

A conveniently placed valve, right behind the shifter. Obviously interior parts will restrict where you locate the knob, but with a bit of creativity, you can end up with a location that falls readily to hand and doesn't get bumped. In this case, the car was used for rallying and the knob had to be adjustable on the fly to deal with changing conditions. Even on a track car, you'd be amazed at how much you can improve your times by being able to dial in the perfect balance for a certain track and day. Note the label so the driver doesn't forget which way is which. Get this wrong, and your brake bias will just get worse and worse.

The brake line routing for the in-cockpit valve. A piece of new brake line was run from the master cylinder and up to the valve. Lengths of pre-flared brake line can be found at any good auto parts store. Any new lines have to be well anchored every 18 inches or less so that they won't fatigue and crack. Here, the line along the top of the transmission tunnel is secured with some clips, but they haven't been added to the vertical section yet.

THE IMPORTANCE OF GOOD BRAKE FLUID

Your brake fluid plays an important role in the braking system. It's what transfers the pedal pressure from the master cylinder to the calipers. It has to deal with high temperatures in the calipers, so it has a high boiling point. It has to compress as little as possible, and it has to prevent corrosion in the steel brake lines.

The temperature resistance of the fluid is important. Fluid doesn't compress significantly, so all the pressure from the master cylinder goes toward pushing your pads into the rotors. But if the fluid boils, air is introduced into the system. As you may remember from high school chemistry, gases do compress. If the fluid acts like a solid linkage, the air will act like a spring. Some of your pedal pressure will do nothing but compress that air, making your brake pedal softer and making it difficult to modulate the brakes properly. The harder you work your brakes and the more heat you dump into your calipers, the more resistance to boiling you need. A good racing fluid will have a boiling point of more than 500 degrees Fahrenheit (260 degrees Celsius).

But brake fluid has a dirty little secret: It's hygroscopic. That means it absorbs water over time. That's good because it keeps any water that gets into the system from freezing or corroding your steel brake lines. But there's a downside: Water boils at a mere 212 degrees F (100 degrees C). So old brake fluid is more likely to boil, leading to a real drop in braking performance.

If you experience brake fade where the pedal drops to the floor and needs pumping to obtain any braking force, you've boiled your brake fluid.

Brake fluids are given DOT (Department of Transportation) ratings by their boiling points, among other characteristics. The chart on the right shows the minimum boiling temperatures of each level. A dry boiling point is with fresh fluid with no water in it. The wet boiling point is with 3.7 percent water absorbed into the fluid. Only 3.7 percent.

Note that these are minimum temperatures, and a fluid has to meet both in order to get a certain rating. For example, Wilwood 570° has a dry boiling point of 570 degrees (thus

As brake fluid absorbs water, it gets darker and darker. It should be the color of white wine. This car is long overdue for a fluid flush. In its current condition, working the brakes hard could easily lead to boiled fluid and an loss of braking capability.

BRAKE FLUID BOILING TEMPERATURES

Rating	Dry boiling temperature	Wet boiling temperature
DOT 3	401°F	284°F
DOT 4	446°F	311°F
DOT 5	509°F	356°F
DOT 5.1	509°F	356°F

system needs to be completely emptied out before making the change. It's simply not a good choice for a sports car. If you need the extreme boiling points of DOT 5, make sure you get a non-silicone DOT 5.1.

Regardless of what kind of brake fluid you use, regular flushing will help keep your brakes in top condition. Fluid darkens as it absorbs water, so once you start to see a color change it's a good idea to spend a bit of time bleeding. A soft pedal is also an indicator that it's time to get into the garage. Because the clutch system uses brake fluid, it's not a bad idea to bleed this oft-neglected fluid as well, although it will turn black quickly without ill effects. It's not exposed to high heat levels, of course. You can find instructions on how to bleed your brake system in *Mazda Miata MX-5 Performance Projects*.

BRAKE LINES

Most of the brake lines in the car are solid steel to avoid expansion; however, because the calipers are mounted at the wheels, a flexible section is required at each corner to allow for suspension and steering movement. The factory flex lines are made of rubber. The problem with rubber is that it can expand, allowing the lines to balloon out from the hydraulic pressure they contain. This has a similar, but much smaller, effect as air bubbles, robbing the pedal of some precision and firmness. This tendency gets worse as the car gets older. A common upgrade is to replace the lines with ones covered in a stainless-steel braid, which cuts the swelling of the lines down to almost nothing. Depending on the age of the brake fluid and the age of the rubber lines, the difference may or may not be noticeable to the driver.

the name), but a wet boiling point of 284 degrees Fahrenheit, thus it barely gets a DOT 3 rating. It's a good choice for racers because a big part of race car maintenance is keeping the brake fluid fresh, but it's a poor choice for a street car that might only get fresh fluid every couple of years.

Sharp eyes will notice the duplication between DOT 5 and DOT 5.1. What about DOT 5? Most brake fluid has a polyalkylene glycol ether base, but DOT 5 fluids are silicone-based. It is non-hygroscopic, so it won't absorb water. It's also not damaging to paint. So why don't we all use it? Because if water gets in the system, it will pool and can cause rust problems. The DOT 5 is more compressible than non-silicone fluid, so you get a softer pedal. It's also prone to frothing under vibration, leading to an even softer pedal. And most important, it will not mix with other types of fluid, so the

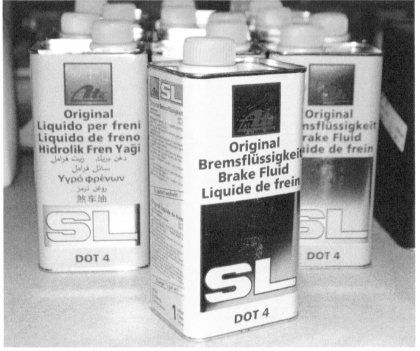

Good brake fluid isn't really expensive, and a single liter (or quart) is more than enough to do a full flush of both the clutch and brake systems. Keeping your fluid fresh and your brake system well-bled is an inexpensive way to keep your braking system in top shape.

One downside to stainless-steel lines is the potential for damage. If the line is allowed to come into contact with anything, something is going to abrade. If the brake line hits the tire, then the line will lose. If it hits a metal part, then typically the other part will lose. Many stainless lines come with a plastic sheath over top to minimize the problem, but a bit of care upon installation will prevent this. Rubber lines aren't immune to damage either, of course.

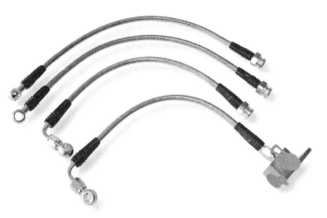

Stainless-steel brake lines with a clear plastic sheath.

PADS

A brake pad has a rough life. It has to deal with a huge range of operating temperatures, last as long as possible, be easy on rotors, operate silently, and not make too much dust. As you can imagine, juggling all of these factors is a real challenge. And like tires, you'll find that no brake pad can do everything. Street pads will stop the car well when they're cold but will wilt under hard use. Race pads will squeal, chew up rotors, and be difficult to modulate when cold but will maintain their composure under high heat. It's important to match your pads to your intended use.

Pads, just like tires, have a coefficient of friction that determines how much braking force they can supply. This coefficient of friction—called μ or "mu"—varies with pad temperature. Above or below a certain temperature, the μ will drop off, leading to decreased braking performance. When a pad overheats, the brake pedal will stay firm, but the car just won't stop. They'll also start to smell, which makes a good early warning system. Make sure you can tell the difference between this kind of brake fade and boiled fluid, as the solution to the problem is different.

So how do you choose a good brake pad? You can measure your brake operating temperature, get your hands on the μ-vs-temperature chart for the pads you're considering, and go that

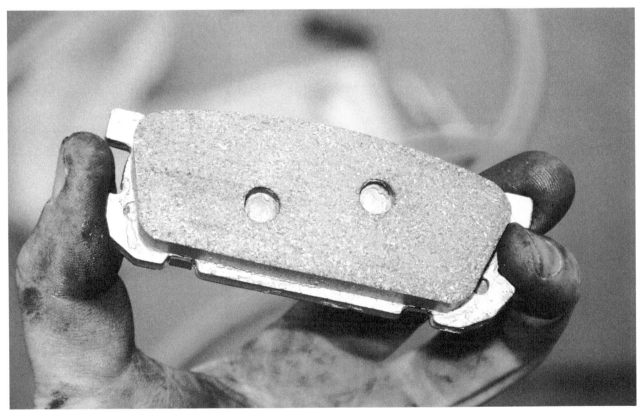

Brake pads are a lot more complex than you might think. The compounds are a real mix of materials, as you can see here. This one even appears to have copper—or is it gold?—in the mix.

way, although it won't tell you much about other aspects of pad behavior such as dusting or rotor wear. So the best way is to talk to brake manufacturers and other Miata owners who use their cars the same way you do. If your Miata is a street car, taking pad recommendations from a Spec Miata racer isn't going to help much. If your Miata sees both street and track use, it might be worth swapping the pads at the track.

One thing that can make a big difference to the performance of your pads is proper bedding. This seasons the pad materials, giving a good initial bite, and prevents them from fading prematurely. It also builds up a thin layer of pad material on the rotor.

Bedding pads is fairly easy to do, but you will need a location where you can perform multiple stops without causing problems with other road users. You need enough room to perform multiple stops from around 60 miles per hour, and this sort of erratic behavior can freak out other drivers.

Basically, you want to get the brakes up to a high temperature, then keep them there for a while. From 60 miles per hour, brake down to about 5 miles per hour. The goal is to prevent coming to a full stop, as the hot pads can transfer pad material to the rotors. You'll do 10 near-stops one after the other without giving the brakes a chance to cool. Start with a moderate braking effort, then increase the severity of your braking until you're braking as hard as you can without lockup or triggering the ABS. You'll start to smell hot brakes, and you might find that all of a sudden you lose braking ability as the pads get to their limit. Finish the set of 10, then drive the car for a while to let the brakes cool down. Repeat the process once everything's cooled off, and you should have some well-bedded brakes. Cars with more aggressive brake setups such as big brakes or race pads will want to go from 80 to 10 miles per hour to put more heat into the system.

ROTORS

The rotors don't affect braking performance much unless you change their size. The heat capacity of the rotor is determined by its mass, which isn't going to change much from manufacturer to manufacturer. The big difference you'll see in rotors is whether they are smooth, slotted, or drilled.

Drilled rotors are a source of some controversy. The theory is that they provide more surface area to the rotor for better cooling and give the gasses produced by the pads somewhere to go. They also make a cool "whir" noise. But while they look fantastic, the holes can be the source of stress risers that promote cracking under heavy use. That's a bad thing, so generally drilled rotors are relegated to the "fashion over function" category.

Slots have many of the same theoretical advantages but without the tendency to crack. This makes them a decent option. However, in the real world, there's little effect from the slots or holes, so many people will simply go for the least expensive rotor available and spend their money elsewhere.

A pair of high-end drilled and slotted aftermarket rotors. The small chamfer around the edge of each hole minimizes the chance of cracking, but it's no guarantee. The black finish will prevent the rotor from getting surface rust, which is more a matter of aesthetics than anything else. If your new rotors don't have this, you can use some BBQ paint to spray the parts of the rotor where the pad doesn't make contact. Some brake cleaner will ensure that there's nothing on this friction surface before you install. You can get a pretty good guide of what to paint and what not to paint from these rotors.

Two-piece rotors used as part of a big brake kit. You can see the bolts joining the aluminum hat to the iron ring. In this case, the two-piece design cuts 1.3 pounds of unsprung and rotating mass from each corner of the car, in return for a fairly high cost.

Two-piece rotors use a cast-iron outer ring with a machined aluminum center section. Thanks to that light center section, they're lighter overall, which has some handling benefits. The fasteners between the two sections should be designed to allow the outside ring to "float" and expand without affecting the dimensions of the friction surface. Due to packaging and parts availability, these rotors start at 11 inches and get larger from there, so they're almost always found as part of big brake kits.

FACTORY PARTS AND INTERCHANGE

At the time of writing, there have been no variations in the NC braking systems fitted from the factory. However, the RX-8 rotors and calipers bolt on, which give a massive 12.7-inch front rotor.

The NA and NB Miatas were equipped with three different brake setups. The first, from 1990 to 1993, used 9.3-rotors in the front and 9.1 inch in the rear. These are often called "1.6 brakes" because all of the cars that used them had the 1.6 engine. In 1994, the brakes grew to 10.0-inch front and 9.9-inch rear. The bracket for the caliper was redesigned to fit the new rotors, and the pad design was changed along with the proportioning valve calibration. However, the rest of the components are the same. This combination is often called "1.8 brakes," and it remained unchanged until 2002 in North America.

The 2001 Miata introduced a new braking system that was full of subtle changes. Because it was part of the Sport suspension package, this setup is often referred to as "Sport brakes." The rotors grew to 10.6 inches in front and 10.9 inches in the rear. The master cylinder bore size went up from 7/8 inch to 15/16 inch. The pistons in the front calipers grew from 2.01 to 2.125 inches, and the rears went from 1.25 to 1.375 inches. The brake booster even got changed. The Sport package was optional for 2001 and 2002, then became standard in North America for 2003–2005. One way to spot these brakes is to look under the car. If it is fitted with the multitude of stock undercar braces, then it will have the Sport brakes as well. Sixteen-inch or 17-inch wheels from the factory are also a clue, and of course you can measure the rotor diameters. All of the 2001 and later Miatas in the United States got the larger 15/16-inch master cylinder. If you want to confirm which one is on your car, the size is cast into the body of the cylinder just under the fluid reservoir.

At the same time the master cylinder changed sizes, so did the specification of the brake booster. The ratio between the force provided by the pedal and the force applied by the booster to the master cylinder is called the boost ratio. Unfortunately, the design of the booster changed, so the 1990–2000 boosters cannot be interchanged with the later master cylinders.

MIATA MASTER CYLINDERS AND BRAKE BOOSTERS

	Master cylinder size	Boost ratio	Amount of hydraulic pressure for 44 lbs of force on the pedal
1990–2000	7/8 in	4.75:1	754–796 psi
2001–2002 non-Sport 2001–2005 with ABS	15/16 in	9.7:1	1,038 psi
2001–2005 Sport without ABS 2004–2005 Mazdaspeed	15/16 in	6.4:1	628 psi

From left to right: Sport, 1.8, and 1.6 front rotors and calipers.

Because it has so many parts in common with the 1.6 brakes, the 1.8 setup is a common modification to the earlier cars. Simply change over the caliper brackets and use the larger rotors and pads. Some people will increase the size of the rear rotors only to gain a bit more rear bias. Autocrossers have also been known to downsize their 1.8 brakes to the lighter 1.6 size to save some rotating mass.

The Sport brakes provide some interesting interchange options due to the changes in the piston sizes. A larger master cylinder will move more fluid for a given amount of pedal movement, so you'll get a firmer pedal. You can choose how much effort is required by switching between one of the two available boosters. You can even fit a 1-inch master cylinder from a Mazda 929 without any difficulty, which firms up the pedal further and requires more effort. The 929 master is only compatible with brake boosters from 2001 to 2005. Going

with larger pistons in the calipers does just the opposite, increasing braking force due to higher pressure on the pads but at the expense of more pedal travel.

The front Sport calipers don't fit on the earlier caliper brackets, so that cuts down on possibilities. They only work in concert with the large diameter discs. The rears, however, can be swapped onto earlier brackets to affect the rear bias. The master cylinder and the brake booster can also be changed independently. The booster, master cylinder, and rear calipers from the Sport brakes, combined with 1.8 parts for the rest of the system, would make a pretty nice street and track setup.

BIG BRAKE KITS

There are a number of big brake kits on the market that offer better braking. How can they be better? Well, they have a few tricks.

This big brake kit for the NC cuts down on unsprung weight by using a lightweight aluminum caliper instead of the stock iron part as well as a two-piece rotor. Overall, the weight savings are around 2.5 pounds per front wheel.

The Wilwood calipers used in most big brake kits have pads that are easy to change. It's like putting bread in a toaster.

An inexpensive way to increase the size of the rotors is to keep the factory calipers, but mount them on a new bracket so that they fit over the larger rotors. This is most common in the rear (that's what this set of brackets is designed to do), but there are also kits on the market that allow you to mount the stock front calipers over an 11-inch rotor from a VW Corrado. In this case, there is an increase in weight, but pad selection remains the same. The larger rotor will deal better with the heat as it can absorb more energy for a given temperature range, and it will also shed heat more quickly due to a larger surface area. The braking torque will also be increased for a given pedal pressure.

First, the larger rotors provide more braking torque for the same pedal pressure. This makes the brakes feel more powerful, but of course the ultimate stopping distance is still determined by the tires. The change in braking torque can also affect the proportioning, which can be either an improvement or a downgrade. Installing larger rotors on the front but leaving the rear alone will increase the front brake bias, which is rarely something a Miata with otherwise-stock brakes needs.

The larger rotors also have more mass, which means more heat capacity. They'll absorb more energy for a given temperature gain and help keep the brakes at a consistent temperature. This extra mass can cause problems with handling, though (see the chapter on wheels and tires). One solution for a heavier rotor is to run a two-piece rotor, which is much more expensive.

Most big brake kits change the calipers as well. This is actually where some significant improvements can be made. Stock calipers are made of iron and are a floating design. This means they have a single piston in them and are allowed to slide side to side (i.e., float) on a couple of slider pins. The floating action means that the pressure from the single piston gets applied to both pads as the caliper moves sideways. Any friction in the system means uneven pad pressure or a loss in braking ability. Racing calipers tend to be a multi-piston design, with one or more pistons on each side of the caliper pressing directly on the pad. The idea is that this gives a more even pad pressure. They're also made of aluminum, which is both lighter and sheds heat faster. On top of this, race calipers tend to have pads that are easy to change and available in a huge range of compounds.

When changing the calipers, it's also possible to change the piston sizes. This will have an effect on braking force and pedal travel. Most big brake kits will match the factory sizes, but not always. Rear calipers are rarely changed because of the difficulty (and expense) of retaining a parking brake and because the rear brakes don't work as hard as the fronts.

Keep in mind that the larger rotors may require a change in wheel size. Fifteen-, 16-, or even 17-inch wheels may be needed to clear the new brakes. This affects a number of other aspects of the car that should be taken into consideration.

How do you know if a big brake kit is a good idea? Well, many people consider them to be useless on a Miata due to the car's relatively light weight, good cornering, and low power levels. Miatas simply aren't that hard on brakes when they're stock. But if you've modified the rest of your Miata, they may be necessary. If you're overheating your brakes on a regular basis and you've already tried ducting and good pads, they're a good solution. If you want to shed some unsprung weight or have access to a greater selection of pads, they might be for you. And of course, there's the fashion aspect, which probably sells more big brake kits than anything else.

Chapter 11
Wheels and Tires

Here it is, where the rubber meets the road. Wheels and tires are a multi-billion dollar industry and represent a large proportion of the aftermarket for cars and trucks. Some of the reason for this is easy to understand. After all, tires are a wear item and have to be replaced regularly, but a big motivator is also fashion. Changing to a set of aftermarket wheels can make a big difference to the look of your car, setting it apart from the masses. Like everything else, however, not every modification is an upgrade. The wrong set of wheels or tires can dramatically affect your Miata's handling and ride.

It all starts with the tires. They're what provide the actual grip your car uses to turn, brake, and accelerate. So they're pretty important. They need to provide as much traction as possible, but they need to be stiff enough to provide quick responses while being flexible enough to absorb road imperfections. They have to grip well on dry pavement and

Here's a comparison of the contact patch of a couple of fictional tires. The one on the left is wider, and both have the same air pressure and overall diameter. You can see how the contact area spreads out and gets wider with the wider tire, but it's not quite as long.

be able to pump water out from under the rubber in the wet. All this while lasting as long as possible. Because many of these requirements are direct contradictions, the trick is to find the compromise that suits your needs best.

Many people assume that because tire pressure is measured in pounds per square inch, that a tire with the same number of pounds on it will have the same number of square inches of contact patch. That's mostly true, although the stiffness of the sidewall will have an effect. Some tires have such stiff sidewalls that it's difficult to tell if they're completely flat. For this reason, a tire with 15 psi of pressure instead of 30 will not have twice the contact area.

So if the contact area doesn't change size, why are people always trying to fit the widest tire they can on a car? What changing the tire width *will* do is change the shape of the contact patch. A wider tire will have a wider contact patch; that's easy enough to figure out. Because the area isn't changing much, it's also not going to be as long. The wider and shorter contact patch will react more quickly to changes in slip angle and will often generate dramatically more cornering force. This can mean a loss in acceleration and braking ability, although generally speaking this is more than compensated for by the extra cornering grip. Almost every racer will choose the widest tire available, with the exception of drag racers who are only interested in straight-line traction. That's why true dragsters have such tall rear tires.

SIZING

Before we get into how to select and evaluate tires, we need to understand the information that's printed on their sidewalls. First, we'll start with the size.

The tire size is a mathematical formula that is a combination of inches, millimeters, and percentages, all of which are important. Let's use a standard 17-inch tire from a 2006 as an example. That's a 205/45-17. There are a few other letters and numbers sprinkled in there, but they're less important.

The number 205 is the width of the tire carcass in millimeters. The carcass width isn't quite the same as the tread width, but in the case of the squat, wide tires found on Miatas, it's pretty close. To convert that width to inches, divide it by 25.4. Our 205 has a carcass width of almost exactly 8 inches. The actual tread width will vary from 7.5 inches on an extremely high-performance street tire such as the Bridgestone RE-01R to 7 inches for an all-season Goodyear.

The number 45 is the profile, or aspect ratio, of the tire. It's the height of the sidewall given as a percentage of the carcass

width. A higher number means a taller sidewall while a lower number means a shorter one. Since it's tied to the width of the tire, the sidewall height is also related to tire width. In this case, our 205/45 will have a sidewall that is 45 percent of 205 millimeters high. This gives us 92 millimeters or about 3.6 inches. Many people will look at the aspect ratio in isolation, but it's a meaningless number without the carcass width.

The 17 is the easiest part to figure out. That's the diameter of the wheel in inches.

A full tire size may read a little longer. For example, our 205/45-17 may have P205/45R17 84W stamped on the sidewall. The P means "Passenger," and that's going to be the case for all tires suitable for a Miata. R means "Radial," also something you'll find on anything but some specialized racing tires. You may also find out if you start reading the manufacturer spec sheets that the actual tires are slightly different than their mathematical ideal. For example, race tires tend to be a little wide compared to what the math says they should be, to make them just a little bit faster than the competition.

The 84W is a speed and load rating. It's pretty safe to ignore the load rating for a Miata. The lower the number, the lower the load, and a little car like a Miata needs less load capacity than just about any other car on the road. Our 84 translates to a load rating of 1,102 pounds or 500 kilograms per tire.

The speed rating is a little more interesting. Speed ratings indicate the maximum safe speed of a tire in good condition. The rating itself isn't all that critical unless you are planning to drive at sustained high speed, but tires with higher speed ratings tend to have stickier rubber compounds and stronger construction. It's one way to get a basic idea of the intent of the tire. Many tire shops will simply refer to this classification to identify a high-performance tire. In reality, most tires found on a Miata will have an H, V, or Z rating. Z-rated tires are indicated a little differently with the Z in the middle of the tire size followed by a letter in the usual place, for example our 215/40R16 86W in the picture.

One of the other useful numbers found on a tire is the UTQG. It stands for Uniform Tire Quality Grade and is meant to illustrate the tire's traction, treadwear, and temperature resistance.

The traction is measured by simply dragging the tire across a surface. It ignores factor such as tread design and sidewall, but it's a test of how well the rubber grips. The scale is AA, A, B, and C, with AA being the most grippy.

Treadwear is pretty easy. Compared to a "standard" tire with a rating of 100, this is an indication of how long the tire might be expected to last. A rating of 200 means the tire will last twice as long as the standard tire. The problem is that this standard tire isn't the same for all manufacturers, making it difficult to compare treadwear across brands. Still, it's pretty obvious that a Toyo with a UTQG of 40 will not last as long as a Yokohama with a UTQG of 250.

TIRE SPEED RATINGS DECIPHERED

Rating	mph	km/h
M	81	130
N	87	140
P	93	150
Q	99	160
R	106	170
S	112	180
T	118	190
U	124	200
H	130	210
V	149	240
Z W	168	270
Z Y	186	300

The mix of letters and numbers on a tire sidewall can be intimidating, but once you can read them it's fairly easy to understand how they affect your car.

Temperature resistance is essentially a variation of a speed rating. Again, it's an A, B, C rating with A being best.

An important number in tire sizing, but one you won't find stamped on the sidewall, is the rolling diameter of the tire. This is more important than the wheel size, as it's what determines your car's gearing and ground clearance.

Going to a taller tire (one with a larger diameter) can also cause problems with tire rubbing. The diameters need to be matched on the front and rear of the car to avoid upsetting your ABS or traction control. So unless you're going for a specific functional change, it's best to keep close to the diameter of the original tires.

You can calculate the diameter in inches from the tire size using the following formula:

$$\text{diameter} = \text{wheel size} + \frac{\text{carcass width} \times \text{aspect ratio} \times 2}{25.4}$$

Remember that the aspect ratio is a percentage: A 45 ratio should be 0.45 in the equation. On an NA or NB Miata, the diameter is 22.8 inches or close to it. On the NC, it's about 24 inches. When looking for a set of tires for your car, you need to look for one that's close to the same diameter. And this is where the interplay between the aspects of tire sizes comes to life.

If you want to run wider tires, you have to adjust the aspect ratio so that the sidewall height doesn't change. For example, a 235/40-17 has almost exactly the same sidewall height as our 205/45-17, but the carcass is 30 millimeters wider.

Increasing the wheel size on a car by an inch is sometimes called a "+1 wheel." When you do go +1, the tire size needs to be chosen to keep the rolling diameter the same. Switching from a 14-inch to a 15-inch wheel means that each sidewall needs to be 1/2 inch shorter. This is done by changing the aspect ratio. Let's go back to our 205/45-17. The sidewall height on this tire is 45 percent of 205 millimeters, or 92.2

millimeters. One-half inch is 12.7 mm, so we're looking for a sidewall that's right around 80 millimeters. The quotient 80 ÷ 205 gives us 39 percent. The closest aspect ratio to that is 40, so the closest equivalent to our current 17-inch size would be a 205/40-18.

But here's a problem. Tires don't come in every possible size. While there are a few options in the 205/40-18 size, there are a lot more in the 215/40-18. There's only 4 millimeters of difference in the sidewall height, which is minimal. So that's a reasonable option.

CHOOSING TIRES

Okay, that's out of the way. How do you choose a tire? I prefer to start by figuring out what compromises are acceptable. Is grip more important than tire life, or does it have to meet a balance? Will the tire have to cope with subfreezing temperatures regularly, occasionally, or never? The stickiest tires tend to lose grip dramatically in cold weather and in extreme cases can even crack. Your choice of compromises will determine what class of tire you're looking for.

The wider the range of conditions you ask a tire to handle, the more compromised it will be in all conditions. If your driving includes snow and cold, a set of dedicated snow tires as well as a set of summer tires can dramatically increase your car's traction over a set of all-seasons. Because you only drive on one set at a time, the overall cost isn't any different other than the cost of an extra set of wheels. The amount of extra traction provided by snow tires in the snow has to be experienced to be believed. If you're going to be taking your

These are all factory wheels that showed up on various Miatas from 1994 to 2004. From left to right, they're 14, 15, 16, and 17 inches. Notice how the diameter of the tire remains the same, despite a 3-inch difference in the wheel diameter? You can get a 205 wide tire in this diameter (or very close to it) for all of these wheels if you want, but the aspect ratio will range from 55 to 40 as the wheel size increases.

HEAT CYCLING

The rubber in your tires is affected by heat. Every time you drive the car, the rubber heats up and then cools off when you park. This is particularly true with hard use, of course. Every time you heat up a tire and let it cool, it's called a heat cycle. With high-performance tires, the lifespan is actually related to how many heat cycles a tire sees instead of how much rubber is on the tire. Racers need to keep track of how many heat cycles their tires have gone through and will often sell their old tires after they've gone off their peak. Sometimes this is after only a couple of qualifying sessions. Hint: This is a great way to get expensive tires for a good price. A tire that is only giving 90 percent of its maximum grip is fine for an enthusiast, but may be useless to a race team.

The first time a tire is heat-cycled is the most important. The tire should be brought up to temperature easily and then allowed to fully cool. This will actually strengthen the bonds between the rubber molecules and make the tire both stickier and longer lived. If the tire's run too hard or too fast the first time out, it will have a shorter, slipperier life. Some tire suppliers will actually heat-cycle your new tires for you under controlled conditions, so they're at their best the first time you drive them.

New street tires may also be slippery on the first drive due to the tread-release compound used to pop the tire out of the mold. Yokohamas seem to be particularly prone to this for some reason. It'll wear off fairly quickly.

These extreme performance street tires still look to be in good shape with lots of life left, but they've been autocrossed too many times and have seen several track days. They've hardened dramatically. They're like driving on bricks. Slippery bricks.

car on the track, a set of race tires—particularly a long-lived and friendly set such as the Toyo RA-1—will deal better with the high loads and temperatures than a normal street tire.

Vendors will often group tires into performance categories. Winter tires, all-season, and summer-only performance are the obvious ones, but each of those have subsets depending on their performance and wear characteristics. In recent years, there's been a real war going on to see who can build the stickiest street tire. They're often aimed at autocrossers, so they tend to have a treadwear rating right around the 140 minimum required by class rules. They're often called ultra high-performance or extreme performance tires, and the party was started by the Falken Azenis. They won't last long, but they're fun while they do. Because the Miata is a light car that's pretty easy on tires, this class is a popular choice among enthusiasts who want lots of grip on the road as well as a tire they can take to the track.

The next step in grip is the R compound. Basically, these are race tires. But they meet DOT regulations, so they're legal to drive on the road. They'll grip better than any "street" tire

will, but you'll pay for it in shorter life. However, some of the super-sticky street tires will now wear out about as quickly as the longest-lived of the R compounds, and some real hard-core performance enthusiasts (such as your author) will use the "R comps" as normal tires. One of the classics is the Toyo RA-1. It's been around forever, and it's not the stickiest of the bunch. But it lasts for a long time, will outgrip anything but another R compound, and has a very friendly behavior, with a wide functional temperature range and an unbelievable resistance to heat-cycling. They'll stick and stick until they cord. The Toyo R888 can also be used as an everyday tire, as can the Nitto NT-01. Expect a set of these to last around 5,000 to 8,000 miles on a street-driven Miata.

Not all DOT-legal R compounds are really streetable, though. Hoosiers are really pure race tires with a slight nod to road legality, and the manufacturer warns not to take them off the race course. They'll stick better than their more robust cousins.

TIRE PRESSURE

Tire pressure is critical to the performance of your car. A tire with too little pressure will be sloppy and won't respond well. Cornering limits are reduced, rolling resistance goes up, and the car's stability drops. That's pretty easy to figure out. High-performance tires with stiff sidewalls may not look underinflated, so you have to check with a good tire gauge. Too much pressure can mean your contact patch gets too small, the ride gets really rough, and you lose grip. An underinflated tire will also wear the shoulders of the tire excessively, while an overinflated one will wear the center.

But there's more to it than simply making sure the tire isn't sloppy. A high-performance tire will grip best at a certain tire pressure. Because tires heat up when you use them, the air inside also heats up and tries to expand. So the pressure will go up, and it's this hot temperature that really matters when it comes to performance. Check with the tire manufacturer to see what they recommend for hot pressures for your favorite tires. If you're at the track, come into the hot pits with the tires at full operating temperature and check the pressure there. Once you've got the hot pressure dialed in, let the tires cool down and see what your cold temps are. They're a lot easier to check, so this gives you a consistent starting point. There's more on determining the correct tire pressure in the suspension tuning chapter, and of course you can always ask other Miata drivers what they're doing with the same tire on their cars.

This tire is only inflated to 20 psi, when it's usually run at around 32 psi cold. Due to the stiff sidewalls, it's not easy to tell. Don't try to use your eyeball as a tire pressure gauge.

Now that you know what sort of tires you're looking for, there are two ways to proceed. The first is to select a size and go from there. This is the usual way of working if you're not changing your wheels. If you have 17-inch wheels on your Miata, then looking at 16-inch tires is pointless. You can either keep the original tire size or go with a wider, lower profile option. For example, you could substitute a 235/40-17 for the stock 205/45-17 tires on many NCs. Once the tire size is chosen, simply look to see what tires are available in that size that suit your criteria. Websites like the Tire Rack will let you input the size and then display the available tires, sorted by category. You can also read the specification sheets for the tires on the manufacturer's websites or (sometimes) on reseller sites like the Tire Rack. These sheets will tell you the actual size of a given tire, including details such as the section width, tread width, diameter, recommended wheel widths, and weight.

The other method is to start by choosing a couple of tire options, then finding out what sizes are available. The correct wheels to make the tires fit are a secondary concern. This is a more functional approach, but it's the way to get maximum performance. Of course, it may require buying a new set of wheels, so it's rarely used. In this case, the manufacturer spec sheets can be quite useful. Let's walk through a couple of examples. Keep in mind that tire manufacturers are in constant battle to produce better tires, so the models in question may be quite dated by the time you read this. Still, it's the process that counts.

These are both Miata tires but built for very different purposes. The tire on the right is a high-performance street tire. It has large tread blocks for more stability under cornering, and the tread pattern is designed to pump water from under the tire for more grip in the wet. It's also uni-directional, meaning the tire is designed to rotate in a particular direction. Generally, the points in the tread pattern should point down when the tire is viewed from the front of the car. The tire on the left is an all-season design. The smaller tread blocks with multiple small grooves in them work better in snow and loose surfaces than big blocks do. They'll also let the tread squirm around under load, making for a less stable design. This tire is designed to work in either direction. If you get stuck in the snow, this is the tire to have. For fun on a twisty back road, the high-performance option will be a lot more enjoyable.

Pure race tires designed for dry tracks don't bother with tread. They're looking to press as much rubber into the ground as possible, with as stable a tread as possible. So they're often pure slicks. The thin grooves on this Hoosier means that it does technically have tread and it's legal for road use, but the tire is so short-lived that Hoosier tells you never to use them anywhere but on a track.

Here's what happens when you abuse a tire. This is an all-season Michelin that was used on the track with a supercharged 2006. The tire wasn't designed to deal with that sort of use, and the rubber literally melted off the tire. The tall and small tread blocks used in all-season tires squirm around more. This not only robs the driver of feel, but it allows the rubber to heat up more. The melted tire wasn't very sticky either. After this sort of overheating, it never gripped very well again.

This Nitto R-compound, on the other hand, is showing a grainy texture. This is an indication of a tire that's been up to full working temperature but not beyond. It's a happy tire. It's rare to get a tire this hot on the street, but if you're on the track this is exactly what you want to see. The small hole in the tread is used for measuring how much rubber is left on the tire.

Car 1: A 2006 MX-5 on the stock 17x7 wheels. The car was supercharged and saw a lot of street use, with the occasional trip to the track. The owner was more interested in traction and a low price than a long lifespan, and winter use was not a factor. The tire chosen was in the "Extreme Performance Summer" category. The owner liked Kumho tires, and they tend to be affordable, so their new Ecsta XS got the nod. In terms of sizing, the standard 205/45-17 was not available but a slightly taller 215/45-17 was. The difference in rolling diameter between these two sizes is minimal. Another option was a 245/40-17 for an extra 1.5 inches of width—but according to the manufacturer's spec sheets, this tire requires at least an 8 inch wide wheel. So the choice was to stick with a 215/45-17.

Car 2: The Targa Miata. You've seen this car in Chapter 1. It would be racing, so maximum grip was a factor. But the race sees a wide variety of weather conditions ranging from cold rain to hot temperatures, along with gravel that gets thrown on to the pavement. In the rain, deep standing water is a real possibility. Because the driver hasn't seen the stages before racing them, a tire with a forgiving nature was required. The regulations at the time stated that only six tires were allowed for the entire race, and all had to meet minimum tread depth rules over the course of the event. The sort of tire chosen was those of streetable R-compounds, race tires that can be driven on the street for long periods. At the time, the options were the Nitto NT-01, the Toyo R888, and the Toyo RA-1. The first two had

If you are fitting oversized tires, it may be necessary to alter the body of the car to make them fit. But how to find out how much alteration? You can get a general idea by comparing the dimensions of the tires with a known set. If a 205/50-15 fits, then a 225/45-15 will need an extra 10 millimeters (approximately 3/8 inch) on each side to clear. Once you have the big tires, you can check their clearance on the car by removing the spring from the suspension and reinstalling the shock and bumpstop. Then use a jack to move the wheel through its full range. In the front, you'll also want to do this with the steering turned to full lock. Wide tires can rub on the fender or on suspension components, while tall tires such as the ones used on *Elvis* can also rub at the top. In the case of a car with extreme suspension travel such as this one, you can even rub with a fairly standard size tire. There's more information on what to do to solve this sort of problem in Chapter 12.

little tread depth to start with, and there were concerns about how quickly they'd wear, so the RA-1 was chosen.

Luckily, this tire comes in a wide variety of sizes. A set of lightweight 15x7-inch wheels was already available, so the size choice was narrowed down to either a 205/50-15 or a 225/45-15. That also gave a useful sidewall height to allow the tire to help absorb the rough roads.

The Toyo spec sheet indicates that these two tires have almost exactly the same diameter, but that the 225/45 is 3 pounds heavier and of course it's wider. Spec Miata racers have found that the added weight and rolling resistance of the bigger tire actually slows down track times on their relatively low-powered cars and narrow 7-inch wheels. The wider tire would also be more prone to hydroplaning, so the smaller size was chosen. A 205/50-15 Toyo RA-1 is a popular Miata track day tire, so this wasn't a surprising decision. In the race, it proved to be effective in all conditions and forgiving. However, tire wear was minimal, so it's possible the stickier R888 or NT-01 would have been suitable as well.

Car 3: *Elvis*, a V-8-powered 2002 Miata with a huge amount of power and torque and a real traction problem. The car gets used on the track and on the street, but doesn't cover huge amounts of mileage. A short-lived, sticky tire was needed, and it needed to be as fat as possible to help keep the car under control. Price wasn't too important, and the car needed new wheels. As with the Targa Miata, the streetable R-compounds were chosen. The next step was to check the manufacturer spec sheets to see what sizes were available. Because the car was fitted with adjustable suspension and the fenders could be modified, the decision was made to allow tire sizes up to 25 inches in diameter. This isn't ideal for handling, but it did give the car a fighting chance of hooking up with more than 400 pounds of torque just off idle.

A 255/40-17 was the widest available, but that width could cause problems in the front. This is where having the spec sheets came in handy. A 235/45-17 is almost the same diameter but gives a bit more clearance, and thus the decision was to go with a staggered setup. One nice thing is that while

these tires are never used on Miatas, they're actually quite common, so a wide range of street tire options is available should a different type of tire be needed in the future. Only one race tire offered the exact combination of tire sizes chosen, so the car was fitted with Toyo R888s.

The tire sizes dictated at least a 7.5-inch wheel up front and an 8.5-inch in the rear, so a staggered set of wheels was chosen. The 17x8.5-inch is an unusual wheel size for a 4x100 bolt pattern, but a couple of reasonable options exist. All four fenders and one wheelwell needed modification to fit the tires inside the body. This is an extreme setup, but it's an extreme car, and it shows the logic behind a tire choice.

WHEELS

Now that we have tires, what about wheels? Wheels are one of the biggest fashion accessories for cars, both in terms of impact and cost. We'll ignore the aesthetic aspect for now and concentrate on function. There are four interesting things to know about wheels: diameter, width, offset, and weight.

The diameter of the wheels is the easiest one to deal with. Basically, they must be the correct diameter to fill the hole in the middle of the tire. A larger diameter wheel will require a tire with shorter sidewalls, as discussed earlier. This will have a number of effects on how the car behaves. The shorter sidewall is stiffer and won't flex as much on bumps and under side loads, leading to more responsive steering, a more stable feel, and a harsher ride. However, different models of tires have varying levels of sidewall stiffness, so it's possible to have a 17-inch setup that rides more smoothly than a 14-inch with the right tire choices. The wheel has be to big enough to clear the brakes, which does limit how small it can be.

The right wheels can have a big effect on the looks of a car, and personal taste is always a factor. Regardless of the specifications, most people won't use a wheel that they don't think looks good.

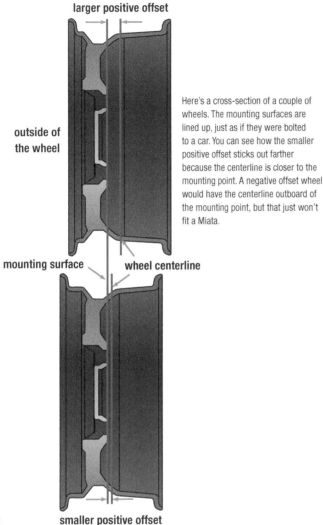

larger positive offset

outside of the wheel

Here's a cross-section of a couple of wheels. The mounting surfaces are lined up, just as if they were bolted to a car. You can see how the smaller positive offset sticks out farther because the centerline is closer to the mounting point. A negative offset wheel would have the centerline outboard of the mounting point, but that just won't fit a Miata.

mounting surface   **wheel centerline**

smaller positive offset

WHEELS AND TIRES

The width of the wheel will affect how the tire works and fairly dramatically. The wheel is basically the foundation for the tire, and a wider wheel will stretch the sidewalls out more and effectively make them stiffer and less likely to deflect. Because the driver controls the wheel and the tire interacts with the road at the contact patch, any extra movement between the two will lead to less precise handling. A better supported sidewall also allows the tire to be run at lower pressure, which increases the amount of rubber in contact with the road.

Generally speaking, for the same size tire, a narrower wheel will be more comfortable and offer less rolling resistance while a wider wheel will handle and grip better. Racers usually choose the widest wheel they can get their hands on. It's telling that racing regulations almost always specify a maximum wheel width, because wider is faster. A 225/45-15 will fit on a 15x7 wheel, but it will be able to move around more than is ideal. On a 15x8, it'll be faster. But on a 15x9—a little bit wider than the manufacturer will usually recommend—it'll be fastest yet. If you're looking for maximum performance, go for the widest wheel you can, but check to make sure you have room under your fenders.

Offset is a measure of the distance between the mounting surface and the centerline of the wheel. The mounting surface is rarely right in the center of the wheel. In the case of a Miata, the suspension is designed to use a positive offset, the same sort usually found on front-wheel-drive cars. This means that the centerline of the wheel is inboard from the mounting surface. Going to a lower offset means the wheel sits farther outboard on the car, a higher offset tucks it in more.

Offset can affect your suspension geometry because it is related to the scrub radius. If you draw an imaginary line between the ball joints on the front upright, that's your

This is what wheel width will do. Both tires are 225/45-15 Nitto NT-01. The wheel on the right is a 15x7; the one on the left is a 15x9. The difference in tire width is dramatic. You can also see the shape of the sidewall on each tire, the wide wheel has the sidewall almost perpendicular to the wheel lip. *Photo courtesy of 949 Racing.*

steering axis. This is what your wheel rotates around when you turn the steering wheel. Now, continue the imaginary line right down to the ground. The distance between this point on the ground and the centerline of the wheel is called your scrub radius. If the wheel is outboard, then you have a positive scrub radius. If it's inboard, it's a negative scrub radius. Miatas were designed with no scrub radius at all. In other words, the wheel centerline is sitting right where that steering axis hits the ground when viewed from the front.

So? Well, a positive scrub radius means the steering wheel will kick more when you hit a bump and will pull side to side if you have traction differences under braking. A negative scrub radius will minimize this behavior but at the cost of steering feel. Generally, sports car drivers will accept a more positive scrub radius up to a point.

Because offset also affects how far the wheel sticks out from the hub, it has a real impact on tire clearance. A lower offset can make a car look fantastic with the wheelwells completely stuffed with tire, but care must be taken not to go too far and get fender interference. The wider track will also cut down on weight transfer in cornering.

Generally speaking, you can decrease offset by up to 15 millimeters without any really evil tendencies coming to light. The stock offsets are +45 millimeters for the NA, +40 millimeters for the NB, and +55 for the NC.

Now, what's this about weight? Most of the Miata's weight is isolated from the road by the suspension and is referred to as "sprung weight." The wheels and tires—along with the brake rotors and calipers and a few suspension components—are referred to as "unsprung weight." That's the weight that has to move up and down when a wheel hits a bump, and it's best looked at as a percentage of the total vehicle weight. If the unsprung weight percentage gets too high, the suspension will transmit more of the bump to the sprung weight instead of letting the unsprung weight move. The greater inertia of the unsprung weight will also make it less likely to follow the shape of the road. In other words, the ride gets worse and the tires are less likely to be in contact with the ground. This is obviously not good.

But wait, there's more! Your wheels and tires also act like flywheels. In order to accelerate or brake, you have to change their speed of rotation.

As with any flywheel, the more mass they have, the more they will resist the change of speed. This means you'll lose acceleration and braking with a heavier wheel and tire combination.

There's still one more effect. The front wheels can have a gyroscopic effect, resisting a change in direction and ruining steering feel.

So what's good about unsprung and rotating mass? Nothing really. It's something that should be kept to a minimum wherever possible, and one of the easiest places to cut down on this mass is in the wheels. Wheel weight can vary drastically. Fifteen-inch wheels, for example, will

If these wheels had a lower offset, the tires would have a real problem clearing the fenders. As it is, the fenders had to be modified to allow them to clear at full lock with the suspension compressed.

With wide tires, you also have to watch the clearance inside the wheelwell. This tire just cleared the spring (removed here for suspension travel testing) and would rub the bulge at the shock tower. To fix this problem, the wheels were fitted with spacers to move them outboard, effectively lowering the offset.

range from under 10 pounds to over 20. Super-light wheels can be expensive but not always. Mazda did a good job of putting light wheels on the Miata from the factory, unlike many cars, so you have to be careful not to install heavier-than-stock wheels when trying to improve things. Unless fashion is the most important criteria in your wheel choice, definitely find out what the weights are of the various wheels you're considering. If nobody can tell you, assume the worst. Anyone who makes a light wheel will be proud of the fact.

As you might imagine, larger and wider wheels tend to be heavier wheels. So going to a 17x7 wheel to replace a 15x6 could add 5 pounds to your rotating mass. It's interesting to note that while tire weights go up with width, the wheel size doesn't have a big effect. So a 205/50-15 typically weighs within a pound or two of a 205/40-17.

Here's a list of factory sizes and weights:
1990–1993 14x5.5 12.5
1990–1997 Steel 14x5.5 18.0
1993 LE (made by BBS) 14x6 10.5
1994 M-Edition 14x6 10.3
1994–1997 14x6 11.8 (hollow backside on spokes)
1994–1997 14x6 10.9 (semi-hollow spokes)
1995 M-Edition (BBS) 15x6 11.6
1996 M-Edition 15x6 14.7
1997 M-Edition 15x6 14.5
1999–2000 14x6 12.5
1999–2000 15x6 13.4
2001 16x6.5 15.5
2002 SE 16x6.5 19.0
2006 17x7 17.0

Actually, there's one more interesting thing about wheels, but it's not something you can really do anything about. Both the bolt pattern and hub bore have to be correct for them to fit on your car. The bolt pattern on an NA or NB is 4x100, meaning it has four lugs that are spaced evenly around a 100-millimeter diameter circle. The pattern on the NC is 5x114.3. Miata wheels are also hubcentric, which means they use a snug fit on the hub to locate the wheel. A wheel used on an NA or NB Miata should have a hole in the center that is 54.1 millimeters in diameter; it's 67.1 millimeters for the NC. Because this measurement varies from carmaker to carmaker, aftermarket wheels tend to have oversize center holes with a "centering ring" inserted to bring it down to size. It's always good to ask if these will be included, or in the case of some Spec Miata wheels, if the wheel is machined to the exact size for the Miata's hub.

It is possible to use a wheel that's lugcentric, meaning the lugs locate the wheel and the hole for the hub is oversized. It takes a lot more care to get the wheel on the hub correctly, and these are very uncommon.

TIRE SIZES TO USE

Want to skip the math? Here are the common tire sizes used on Miatas. It's not an exhaustive list, of course. Some tires come in unusual sizes that can work nicely. The ones in bold were used from the factory and may be easier to find. Bolds denote a size that will fit but is a little larger. The measurement afterward is the diameter of the tire. These certainly aren't the only options, particularly if you're feeling a bit adventurous. If you're willing to go an inch taller, the options open up, particularly for the NC. An example is 255/35-18.

NA/NB
185/60-14 (22.8 inches)
195/55-14 (22.4 inch)
205/55-14 (22.9 inch)
195/50-15 (22.7 inches)
205/50-15 (23.0 inch)
225/45-15 (22.8 inch)— often the size of choice for very
                                                high performance
205/45-16 (23.3 inches)
215/40-16 (22.8 inch)
205/40-17 (23.5 inches)

NC
205/50-16 (24.0 inches)
225/45-16 (23.9 inches)
205/45-17 (24.3 inches)
215/40-17 (23.8 inches)
235/40-17 (24.4 inches)
245/40-17 (24.7 inches)—popular race tire size
215/35-18 (23.9 inches)
225/35-18 (24.3 inches)

These two wheel-and-tire combinations are pretty similar. Both wheels are a +30 millimeter offset 15x7 mounted with Toyo RA-1 tires. The light white SSR Competition wheel is fitted with some 205/50-15 tires, while the gray Kazera KZ-M has 225/45-15s. However, there's a big difference you can't see. Due to the extra weight of the wider tire and a heavier wheel, there's 6 pounds of weight difference between them. If you believe the published weights for the wheels, you'd actually expect even more. The Kazera is a Spec Miata wheel, and thus has to conform to the minimum wheel weight of 13 pounds. The SSR does not, and it's both a fair bit lighter and approximately three times the cost.

RECOMMENDATIONS

After all those details, what's the preferred setup? It comes down to tire availability. As time goes on, smaller wheels are becoming less common, and the selection of high-performance tires in those sizes is evaporating. But the extra weight of a larger wheel and tire combination hurts the Miata.

For many enthusiasts, the sweet spot for an NA or NB is the 15-inch size. Thanks in part to a large number of racing classes, the slightly oversize 205/50-15 has a good range of options for performance tires, and there are some good tires in the wider 225/45-15. Both of those sizes will fit under stock NA or NB fenders with little or no modification, depending on offset and wheel width. The 15-inch wheels will fit over any factory and almost all aftermarket brake systems. Because Spec Miatas use a 15x7 wheel, there are a number of inexpensive,

strong, and reasonably light wheels on the market. Wider wheels are becoming available, and these are preferable for track-based cars to give the sidewall more support.

Currently, some of the fastest Miatas are running a 225/45-15 stretched over a 15x9-inch wheel. Autocrossers are going even wider, with race-only 275/35-15 tires stuffed into the wheelwells.

The NC has a bunch more room in the fender wells than the earlier cars. A 235/40-18 on a +48 offset is about as aggressive as you can go without having to modify anything. With a bit of careful fender rolling a 245/40-17 or even a 225/40-17 will fit. With enough fender massaging or flares, you can even fit a massive 295/30-18. Keep in mind that the tire is more important than the size, though. A superior tire in a slightly smaller size is a better choice than a poor tire in a larger size.

Looking for more fun and style on a budget? While it's fun to pick out $300 wheels from a catalog, a bit of paint can make even stock wheels stand out from the crowd. This 1990 is running on the stock 14x5.5 wheels. They were stripped of paint, the lips were polished by hand, and the centers were painted black with an off-the-shelf wheel paint. The total cost was around $30 for materials, and the car has a set of light, stylish wheels. They're mounted with 205/55-14 Toyo RA-1 tires for track and high-performance street use.

Chapter 12
Body and Chassis

With all this talk of horsepower and suspension, we need something to hold it all together and cover it all up. That would be the body and chassis. There's a big industry in body kits to make your Miata look different from all the others, but we're going to concentrate on functional changes. Miata doesn't have a separate body and chassis but a unibody structure that combines big parts of the two. However, for clarity, I'm going to refer to the external sheetmetal as the body and the structure as the chassis.

RIGIDITY

In order for the suspension to be able to work at its best, it needs a good solid platform. A flexing chassis acts like a big undamped spring, which takes precision out of the handling and undoes a bunch of that careful suspension tuning you worked so hard on. A stiff chassis lets the moving parts of the suspension deal with bumps and cornering forces, just like they're supposed to. It means you can run higher spring rates and more aggressive damping. There are no downsides to a rigid chassis, either, other than potential weight gain. A car with a solid structure will ride better, handle better, and be quieter than a loose one. That's why manufacturers work so hard to bring up the rigidity of their production cars.

Mazda tried, too. The Miata used state-of-the-art CAD modeling when it was originally designed, and it was a pretty stiff little car in 1989. The NB was based on the same platform with a number of changes, increasing stiffness by as much as 35 percent thanks to more sophisticated modeling. In 2001, Mazda added on a number of underbody braces as part of the Sport package designed to improve the car further, coming up with the stiffest Miata to date. These braces are often referred to as the Sport braces and became standard for American Miatas in 2003. But by 2005, that original NA platform was starting to show its age. The fundamental design needed a rework. And with the NC, it got one. The new car is substantially stiffer than before.

There are a wide variety of braces available on the market for all three generations of car. In the case of the early cars, many of the available braces duplicate (or anticipated) those added by the factory in later cars. There are two basic types: those intended to keep the suspension geometry consistent and those designed to stiffen the rest of the chassis.

The suspension pickup points are where the cornering loads are fed into the chassis. If they're allowed to flex, the Miata's precise suspension geometry goes out of whack. So the initial factory braces were found in this area. The lower

pickup points weren't well supported, and both cross and longitudinal bracing helped. In the front, a simple crossbar was used to reinforce the rearmost lower control arm pickup points. In the rear, all four lower control arm pickups were fairly unsupported, so the braces started off as simple crossbars and grew into beefy ladder frames that tied the pickups directly to the floorpan of the car. Over the years, they got stronger and stronger. Unfortunately, the NB rear braces cannot be bolted to an NA subframe.

An example of how a little change can make a big difference, this gusset straddling the top of the transmission tunnel made such a difference that the steel in the bulkhead could be made thinner. A similar patch is used at the firewall. Changes like this improved the dynamic torsional rigidity of the NB by 35 percent over the NA.

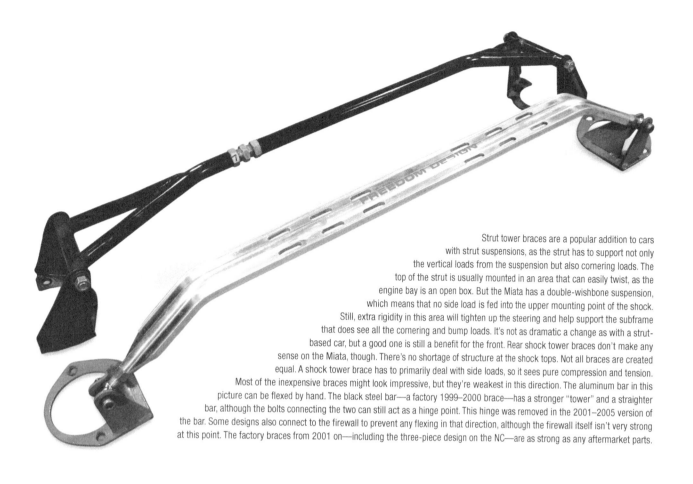

Strut tower braces are a popular addition to cars with strut suspensions, as the strut has to support not only the vertical loads from the suspension but also cornering loads. The top of the strut is usually mounted in an area that can easily twist, as the engine bay is an open box. But the Miata has a double-wishbone suspension, which means that no side load is fed into the upper mounting point of the shock. Still, extra rigidity in this area will tighten up the steering and help support the subframe that does see all the cornering and bump loads. It's not as dramatic a change as with a strut-based car, but a good one is still a benefit for the front. Rear shock tower braces don't make any sense on the Miata, though. There's no shortage of structure at the shock tops. Not all braces are created equal. A shock tower brace has to primarily deal with side loads, so it sees pure compression and tension. Most of the inexpensive braces might look impressive, but they're weakest in this direction. The aluminum bar in this picture can be flexed by hand. The black steel bar—a factory 1999–2000 brace—has a stronger "tower" and a straighter bar, although the bolts connecting the two can still act as a hinge point. This hinge was removed in the 2001–2005 version of the bar. Some designs also connect to the firewall to prevent any flexing in that direction, although the firewall itself isn't very strong at this point. The factory braces from 2001 on—including the three-piece design on the NC—are as strong as any aftermarket parts.

The factory undercar brace on an MSM. This is an interesting piece, as it's obviously designed to crumple in a crash. The MSM version has some extra heat shielding and is configured to clear the MSM's unique exhaust. The version off the non-turbo cars can be fitted to any non-turbo 2001–2005 NB.

The final evolution of the NA/NB rear subframe brace. Not only are the tubes beefy, but they're attached to each lower control arm mounting point with some very strong bolts. Two pairs of bolts are used to attach it to the floorpan. This brace can make a big difference on high-power cars in a straight line as well as cornering for any Miata. This particular design can be retrofitted to any NB, although you may have to leave off two of the floorpan bolts. The NA had a design that was similar but not as strong. You can tell a lot about how effective a factory brace is by how solid the mounting points are. The rear subframe braces are held in with eight beefy bolts. The cross brace visible at the bottom of the picture has two fairly small 8-millimeter bolts, and it has a couple of bends in the bar. Obviously, the subframe braces are dealing with much higher loads.

To stiffen the rest of the structure, the main focus is on the area around the cockpit. This big open hole is a real problem for convertibles. Just open the doors and have a look at your car from the side to see why. One popular solution developed by Flyin' Miata has been to add an extra layer of steel around the box sections that run from front to rear under the floor. This makes a dramatic difference to the rigidity of the car with little weight gain. A number of similar products have hit the marketplace. The factory pseudo-frame rails are made of thin metal and are easily crushed by speed bumps, improper jacking, or other mishaps. Most Miatas have damaged frame rails.

Adding cross bracing from one side to the other helps out quite a bit as well, and both commercial and home-brew solutions have proven effective here. The best will cross under the transmission tunnel diagonally. It can be difficult to arrange good exhaust clearance without affecting ground clearance.

A roll bar will help out with chassis stiffness as well as the more obvious benefits of protecting the occupants (just in case you needed another reason to add a roll bar to your Miata). Better yet is a full roll cage, which effectively turns the open Miata into a coupe. It's not a good solution for street driving, but the difference in chassis rigidity has to be felt to be believed.

Claims as to the effectiveness of the NA/NB hardtop in chassis stiffness vary. Some sources inside Mazda claim no difference, while Takao Kijima (the Miata program manager) has claimed a 10 to 15 percent improvement in stiffness. I'm biased toward believing the latter, as a hardtop can make a discernible difference to the car. Bolting the hardtop in using a set of Spec Miata plates will help even further. As an added bonus, the hardtop also makes the car more aerodynamic. The weight is close to that of the soft top, so bolting on the hardtop and removing the folding top is a good way to make the car both slipperier and stiffer—and to add a surprising amount of room inside behind the seats.

NA and NB Miatas are prone to rust in one place, and it's a bad one. The side sills are responsible for much of the car's structural rigidity, and they can rust out from the inside. When they do, the car loses a lot of strength. This rust should be repaired properly with a patch panel, not simply sanded down and resprayed.

SEAM WELDING

One way to improve the stiffness of almost any car is to seam weld or stitch weld it. When cars are produced, pieces of sheet steel are bent to shape and welded together. Almost all of these seams are spot welded, which are structurally similar to rivets. More welds are stronger but take longer to do, and when you're a big manufacturer popping out cars, time is money. Stronger still is a stitch-welded chassis, where the spot welds are replaced or supplanted by short lengths of weld to keep those panels well and truly stuck together.

You can improve the rigidity of a Miata by seam welding it. A word of warning, however: Production cars are designed to deform in an accident, and this is carefully engineered into the unibody. Those spot welds are designed to come apart. By adding more welds, it's possible that you could affect the crumpling and make the car less safe. Exactly how this will affect the car we don't know, and Mazda doesn't want to say. So keep this in mind. Of course, the same thing applies to undercar bracing, door bars, and the like.

If you do decide to stitch weld the frame, make sure you clean off the seams as well as possible with a wire brush before you do it. They're usually covered with seam sealer, and it doesn't weld well. The easiest area to access is the door opening, and it can make a noticeable difference to the rigidity of the car. The other areas are underneath the front fenders and in the engine bay. When welding, weld a short bead (an inch or less) and then skip ahead an inch or two. If possible, move around the car frequently to avoid heat distortion. There's no need to completely weld each seam.

Suggested seam-welding locations under the front fenders.

Suggested seam-welding locations under the hood. The amount of bracing around the shock tower makes it clear how much loading is run through this area.

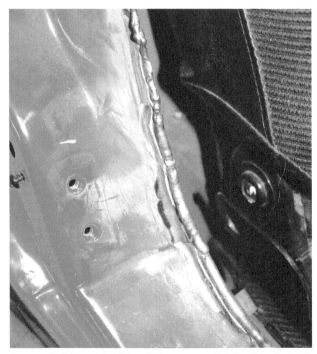
A seam-welded door opening. This particular car was welded along the entire length of the seam, which is overkill. All of this welding is covered by the factory trim.

These Frog Arms from Boss Frog give much the same benefit of seam welding under the fenders, but they simply bolt on. There's a weight penalty compared to the welded version, but it's far easier to do.

BODY
Fender Flares

A car with big fender flares or a wide body just screams performance. Most wide-body kits are sold for looks alone, but they do serve a purpose. If you've fitted really wide rubber or pushed the track wider with low-offset wheels, then you need to cover those tires so that they don't stick out past the bodywork. That's the real purpose of fender flares. Usually, wide-body kits are installed for looks and then the owner goes looking for fat rubber to fill them up.

Sometimes, you need just a little more room to fit your tires under your stock fenders. It's often possible to get that extra space by rolling the fenders. Basically, you end up folding the lip inside the fender flat against the inside of the sheetmetal. The downside is that this sometimes will prevent you from installing the plastic fender liners that help protect all those little crevices inside the wheelwells against rocks and general road goo. Racers generally don't care though.

The classic way to roll your fenders is with a baseball bat. Lever it against the tire and roll it around, forcing that inner lip flat. A more sophisticated method is to use a dedicated fender rolling tool. This is a lot easier to control and you can even stretch the fender outward a little bit if required. They're a bit expensive for most home garages, but some clubs will get together to buy one. Regardless of how you roll the lip back, use a heat gun to get the paint nice and toasty warm. That will help avoid cracking.

This dedicated race car runs the same wide slicks used in E Production with a low offset wheel. The wide body completely replaces the front fenders with lightweight fiberglass. The new body panels are bonded to the stock unibody in the rear, with the stock fenders cut away underneath.

Need to cover 295/30-18 tires? Then you'll need more room under your fenders. These flares serve a distinct purpose.

A commercial fender-rolling tool at work. With careful heat application, this fender was stretched outboard quite a bit without any paint damage and with a nice smooth curve.

WEIGHT LOSS

One of the least expensive ways to gain performance is to drop some weight. A lower weight will not only help you accelerate better, it will also improve cornering ability and braking. There's a reason that race classes specify a minimum weight.

Unfortunately, the Miata is a fairly lightweight car, so dropping massive amounts of weight isn't all that easy. Weight loss claims also have to be taken with a grain of salt, as there's often some creative math at work. In my opinion, cars should only be weighed full of all fluids, as it's far easier to be repeatedly full than it is to repeatedly have 2 gallons of gas in the tank. If you're serious about tracking just how much weight you've removed from your car, make sure you weigh it in the same condition every time.

There are a few obvious big things that can be removed to shed some weight. The bumper supports under the skin, for example. The spare tire and jack. This sort of thing won't affect the car's day-to-day driving experience, but it can let you dump a surprising amount of weight in a hurry. Depending on how you feel about driving in weather other than "sunny and warm," you can remove the soft top, the wipers, the heater and AC components, and the side window glass and associated mechanisms. For a real race look, strip out as much of the interior as you can. By this point, of course, you've got a car that can only be driven in the dry and that will be noisier. It's all about choices.

Once you've run out of big things to unbolt and set aside, it's time for detail work. As every hiker knows, the easiest way to lose a pound is to find an ounce 16 times. Are there extra brackets on the car you don't need? Cut 'em off. Some racers have gone to the effort of grinding extra metal off the intake manifold. Others will recommend cutting the exposed threaded ends off bolts, a technique that can drop a few pounds but has the potential to damage your threads.

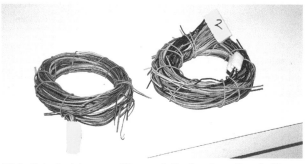

A high-effort option is to remove all the unused wiring from the car. If you don't have a radio, power windows, airbags, or a heater, you don't need the fairly hefty electrical system required to support them. This is not something to undertake without a factory wiring diagram. The wires in the picture are what was removed when the ECU was moved from behind the passenger's seat to under the dashboard in a 1994.

A minimum-weight interior. The 1990 dashboard has been cut in half and much of the structure underneath was been removed. All extra wiring is gone, and the big heater fan has been replaced with a bilge blower to defrost the windshield. A hand-made aluminum switch panel covers a hole in the center of the dash, a nice combination of aesthetics and accessibility. They can't be seen well in the picture, but the factory seats have been replaced with a pair of racing shells bolted directly to the floor. The doors haven't been stripped much because of the need to retain side windows in this particular car.

Extreme weight loss at work. This factory door was reduced to a simple skin, and the door latch is opened with this thin cable. The door will no longer support its own weight when opened, but it's about as light as it can get. The rest of this car was treated to a similar weight loss regimen, with the dashboard later replaced by a simple panel to support the gauges and a polycarbonate windshield.

Your battery is a major chunk of weight. The Odyssey PC680 at left is about 10 pounds lighter than stock but will crank just as hard. Where it suffers is in reserve capacity, so it's not a good option for a car that's difficult to start.

Look at interchange options as well. Switching from a 1994 dashboard to a 1990 one will shed some weight and should bolt straight in. The soft top from the NB not only has a glass window and better sealing, but it's 6.6 pounds lighter than the NA version and bolts right in. Even converting from power to manual windows will save a pound per door, not including wiring. If you don't need a lot of heat capacity in your 1994 to 2002 brakes, consider installing a set from a 1990 to 1993.

And, of course, you can spend money on lightweight parts. The most useful area is probably the seats, as you'll not only cut some weight, but you'll also have the option to improve the ergonomics and potentially even the safety of the car. More on that in Chapter 13. Carbon-fiber body panels are available, but watch yourself here. Mazda did a pretty good job of keeping the removable panels light. The hood is aluminum, and the front fenders are made of very thin steel. Nevertheless, the trunk lid on the NA and NB models is surprisingly heavy and so are the lids for the pop-up headlights on the NA.

If you do want to spend money to make your Miata lighter, look at options that will have secondary benefits as well. The wheels, for example. Saving 4 pounds off each wheel will take 16 pounds off the entire car, but it's also rotating unsprung weight—the worst kind. A lightweight flywheel can drop as much at 10 pounds from the car, but it will feel like far more. A big brake kit with Wilwood calipers will often weigh less than stock.

Spec Miata races are required to bolt their hardtops in place. A bolted-on top is not only more secure, it's difficult to steal and will impart more rigidity to the chassis than a clamped-on one. These aluminum plates are also significantly lighter than the normal latches and can be removed quickly when required.

Extreme weight loss! This CSP autocross car runs a smaller and lighter alternator. Weight is critical in autocross, so the whole car had been examined from top to bottom.

Glass can be replaced with a polycarbonate such as Lexan. Make sure not to use acrylic such as Plexiglas. Replacing glass is actually quite easy to do; make a template of your original glass on paper and transfer it to a sheet of plastic. Even if you have a broken window, it's not that difficult to get close. Cut the plastic a bit oversize and then trim to fit. For this rear hardtop window, ⅛-inch thick polycarbonate was used. It was attached by rivets, starting in the middle and moving to the ends. The polycarbonate is flexible enough that it will simply conform to shape, and it saved approximately 6 pounds in this case. The triangular side windows can be changed for plastic with no visible sign. As with many other weight-saving methods, however, check to make sure they're legal for road use in your area.

AERODYNAMICS

Cars spend a lot of effort pushing through the air. In fact, in most naturally aspirated Miatas, it's aerodynamic drag that limits the top speed of the car. The power needed to overcome drag rises with the cube of the speed, so it takes eight times as much power to drive at 100 miles per hour as it does at 50. Mazda didn't really spend much wind tunnel time on our little roadsters, and they're aerodynamically fairly poor. But there's more going on than just drag. We can put all this air to work for us.

The science of aerodynamics is all about air pressure. That's how wings on airplanes work. The air going over the wing is forced to travel farther than the air underneath, which means there's less pressure above the wing than below. This creates lift so you can fly. Of course, we don't want our Miata to actually take to the air. Even a bit of lift at speed will start to unload our tires, making the car less stable and costing us grip. What we really want is no lift, or even better, negative lift or downforce. This will press our car into the surface of the road, increasing grip without extra weight. This is, of course, the sort of thing you can spend your life studying, so this will not be a comprehensive rundown of what can be done but more of a general introduction.

Some heavily managed airflow. The low front air dam keeps air from getting under the car. Intakes just above that feed cold air to the brakes with a big one for the radiator and intercooler. The turn indicators have been replaced with inlets that feed an oil cooler on one side and the engine air intake on the other. Above that, NACA ducts in the headlight covers do the same. The hood is fitted with an extraction vent to pull air out of the engine bay. NACA ducts in the windows shoot cool air at the driver. Meanwhile, at the back, a wing provides downforce to keep the car planted in corners. There are even vents in the rear window to help manage the airflow, and a transmission oil cooler is embedded in the rear bumper to take advantage of the air trapped by the bodywork.

Laminar airflow refers to air all moving in much the same direction. Turbulent flow is when the airflow is all scrambled and moving in many different directions.

As air moves around your Miata, it usually follows the shape closely. This sort of airflow is called attached flow. If the air can't stay close to the surface, it's called detached flow. Typically, this will also be turbulent. Attached, laminar airflow we can use; detached turbulent air will cause a lot of drag without giving us much benefit.

Unfortunately, downforce is hard to arrange. Mostly what we'll be able to accomplish with a Miata is less lift. One of the best ways to do this is to keep air from getting under the car. This forces more air to go over the top of the car, which raises the pressure on top and drops the pressure underneath. This is what air dams and splitters are intended to do, and they can make a dramatic difference in high-speed stability. Mazda even put a subtle air dam on the bottom of the nose of the NB to manage airflow. The biggest problem with a deep air dam is that it's prone to damage.

Wings are pretty easy to understand. They work like aircraft wings but upside down. That's why they're used on every race series that allows them. Airplanes have an advantage, though. They're (usually) flying through clean air, while wings on cars have to deal with the perturbed airflow from the body of the car itself. There's a lot of science in the shaping of wing cross-sections. It can be difficult to distinguish between an effective design and one that was simply styled, but some conversations with the vendor should clarify that fairly quickly.

Spoilers are different from wings in that they're designed to actually spoil the airflow in carefully chosen spots. By putting one on the rear deck lid, the transition from the attached airflow on the trunk lid to the detached turbulent air behind the car is made sharper and can decrease lift. Most of the rear spoilers installed on Miatas are for looks only.

A fairly simple but effective wing. In testing, this setup made up to a 2.5-second-per-lap difference on a medium-speed track, depending on the angle of attack. The wing probably would have benefited from larger end plates and a slightly taller lip along the trailing edge, called a Gurney flap.

Tuft testing involves taping short pieces of string to the car to see what the airflow is doing at various locations. Smooth, attached airflow will lie the string down in the direction of the flow, while detached or turbulent flow will stand the strings up or point them in odd directions. In this case, you can see the airflow is nice along the sides of the hardtop and the rear fenders, but it detaches as it drops down the rear window. A couple of the tufts on the window are actually pointing directly against the main airflow. As expected, there's a lot of turbulence underneath the spoiler. This inexpensive testing is easy to do and interesting. Combine it with some cardboard spoilers, and you'll learn all sorts of things.

A simple front splitter from Track Dog Racing. It simply extends out from the bottom of the bumper by 1.75 inches and provides a good benefit for such a simple part. Just watch for curbs.

An aftermarket air dam for the NC. While it's probably never been in a wind tunnel, it should be fairly effective. It would help with cooling as well, ramming some extra air through the radiator.

The attached airflow around the body of the car means the air is moving in a different direction as it comes off the roof than the clean air around the car. This wing from 949 Racing is designed with a different shape in the center to allow for this and to make maximum use of all the air. A wing like this will still trade downforce for drag. Generally speaking, you keep adding downforce until your lap times start to go up from the extra drag. *Photo courtesy of 949 Racing*

NACA ducts (developed by the predecessor to NASA) were developed as a low-drag intake for surfaces with attached airflow. If shaped correctly, they're amazingly effective. They are not designed to be exhaust vents, though, and are often misused. If you're willing to do a bit of measuring and cutting, you can make your own as done here. The edges where the duct meets the flat surface have to be sharp and square; that's important. The ideal dimensions can be found online easily, these particular ducts were shortened to make them fit on the headlight covers. Notice the hand-made extraction vents on the hood as well. This car has quite a bit of aerodynamic cooling.

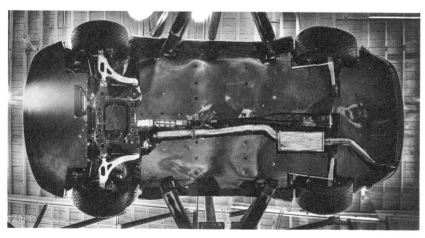

A smooth undertray will drop your aerodynamic drag and can open the door to some significant downforce if done properly. You may have to watch the temperature of your transmission and differential, and you'll definitely have to make sure the exhaust can get some airflow, but the potential is good. This particular car is a rotary Miata with the suspension from a 1993–1995 RX-7, so it looks a little different than most Miatas from underneath. *Kris Eidnes*

Because there's so much surface area on the bottom of the car, you can use it to build some serious downforce. Just a small pressure differential will mean a lot of aerodynamic "weight" to keep those tires pressed into the pavement. Unfortunately, it's also fairly difficult to arrange on a production car. A front air dam is going to be the most effective way to keep the air pressure under the car low, but a diffuser at the rear can help suck the car down into the ground. To make a diffuser, the bottom of the car needs to rise so that the space between the ground and the car gets larger as you head toward the back of the car. Of course, there are awkward things like mufflers and differentials to deal with that can spoil the fun, but the potential is there to add a lot of downforce without a significant drag penalty if you're willing to build a custom exhaust system at the very least.

Even if the car isn't fitted with a diffuser, the rear bumper can act like a sail and catch the air under the car. Drilling some vents or cutting the bottom portion out as seen here can make a big difference in drag.

An example of low-speed aerodynamics. Bill Schenker's CSP autocrosser runs this massive rear spoiler to help keep the rear end planted. He can adjust the angle as needed. Note the small bracket at the end above the taillight. Without it, the ends of the spoiler deflect and spill air out the side. The odd shape along the top is due to regulations that limit the height of the spoiler over the bodywork, so it follows the shape of the trunk lid. This design would add a large amount of drag and wouldn't be ideal for a track car, but for the relatively low speeds found on the autocross course it's very effective. Wings are not allowed in this race class, and for the sake of regulations a wing is described as having airflow on both sides. Because this piece has no gap between the body and the large surface, it's a spoiler.

The front air dam from Bill Schenker's car. Not only does it stop air from getting under the car, it helps smooth out the air that does and provides some radiator ducting. The nose of the car is so low that the air dam has to be removed to put the car in the trailer.

UNDERHOOD FLOW

There's another area of airflow we're interested in, though. A high-power Miata makes a lot of heat and all the heat exchangers in the front of car need airflow to work at their best. There are two aspects to this: getting air in and out. An air dam will help here, forcing more air into the mouth of the car. But once it's in, we need to make sure the air is forced to go through the radiator and intercooler. As I said earlier, air's lazy, and if you give it an easy way around something it'll take it. Some time spent with ducting inside the nose can make a huge difference in cooling efficiency for little effort. Mazda knows this; that's why there's plastic ducting all over the place.

Once you've managed to get air in, you need to get it out. That's what extraction hoods and vents do. They're set up with a vent at a low-pressure area to pull air out from underhood. Because the pressure underhood drops, it's easier to pack more air in there from the high-pressure area at the nose and voila! More airflow through the radiator. These can make a dramatic improvement in cooling effectiveness.

A grille might seem like a good idea, but they're terrible for airflow. A typical tight mesh will use 0.025-inch wire with 10 openings per inch. Sounds pretty open, but if you do the math, you'll discover that 44 percent of the surface area is now steel wire. Even a more open mesh will still be 25 percent wire. On top of that, the wires cause a lot of turbulence, which impedes airflow. The good news for this NC owner is that the air dam below the grille functions as an intake, and it is unaffected.

You can also get more air in by making the opening bigger. That's where many body kits get it right, but you don't have to go with the latest Godzilla face to make it work. A popular modification is to simply cut some of the front bumper cover out. On the NA and NB, there's nothing above the bumper itself, so a well-placed hole can help out a lot. It will expose some black plastic and the artistic qualities of the hole do depend on the cutter, but the price is right.

Who says aerodynamic modifications have to be big and obvious? Myron Ybarra's car is subtle but effective. The front air dam is a factory accessory that does a good job of cutting down the amount of front-end lift at speed. The turn indicators have been replaced by air inlets. On most cars this wouldn't make sense, but this turbo engine has its intake in a sealed box right behind one of these inlets, so this feeds lots of high-pressure cold air to the engine for more horsepower. The hood has been modified with louvers to help pull air out from underhood, encouraging airflow through the radiator and intercooler.

A vented hood to help pull air out of the engine bay. These vents work well because they're placed where tuft testing tells us is the lowest pressure area of the hood. The big bulge in the middle is primarily for show. In fact, it works as an inlet into the engine bay due to the high-pressure area at the base of the windshield.

Chapter 13
Safety Gear

It would be irresponsible to spend a whole book discussing how to make a car faster without talking about how to keep it safe. Of course, excellent handling, braking, and driver ability are safety items. The easiest way to survive an accident is simply not to be in one, but if it all goes wrong, what next?

ROLL BARS

One of the basic safety upgrades to a Miata is a roll bar. It's fairly easy to imagine what they're for, of course. The windshield frame can collapse easily if the car ends up with the shiny side down, and that's not usually healthy for those in the car. Almost every track day will require some sort of rollover protection, and it's mandatory for just about any sort of racing. As an added bonus, they'll stiffen up your Miata's structure.

If you are buying a roll bar to meet some sort of regulations, find out what the regulations are. Any roll bar manufacturer will be able to tell you the specifications of their bar, but they may not know offhand if it meets the rollover protection regulations for your local track day organizers. Generally speaking, most groups in the United States will simply go off the SCCA rules. Other countries will have an equivalent ruling body.

Do not try this at home. *Photo courtesy of Hard Dog Fabrication*

A real roll bar will tie into the car's structure in at least four places. There are a lot of bars on the market that simply bolt to the top of the seatbelt towers and are designed to look cool without offering any protection. They're called "style bars" and don't really belong in a chapter about safety. A real roll bar like this one will have legs extending forward or, more commonly, back that are bolted straight to the frame rails of the car. The diagonal braces keep the bar from collapsing sideways if it's hit on one side.

Keep in mind that the SCCA is a fairly major organization and sanctions a huge range of racing. SCCA autocross does not require roll protection in any but the most extreme classes, while Spec Miata requires a full cage with door bars. The typical class used for rollover specifications of sports cars is Solo 1. In that case, it means a bar made of 1.75-inch DOM tubing with walls at least 0.120-inch thick, formed to a particular shape. The bar will have to be fitted with fore-aft bracing and usually a diagonal. It's easy enough to find an SCCA-legal bar. Simply ask the manufacturer for one.

There's one aspect they won't be able to guarantee: The top of your helmet needs to be 2 inches below the top of the bar. For a lot of people in an otherwise-stock Miata, this can be quite difficult to do. There's a limit to how tall the bar can be and still fit under the top. It may be necessary to do something with the seat. For maximum protection, you're also going to want a bar that's as wide as possible.

For a particular look, many people want a pair of roll hoops behind the seats, sometimes called a double-hump bar. They look cool, but beware. Most of the available double-hump bars are style bars only. There are a couple of exceptions, such as this one from Hard Dog and another from Boss Frog, but even these aren't as effective at protecting the occupants as a standard single hoop and may not be accepted by track day organizers. If you make this particular choice, be aware of what you're trading off.

Naturally things are a bit different for the NC. Due to the way the top folds down, it's pretty much impossible to come up with rear bracing for the roll bar that lets you keep the roof.

One solution to the bracing problem for the NC is a set of removable rear bars. Obviously, it's not reassuring if you're not sure about the weather and it means the bar is always unbraced when the roof is up, but it's an option. Extra bracing does need to be added inside the trunk. Another choice is a Petty bar, which runs down into the passenger's footwell. It's not passenger-friendly, however.

The factory hoops in the NC are well tied in to the car's structure—as you'd expect from a set of bars designed at the factory—but there still isn't any fore-aft bracing for those hoops.

Of course, things are a bit different for cars that are primarily used on the street. Step back and take a look at your Miata. See how the roof arcs downward? SCCA-legal bars are designed to be as tall as possible, which means they have to be fairly far forward. This means they're quite close to your head. If the bar's properly padded and you're wearing a helmet, that's acceptable if not ideal. But an unarmored skull doesn't do as well against one. So a car that sees primarily street use might be better off with a lower bar that sits farther back. Not *too* far back, of course, because then they're not tall enough to do much. A good vendor should be able to help you figure out what works best for you, or you can go to a club meeting or track day and sit in as many cars as you can. Pay attention to the rear vision as well. A low bar or a carelessly placed diagonal can make the center mirror almost unusable. The 1990 to 1995 cars have the hardest time with this because of their rearview mirror design. The double-articulated design used from 1996 can be moved up and down, and this mirror can be retrofitted to earlier cars easily.

Street cars will also have to use a roll bar that's compatible with whatever top is fitted to the car. If you have an NB, you'll need a bar that will work with your glass window. If you have an NA and you've installed an aftermarket glass window, you're going to have to make sure your bar will fit with your top. Because aftermarket tops tend to have rear windows that are larger than the stock NB part, this can be a problem. If you run a hardtop, you're also going to want to make sure the bar fits under that and doesn't interfere with the side latches. There's a lot to keep in mind, but a good vendor should be able to take your criteria and help you pick the appropriate part for your need.

Installation of a roll bar usually takes most of a Saturday, and it's easiest if you have a friend handy to help. Check out *Mazda Miata MX-5 Performance Projects* for a how-to.

Anywhere your head can hit a bar, you need padding. Here are a few examples. On the left is pipe insulation, cheap and easy to find at a local hardware store. Unfortunately, it's far too soft to offer any protection at all. It doesn't really belong in a car. Next to it is some padding designed for a roll bar. It's offset so that you can put the thickest point close to your body. It's better, but still too soft to deal with the impact from your head on a metal bar. The thin C-shaped piece is a proper SFI-certified pad. This is the sort of stuff you're required to have anywhere your helmeted head can make contact with the bar. It's hard, but it's softer than the steel bar. You don't really want to hit your unhelmeted head on it if you can help it. On the right is a dual-density pad. The inner piece is SFI-certified padding, surrounded by a softer outer layer. The large surface area and softer material make this suitable for locations where a bare head might whack into a bar. It's thick stuff, and it can be awkward for space in a Miata. Because the outer layer is separate, it's possible to pull it off when you're wearing a helmet. This is a good solution for a car that sees both street and track use, especially one with a cage where there's a bar close to your head.

Here's a good street setup from Hard Dog: There's formed SFI padding underneath a vinyl cover. The cover makes it look good and protects the padding from damaging UV radiation. These 2004 seatbacks are pretty high, but you can see how a tall driver could have trouble staying clear of the bar in this case as well.

ROLL CAGES

Full-on wheel-to-wheel racing requires a roll cage. The rear section is similar to a roll bar, but there's also a hoop around the windshield frame and bars joining the two. There are often bars crossing the door opening as well. If you need a cage for racing, read the rule book carefully. That's your most important criteria for choosing one. A cage designed for SCCA use may not meet NHRA requirements, and different classes in the same organization will have different rules.

There's a side benefit to a cage. They have a massive stiffening effect on the chassis of the car. So much so that some racing classes will limit just how much of a cage you can put in to prevent too much of a performance increase. Tying the cage to the windshield frame and the upper shock mounts can make a big difference.

Cages can bolt in with backing plates, similar to the way roll bars are attached, or they can be welded in. In both cases, the ends of the tubes will be fitted with large plates to spread the load. The welded-in type are more of a hassle to install, but they do give more room inside the car. Because Spec Miata racers are both numerous and required to run cages,

there are a number of suppliers who cater to this market. It's where I'd recommend starting. They can help guide you in finding the right cage for your class requirements.

At the other end of the scale is a custom cage. A good race shop should be able to design and install a cage that meets your particular requirements. Typically they'll also be more closely fitted to the shape of the car and to your own particular physical requirements as well as the best harness mounting points. This gives you as much room as possible inside and a safer car. The best way to find a good local shop is to ask the racers in your area. Again, hanging around in the paddock at the track will let you see a number of different examples of cage design and the quality of work. Find one you like and get the builder's contact information.

A word of warning, though. While cages offer great protection in combination with a race seat, harnesses, and a helmet, they're not good for road use. Some of the bars run close to your head. Also, in order to run some of the door bars, the door has to be gutted. This means no side windows. It's cool to think about a caged street car, but unless you need it for the track, it's not really a smart idea.

This is a basic Spec Miata cage with a single door bar. This particular cage is also welded to the windshield frame, which isn't legal in Spec. Obviously, a cage installation tends to be permanent and is most easily done on a bare chassis like this one.

Harnesses are given either an SFI or FIA certification. The SFI belts expire at the end of the calendar year after their second birthday. This January 2007 set expired at the end of 2009. The reason for this is the nylon will degrade due to UV radiation. After a year of outdoor exposure, it's lost fully half of its original strength. FIA certified belts are good for five years thanks to a polyester belt material. The FIA certification is almost always more expensive, but remember that over a decade you'll either need two sets of FIA belts or five sets of SFI ones. It's amazing how quickly a two-year certification goes by. You can often get the belts re-webbed and recertified, reusing the expensive latching hardware. For street use or even most track days, it's unlikely anyone will ever check, and there's no expiration on stock seatbelts. But you're the one who's going to be strapped into these.

HARNESSES

Don't even think about running a harness without a real roll bar. Period.

Now that that's out of the way, a harness is designed to do the same thing as your seatbelt: hold you in place. The factory seatbelts are designed to be easy to live with, but they're nowhere near as effective at keeping you in place during an accident or even hard driving. In fact, having a harness to restrain you while driving frees you up to concentrate on the wheel, gearshift, and pedals instead of bracing yourself. Keep in mind that harnesses may not be street-legal in your area, although this isn't always something checked in a typical safety inspection.

There are two basic types of harnesses, 4-point and 5/6-point. A 4-point harness has two shoulder straps and two lap belts. Those are mounted to the chassis at four locations, thus the name. A 5/6-point will add a sub or crotch belt, which is anchored at either one or two locations on the chassis. In

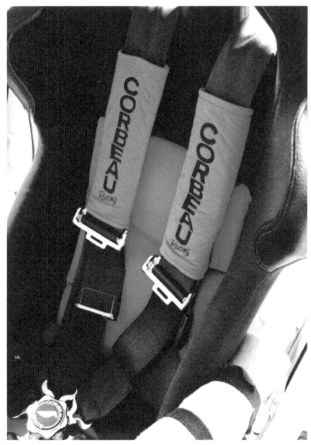

Belts typically come in 2- and 3-inch widths. The thinner size is easier to live within a street car, but it's not as comfortable. Remember that you're going to be putting a load on these, and a 3-inch belt has 50 percent more surface area. If possible, run the larger size. You can also pick up pads like the ones shown to make the belts a bit more cushy. If you are using a HANS device or similar, check to see what size belts it's designed to use. Some people find that 3-inch belts don't stay on the devices well. HANS-compatible harnesses with narrower webbing in the appropriate places are becoming available.

You'll find a couple of different latch designs for belts. The most expensive and easiest to use is a camlock like this, which has a round central latch. Twist the top and the entire harness falls away so that you can easily get out of the car. There's also a latch-and-link design, which is a bit harder to assemble but less expensive. If you're planning to use the belts in competition, check the regulations as some classes will only accept camlocks.

order for the harness to work as well as designed, the lap belt needs to be low on your hips so that your pelvis takes the load. If it sits up too high, it's over top of all sorts of delicate squishy internal parts. In a crash, the shoulder belts will tend to pull the lap belt upward with unhealthy results. Thus the usefulness of the sub-belt: It prevents the lap belt from riding up in a crash. Many people think it's also to prevent the driver from sliding out from underneath the lower belt, but this is more of a concern with a formula car with a very reclined seating position. The end result of a sub-belt is that the harness is much safer and actually more comfortable, in my opinion.

Ideally, a harness should be used with a race seat that has cutouts for the straps. Unless you have particularly wide shoulders, the stock seat forces the shoulder belts to be too far apart. It's possible for you to pop out from between them. To minimize this risk, you can cross the belts behind the seat. They won't be tempted to wander off, but it's still best to use a proper race seat. The sub-belt should really come straight up from below, which means there needs to be a hole in the seat. Another option is to mount the sub-belts behind the seat and slip them between the back and base of the seat so that you're sitting on them.

There is a 4-point harness on the market from Schroth that uses controlled stretching to prevent the lap belts from pulling upward. If you don't like the idea of a sub-belt, this is an alternative.

It's pretty easy to figure out where to attach the lap belts for a harness. Use the factory locations. All NA cars have a threaded hole on the transmission tunnel for the inner mounting, even if the stock belt is attached to the seat. On the NB and NC, you will need to drill a hole in the transmission tunnel. The area indicated here has a couple of layers for extra strength, and you'll have to use a backing plate. For the sub belt, there's a square cover in the floor that is glued down with seam sealer. Pry this up, and you'll gain access to the inside of the frame rail. This lets you put a backing plate under the floor for a center-mounted single sub belt. There's also a section of floor at the base of the rear bulkhead that is about four layers thick. When you're done, simply glue the plate back in to place with silicone sealant or seam sealer.

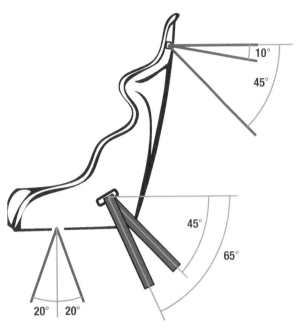

This diagram shows the recommended mounting locations of a set of harnesses according to the FIA, and these locations are also used by most other racing groups. They prefer an angle of 0 to 10 degrees down for the shoulder straps, but as much as 45 degrees is acceptable. The SFI has a different range of acceptable angles for the shoulder straps, ranging from 5 degrees down to 30 degrees up.

The shoulder harnesses can either be looped around a harness bar on the roll bar or attached to eyebolts on harness tabs. Ideally (and to be SCCA legal), the two shoulder straps should not share a single eyebolt. A glass window can cause problems with a harness bar, so definitely check with the manufacturer. The factory crossbar in the 1994–1997 cars is tempting, but it isn't suitable for harness attachment. The sub-belt is best installed by drilling a hole through the floor of the car and bolting it in, with a big washer or plate on the back side to spread the load around.

Note that it's possible to keep both harnesses and stock belts in the car, or simply attach the harnesses to eye bolts so that they can be quickly removed. It's not a bad setup for a dual-purpose car.

HELMETS

When doing just about any sort of motorsports, you'll need a helmet. And for good reason, they work.

Helmets in North America are rated by the Snell foundation. They're rated for motorcycle use (M), auto racing (SA or SAH), and other options such as karting. There's also a number involved, the year the standard was last updated. For example, an SA2005 helmet is a car helmet that meets the SA standard laid down in 2005. The standards are updated

There are two basic types of helmets: open and closed. The former is less expensive and cooler to wear, but it doesn't provide as much protection from flying debris. There's also been some debate about the compatibility of closed-face helmets and airbags. If you do decide to go with an open-face helmet, eye protection is a good idea whenever you're driving on track with the top down. This particular open face has been fitted with an intercom system.

every five years for car helmets, and most race organizations will accept a helmet that meets the last two ratings. This means that, in 2011, both SA2005 and SA2010 would be acceptable. Once the SA2015 helmets become available, the SA2005 one will no longer be accepted. Sometimes the last three ratings are allowed.

A common question has to do with the difference between SA and M helmets, as the latter is so much easier to find. Basically, SA helmets are required to pass a flammability test and a roll bar multi-impact test while the M do not. Also, SA helmets are allowed to have a smaller field of vision. As with any piece of safety equipment, check the rules. An autocross group may allow M class helmets, but a track organization may not. Helmets do degrade with time, so an M1985 helmet might not be a good choice even if it is allowed by the organization.

Helmets need to fit you well. They need to be snug enough so that they don't move around on your head, but they shouldn't pinch. Even light pressure can give you a real headache over the course of a 25-minute track session. When trying on a helmet, keep it on for a while so you can get an idea of how it feels. Different helmet manufacturers have varying ideas on the shape of the human head, so make sure you try on a few different makes. This is another good item to try out at a local track day.

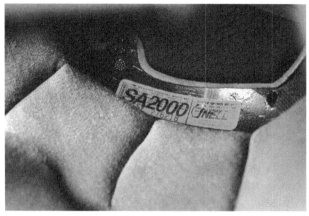

The Snell certification label is found inside the helmet. You may have to pull the inner lining out of the way to see it. Other organizations such as BSI may put their labels on the outside.

Here's what the Snell label looks like inside the helmet.

Head restraints, sometimes called HANS devices after the most popular brand, are intended to keep your head from getting whipped forward in a crash, which can lead to a basilar skull fracture. This particular type of injury came to the public's attention when NASCAR driver Dale Earnhardt was killed, and it's estimated that it's involved in as many as half of all racing deaths. While expensive, head restraints are becoming more popular among the track-day crowd and are required in most high-level motorsports. A HANS device sits on your shoulders and is attached to your helmet with a couple of straps. In most cases, these tethers are allowed to slide side to side in order to give you complete freedom of movement. Various models are available depending on weight and cost. The 2010 Snell helmet certification is the first to include an SAH rating, intended for helmets fitted with head restraint fixtures. An inexpensive doughnut-shaped neck brace may not provide the same protection as a HANS, but it provides some added safety at a low price.

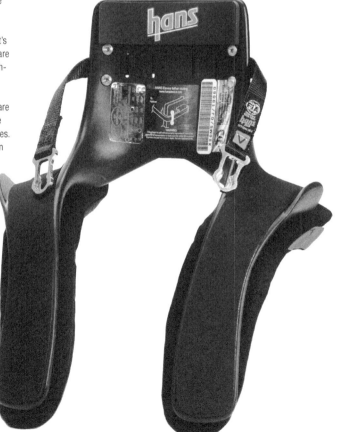

SEATS

Seats are important in a number of ways. They have to keep you in place while driving. They have to position you well to drive the car. And, of course, they have to be comfortable. The factory seats fail on at least one of these counts for many people.

Race seats are excellent at the first criteria and tend to do very well on the second as well. A real race seat will have a fixed back, deep bolstering, and cutouts for a harness. If at all possible, pick one up with FIA approval, as this means it is tested to withstand a minimum impact of 15 g acceleration from the side and 20 g from behind. Ideally, you'll want a seat rated for even more if possible, and some manufacturers will release their test data. Any harness cutouts need to be well positioned with respect to your body so that your harness can be properly mounted.

Most race seats won't work well with stock belts, as the latches tend to end up in awkward locations. One thing to keep in mind is that seats have an expiration date as well, so check with your organization to see if expired seats in good condition are accepted.

The mounting is important. The strongest mounting bolts the seat directly to the floor, preferably to the factory mounting holes. If you need adjustability, you can often buy sliders from the seat manufacturer. If you need to get yourself as low as possible in the car, you can cut the factory mounting points off and bolt the seat through the floor. Use nice large backing plates if you do this, however.

Construction has an effect as well. The best seats are made of Kevlar or carbon fiber. They're a bit on the expensive side, but most people don't mind spending for safety. Next is fiberglass, which tends to be much more

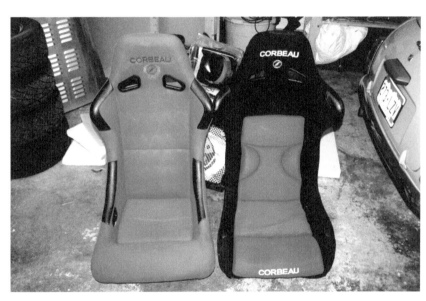

The seat on the left uses a tubular frame, the one on the right is a fiberglass shell. They look a lot alike, but there's a big difference in comfort. The shell can also be mounted with side mounts, which give more options for installation.

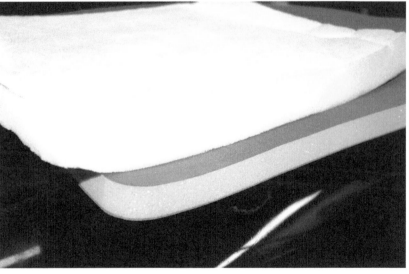

Two types of memory foam were tried as a replacement for the standard foam in some Corbeau seats. The off-white foam was cut from an inexpensive mattress topper, while the blue is a "Backsaver" sourced from a racing supply store. The cheap foam was better than the standard, but the military and medical grade "Backsaver" was far superior. With the cheap foam, both occupants were complaining after 30 minutes. With the good stuff, the team was happy for 13-hour days in the car. Even race seats might need a bit of extra tweaking to make them work.

affordable. The third choice from a strength perspective is a tubular steel frame. Unfortunately, these also tend to be inexpensive, so they're quite popular. Many racers will also use aluminum seats welded up from flat plates, which can be amazingly cheap. However, they're about as comfortable as you might imagine and have to have a back support, a bar extending from the roll cage to support the back in order to be strong enough and to meet regulations in most classes. Reclining seats are not race seats.

When choosing a seat, have a look at the material used to cover it. Typically, it's a fabric of some sort. High-wear areas should have some vinyl or leather reinforcement to keep the seat in good condition for a long time.

Seats are a bit like shoes, you need to find one that fits your particular physique. And the best way to do this is to sit in as many seats as possible. Yet again, track days are a good place

for this. Sit in the car for as long as you can, as a seat that seems comfortable on initial introduction can be quite uncomfortable after a longer period. Some seats offer a split bottom cushion, to provide different levels of support for your clutch leg. Check the position of the holes for the shoulder harnesses and make sure they're not too low for your build.

There's another aspect to buying a seat, and that's the difficulty of finding one that actually fits in a Miata. The cockpit of the NA and NB isn't all that large. The base of the seat needs to be no more than 19.5 inches wide, and the shoulder area shouldn't be more than 21 inches. In the NC, there's about 20 inches available top and bottom. Seat dimensions are quite easy to find from the manufacturers though.

So that's the high-end option, but what if you simply want to make your own seats a bit more comfortable without spending a bunch of money or making it difficult to get in

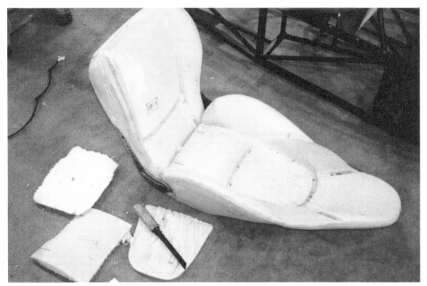

Halfway through a foamectomy. Some foam has been removed from the back of the seat as well as the bottom where you can't see it. After some more test sitting, foam was also removed from the shoulder area.

For a real custom touch, you can have a local upholstery shop alter your seat covers. In this case, the center sections of this leather seat were replaced with suede to hold the driver in place better. Combined with some custom foam shaping, the end result was a pair of classy seats that gripped far better than stock for less than $300 total.

and out of the car? A popular way to improve on the Miata's seats is to perform a "foamectomy." Basically, this involves removing the upholstery and reshaping the foam to fit you better. This works well on the NA and NB. The NC's seats have airbags, so this is not a recommended procedure due to the potential for explosive seat disassembly.

First, remove the seat by unbolting it from the floor. Separate the top and bottom halves from the reclining mechanism. Remove the upholstery from the parts of the seat you'll be modifying. Typically, people will concentrate on the bottom cushion of the seat to lower themselves, but I prefer to do a bit of shaping on the top as well. The upholstery is held on with metal loops called hog rings that can be cut off with a strong set of pliers. Eye protection is a must here. The foam can be removed from the bottom seat pan completely, but watch for the ridiculously sharp edges on the steel pan. Gloves are a good idea.

Once the seat is naked, you can shape the foam with a sharp or serrated knife. An electric carving knife does the job well. The best place to remove foam from the bottom cushion is actually on the bottom, between the foam and the pan. Take it off a bit at a time. Personally, I like to reassemble the seat without the upholstery so that I can test-fit it and make sure the shape is bang on. Once I'm satisfied, it's simply

a matter of reskinning the seat. You can either use new hog rings to secure the upholstery—any upholstery shop or good hardware store should be able to help out here—or you can actually substitute zip ties for a much easier job.

FIRE EXTINGUISHER

It's such a simple thing, but it can make a big difference. While it's not a great idea to risk life and limb to put out a burning car, most fires start off small. Having an extinguisher on board can make the difference between watching your baby go up in smoke and having to simply deal with some singed wiring. It doesn't even have to be your car you use it on.

Look for one rated for B:C fires (fuel and electrical). That's the sort of thing you'll need for car fires. These are often sold as kitchen extinguishers and use a sodium bicarbonate agent. The monoammonium phosphate found in A:B:C (solids such as wood as well as fuel and electrical) extinguishers is a lot more difficult to clean up and corrosive. Ideally, a halon extinguisher is best, but they're expensive. Get one rated for at least 10-B:C. The cute tiny chrome ones sold by some "race" shops are mostly for looks. You can pick up a budget extinguisher at just about any home or hardware store. These are made with plastic parts. For the professional level, go to a fire protection supply shop and pick up one with a metal nozzle.

My favorite place to mount extinguishers is in front of one of the seats. It's out of the way but immediately accessible. Use a bracket with one or two metal straps to hold it in place; the plastic ones that come with the extinguishers aren't much use. If you mount the extinguisher so that the gauge is readily visible, it's easy to check it once in a while to make sure it'll be working when you need it.

Chapter 14
Engine Swaps

About five minutes after the Miata was announced, someone thought, "I wonder if a rotary engine would fit?" At the same time, someone else thought, "Wow, that car needs a V-8!" And shortly afterward, both came into existence.

Monster Motorsports started selling cars with a 5.0 Ford V-8 almost immediately, and the result was so memorable that people who can't recognize a Miata know about them.

Obviously, ripping the stock drivetrain out of an unsuspecting Miata and shoehorning something completely different inside is a major step. It's not something you're going to do over the course of a weekend, and definitely not without some mechanical skills. But the end result can be mesmerizing, and not just to drive. While undoubtedly some of these conversions are quick and dirty jobs, the amount of creativity and care that goes into most is fantastic to see. No two are alike.

Just what's involved in an engine swap? There are two basic ways to do it. The first is to buy a kit. The more popular swaps are well supported by the aftermarket, so fabrication and problem-solving is kept to a bare minimum. Generally speaking, this means either a Ford or Chevy V-8, although rotary kits are sporadically available. Typically, a kit will consist of a new or modified front subframe, transmission mounts, differential mount, driveshaft, half shafts, and other necessary parts needed to complete the swap. More important, the supplier should be able to tell you just what you need to finish the job. This is the path of least resistance, and it'll get your repowered Miata back on the road as quickly as possible.

The quality of the kit will vary from supplier to supplier, of course, as will the quality of the support they can give you. If possible, talk to other builders who have

Landon Veith

used the same parts and get an idea of what you're dealing with. The amount of fabrication remaining will vary as well. Some will require you to alter the transmission tunnel and build an exhaust, while others will be as close as possible to a bolt-in. Of course, most people know what engine they want to install before they start doing any research at all into exactly how they're going to make it happen, which is going to limit the number of kit suppliers to only one or two for a given engine option.

But what if you want something different? For many people, the purpose of a re-engined Miata is to make a car unlike any other. As the old saying goes, anything's possible if you have a welder.

The first step is to get the new engine and transmission in the car. Depending on the size of the engine, this could be easy or it could get complicated. V engines can be tall, and this can be a real problem for height. Of course, they're always wider than a Miata engine as well. The subframe will probably have to be modified or you can replace it with a tubular version for more space. The firewall or transmission tunnel may have to be reshaped. The hood might have to be altered. The steering column or rack might need to be moved. The oil pan may have to be altered. And so on.

It's a good idea to spend some quality time with a tape measure before you start to hack things apart. Because most engines have seen use in multiple cars, knowing what's available to solve your problems goes a long way. Instead of a custom oil pan, it might be simply a matter of installing one from a different version of the same engine. Do your research.

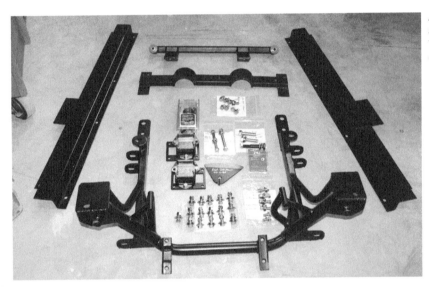

An example of a kit from V8 Roadsters. The driveshaft, axles, and new hubs for the rear are not shown. This particular setup does not include any exhaust components, so there's some fabrication ahead there.

If you're retaining the stock differential, you'll have to do something to replace the PPF that originally joined the nose of the differential to the rear of the transmission. Some people will build a PPF substitute running up to the new transmission; others will find a way to mount it to the rear subframe. There's a lot of vertical force on the nose. Bill Hingston used a solid bar with a bit of length adjustment to support his. *Bill Hingston*

There are a couple of ways to source your engine. A crate engine is exactly that: a brand-new engine that shows up in a crate such as this 480-horsepower Chevrolet LS3. In this case, the engine even has a factory warranty. It's not the cheapest way to get a motor, of course, but if you're looking for peace of mind, it may be the best option.

Another engine option is to rebuild one, either yourself or to have a shop do it. The cost here can vary widely, of course, depending on what you stick inside. It's actually a fairly common route to take, making the end result just that much more special. Here, Chad Kennedy from Kennedy Performance sets up a Ford 331 for Lee Bohon.

One way to simplify the wiring and plumbing considerably is to use a carbureted engine with a distributor like this one. The complexity of the engine management wiring is reduced to almost nothing at all. Packaging can be a problem with a V engine in this case because of the height of the resulting intake. An easy solution to this is to use a different hood such as the cowl induction hood from Simpson Design. *Lee Bohon*

One of the biggest problems with any swap is making sure there's enough ground clearance. A stock Miata engine is approximately 24 inches from top to bottom. The factory oil pan is level with the bottom of the front subframe and is thus protected from damage. When the pan protrudes below the subframe like this, it can be a real liability. A good solution is a skid plate or even a bar in front of the pan so that something else will take the initial impact. *Lee Bohon*

The cheapest way to get a drivetrain is to pull an engine out of a junked car. It's a bit more of a risk, but if you check it out carefully, it's a big money saver. Buying a running donor car will let you test-drive your drivetrain before you install it, so you can be sure it's in fine shape before you pull it out of its original home.

Once the big mechanical bits are in, there are still a few hurdles. Some creative plumbing will let you hook up the cooling system. The exhaust will almost definitely have to be a custom job for at least part of its length. The fuel system may have to be adapted to match both the fuel delivery and fuel pressure needs of the new engine. If your new engine is much stronger than a Miata one (and hopefully it is), then the rear end may need to be upgraded as well.

And then there's the electrical. Here's where it can get tough with a modern engine. If you have an old V-8 with a carburetor and a distributor, you only need to hook up one or two wires. These days it's a different matter. The best you can hope for is that the engine has separate engine management that's not tied into the rest of the car. In the case of engines that are popular to install in the wrong car, such as the ubiquitous Chevy and Ford V-8s, you can often buy wiring harnesses designed for hot rods that are simplified and easy to hook up. The worst case is a factory computer that's tied deeply into the rest of the car. For example, with the Honda S2000 engine, you need to use the S2000 gauge cluster to keep things working. ECUs out of OBD-II cars may need a bit of extra work to avoid check engine lights, although the extra diagnosis ability provided by the OBD-II system can be helpful.

Regardless of whether you decide to use a kit or to roll your own conversion, cost obviously has to be taken into consideration. Completing an engine swap for under $10,000 is a real feat. You might be able to pick up a running 5.0 Mustang for $200, but there are a lot of extras involved and you're going to get almost every aspect of the car involved. Wiring, fuel, exhaust, differential, driveshaft, axles—the list is pretty long. In fact, it's probably fair to say that the initial cost of the engine isn't really important. The commercially available conversion kits usually cost right around $4,000.

There's also the matter of legality. Call your local DMV or registration authority. In some areas, anything goes. In others, the engine cannot be newer than the car it goes into in order to meet emissions regulations, or the car will have to meet the emissions standards of whichever is newer, chassis or engine. Some areas even restrict the size of the new engine relative to the weight of the car. It's important to check this first. While Internet forums are an easy way to get information, 'they are not always accurate. The best thing to do is to call the DMV directly. They'll know, and if you call the central office instead of a branch, you'll often find you'll get an answer quickly.

'That's out of the way. Now, what's been done?

One of the biggest challenges to any swap can be dealing with the accessory drives. When you're dealing with an engine that has only been used in one application such as the Honda S2000 motor, you're limited to the original off-the-shelf solution or a custom setup. A popular engine such as this Ford or a Chevy V-8 has a wide variety of both original equipment and aftermarket options to make life much easier. In this case, the parts from a 1994–1995 Mustang were used with a bit of modification to clear the large aftermarket valve covers. Having contact with an expert in your engine can make life much easier, as they'll know the tricks. *Lee Bohon*

The front subframe of the Miata can be unbolted and a tubular one installed in its place. This one, from V8 Roadsters, can be supplied with either motor mounts for an LS motor or with none at all. This makes life a lot easier when doing a swap. This piece is sometimes called a "K member" by swap enthusiasts, a piece of nomenclature that's come over from other cars. In this particular case, the subframe is fitted with Miata motor mounts, as it'll also drop 10 pounds of weight from the front of the car.

The differential usually has to be upgraded with a high-torque engine—not just for strength, but also for the tall gear ratios often needed. The Cadillac CTS-V has been used a number of times with Chevy-based cars, but the Monster kit uses this 7.5-inch Ford found in cars such as the Thunderbird. For maximum strength, an 8.8-inch Ford is sometimes used, although it's a bit heavy. Both of the Fords have a wide range of rear-end ratios available. *Lee Bohon*

ROTARY

The rotary swap is the one that all the Mazda fans want to know about. After all, the car's a Mazda, and the rotary is a Mazda engine, so it must be easy, right? Well, no. Even though the rotary is a small engine, packaging is a problem. The eccentric shaft (the equivalent to a crankshaft) sits higher in the engine, so the whole engine has to sit lower. This causes problems with ground clearance. Not to say it can't be done, but it does make things more difficult.

Rotaries are also hot and loud, leading to some real challenges with the exhaust and cooling system. In fact, most rotary Miata owners identify the cooling system as one of the most difficult aspects of a swap. Despite the appeal of the end result, the rotary NA or NB Miata remains a rare beast, not commonly seen and causing excitement whenever it is spotted.

That's liable to change, though. The NC is based on the same platform as the RX-8, and it turns out the Renesis rotary and associated pieces fit nicely under the sports car. Very nicely. Get your hands on the front subframe, engine, and transmission from an RX-8, and it'll literally bolt in to the NC. Even the normal NC driveshaft will fit. As engine swaps go, the basic mechanical aspect is straightforward.

There are still some hurdles to overcome, of course. The PPF needs just a little bit of tweaking to fit. More important, the wiring is difficult. Both the NC and the RX-8 have ECUs that are fairly easily upset, but with an aftermarket ECU or with a lot of time spent with wiring diagrams, it should be possible to do a seamless job.

Steve Moore owns this turbo rotary Miata with a very clean installation. The center of the subframe was cut out and replaced with a tubular crossbar, then a custom oil pan with a rear pickup was fabricated to fit around this. Some redesign of the upper half of the subframe was required as well. It was a labor-intensive piece of work, but effective. The stock ground clearance is retained and the transmission tunnel didn't need modifications at all. A cross brace was added behind the transmission to support it. The end result is well done, although the overall weight is much the same as a V-8 car. Then again, V-8 cars don't have a 9,000-rpm redline. *Steve Moore*

ENGINE SWAPS

A carbureted 13B rotary in a Miata. The cooling system shown here was the final design after multiple iterations. The end result was a large radiator with an oil cooler underneath in a V layout. This particular car was a fairly successful racer, and because of its race application niceties such as a heater, wipers, and bumpers were ditched. The air intake also stuck through the hood, not what's considered acceptable for every street car. *Alan Branch*

Here's one way to make a rotary Miata. Composite Envisions basically stuffed an entire 1993 RX-7 inside (well, mostly inside) this Miata. Subframes, the entire drivetrain, instruments, electrics, even the windshield wiper motor is from the RX-7. That's a bit further than most are willing to go, of course; but it shows what's possible if you really set your mind to something and have the ability to carry through. *Kris Eidnes*

THE V-8S

For those who aren't Mazda fans, the obvious engine to put in a small sports car is a big V-8. There's a long tradition of this sort of thing, resulting in cars such as the AC Cobra and the Sunbeam Tiger. The appeal is logical: Mate one of the world's best handling cars with a lot of power. The common complaint is that this will somehow wreck the Miata and take away its soul. Well, the former is simply a matter of engineering. The latter is a matter of viewpoint and is usually a poor justification for not liking an idea.

The compact size of the Ford 302 has made it a favorite for Miata engine swaps since the beginning. *Lee Bohon*

A 302 hooked up to a T5 transmission. There are a number of variations of this transmission available, and a stronger aftermarket unit is required in many cases. It's a nice small unit though. *Lee Bohon*

The LS series of engines, also known as the Generation III and IV, are beautifully packaged. They all share the same external dimensions and everything is cleanly tucked away as you can see here. This cammed LS3 is rated at 480 horsepower and will get more than 30 miles per gallon on the highway in a Miata.

FORD V-8

For years, the Ford 302 or 5.0 has been used in the NA and NB. It's a fairly compact engine and goes into the car well. Monster Motorsports led the way, and now just about any V-8 Miata is called a "monster." For those with a truly short attention span, adding a supercharger makes the car into a Mega Monster.

Thanks to the amount of experience with this swap and the existence of various kits, including the one from Monster, it's still a popular conversion. In stock form, most of these engines run around 200 horsepower, but a massive aftermarket exists to push the engines well beyond that range. Because the basic engine was used in millions of Fords, they're relatively inexpensive and easy to find. The typical transmission is a T5, which packages well in the Miata.

The biggest difficulty seems to be in hood and ground clearance, particularly in cars retaining a carburetor. The oil pan does hang below the crossmember. They're also a bit on the heavy side in stock form, but some aftermarket aluminum heads help out there. In terms of bang for the buck, the straight 302 conversion is high on the list.

CHEVY V-8

At the moment, the biggest excitement in the Miata conversion community is about the LSx engines. The classic small-block Chevy was usually ignored for the Ford because it's a bit larger and more awkward to fit, but GM changed that when it redesigned the engine in the late 1990s. The LS family of engines has cleaner packaging, a lightweight aluminum block, and makes completely ludicrous power. When first introduced, the base LS1 made 350 horsepower or so. Ten years later, the LS3 in the Corvette was rated at 430. Of course, the aftermarket will help you move well beyond that point.

The engine's been used in many applications, so there are a bunch of parts available to make fitment easier. When used with the oil pan from the 1998–2002 Camaro and Firebird, the oil pan sits no lower than stock and the engine clears the stock hood. For a real budget build, the inexpensive 5.3-liter version used in many trucks can be used if the right oil pan and intake manifold are bolted on. The transmission usually paired with this beast is the T56, a six-speed with loads of internal strength. It's a big transmission, though, which can mean some transmission tunnel widening is in order, depending on the engine location.

There are a couple of kits available on the market at the moment to make this a simple swap, and there's an arms race of development going on. The first LS- powered NCs have also made an appearance. The NC appears to have more room for engine swaps because there is more space between the frame rails, and it has a more bulbous nose.

ENGINE SWAPS

BEFORE-AND-AFTER SWAP DETAILS

Here's a closer look at a LSx swap into a 2003 Miata, performed by Flyin' Miata. The amount of work that had to be done is representative of what needs to be done for most engine conversions.

The LS1 engine and T56 transmission came out of a 2001 Pontiac Firebird. The front and rear subframes were removed from the Miata along with the interior. The corners of the frame in the engine bay took a bit of trimming, a common alteration no matter what swap is being performed. The transmission tunnel was opened up by cutting a couple of slits, hammering the tunnel, and welding it back up again. The carpet was removed so that it wouldn't catch fire with the welding. The transmission tunnel alterations aren't noticeable from inside the car at all, but they do allow the big T56 and engine to sit a bit farther back. This improves the weight distribution, puts the shifter in the right place, and gives more room up front for a sway bar. While the welder was out, the oil pan was modified to give a little room for the steering rack.

With the body modifications done, a tubular front subframe was installed along with the engine and transmission. New frame rail supports were bolted on along with a crossmember to support the transmission. At the back of the car, a new mounting tab was welded on the subframe and a differential from a Cadillac CTS-V was installed along with new half shafts. It was all joined together with a custom driveshaft. A custom exhaust was welded up using a couple of "block hugger" headers to start with and running back to a muffler designed for high-power turbo Miatas. Clearance between the exhaust and the stock steering column is tight.

A new 3/8-inch fuel line was run from the tank to make sure the engine had enough fuel, and it was fed with an upgraded fuel pump. The GM ECU is mostly only concerned with the engine, so it was wired in carefully. A few tweaks were needed in order to get it to play well with the tachometer and speedometer in the stock Miata instrument cluster. For cooling, a Miata race radiator was hooked up to the LS, and particular attention was paid to the ducting in the nose to optimize cooling.

When all was said and done, the car had gained just under 200 pounds and the front weight distribution had gone from 51.4 to 52.6 percent. The same car had been run as a high-power turbo car in the past, and the weight and balance were almost the same then as when the V-8 was installed.

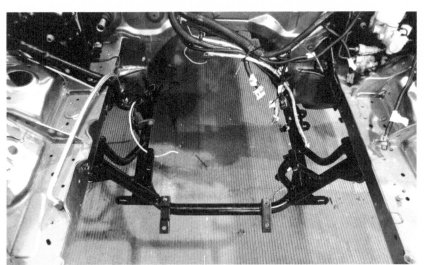

The amount of extra room allowed by the tubular subframe is dramatic. This is another car, and the transmission tunnel has already been extended and the engine bay repainted.

Almost every conversion requires this same modification to the frame rails in the engine bay. This picture was taken after the initial cut, before some extra metal was welded in for extra strength and to close off the frame rail. Seam sealer was used to finish the job.

Bill Cardell adjusts the transmission mount on the new crossmember. The semi-circular cutouts for the future exhaust can be seen, as can the reinforced frame rails that the crossmember bolts to. Almost every conversion will need a similar transmission support.

OTHER ENGINES
S2000

One engine that gets a lot of attention and that has been used a couple of times is the one from the S2000, known as the F20C. It's a beautiful piece of work, with a 9,000-rpm redline and an aluminum block. In fact, the end result is often a bit lighter than the original Miata was and the character of the engine suits the car perfectly. It's more of an evolution to the Miata concept than a reinventing. It's not a bolt-in swap, as the Honda engine is tall and a lot of surgery is required to the subframe. The oil pan sits about an inch lower than the stock one and should probably have a skid plate. The Honda ECU requires the instrument cluster to run, so a bit of creativity is required to fit that into the Miata dashboard. Unlike most swaps, you can keep the stock rear end without being concerned about tearing it apart, and the S2000 actually uses a ring-and-pinion that's interchangeable with the Miata one to bring the gearing into line. If a vendor ever comes up with a kit for this swap, it may prove to be very popular.

While most of the Chevy engine conversions use the later generation LS motors, some still use the classic small-block. This super-clean installation is by Landon Veith. It's a 409-cubic-inch mill (that's 6.7 liters for those who prefer metric), and you can imagine what it does for performance. There's some nice attention to detail here. *Landon Veith*

It looks as if it belongs there, doesn't it? Bill Hingston's S2000-powered Miata required a fair bit of work, but it's a joy to drive.

1.8 CONVERSION

Despite what it says at the beginning of this chapter, one of the most common swaps *is* one you can do in a weekend. The 1.8 BP engine can be swapped into a 1.6 Miata with minimal fuss. This is detailed in *Mazda Miata MX-5 Performance Handbook*, and it's a fairly simple job. There is even an off-the-shelf conversion kit that means no fabrication is required, just a few wires that need to be extended.

The basic rule is that mechanical parts come from the 1.8, while electrical parts come from the 1.6. The 1.8 provides the engine, motor mounts, exhaust manifold, intake manifold, and injectors. The 1.6 provides the throttle body, all wiring including the ECU, all sensors, the coils, airflow sensor, and a cam angle sensor. Many of the 1.8 engines have extra sensors; these can be ignored as the 1.6 computer doesn't know what to do with them. The EGR system can be removed and plugged or simply left alone. The 1.6 has a thermosensor in the thermostat housing that triggers the main fan. The 1.6 thermostat neck and housing can be transferred over to the 1.8, or the 1.8 housing can be modified to take the sensor. Another option is to simply run this wire to ground, and the fan will run whenever the ignition is on. The trickiest part for most people is dealing with the exhaust and the intake.

For the exhaust, if the donor engine is from an NA, you can simply use the lower half of the 1.6 downpipe mated to the 1.8 exhaust manifold. This will require an O_2 sensor bung to be welded in to the downpipe, however. Alternately, you can use the cat from a 1.8 NA with the 1.8 manifold and downpipe, and it's all sorted out. This will let you use an aftermarket header. If the donor's from an NB, then the easiest thing to do is either source the NA downpipe or use an NA header with a 1.8 NA cat.

The intake piping seems to cause some trouble, but anything that simply delivers air to the throttle body will do the job. Stock parts can be used, but depending on how the throttle body was mounted and which thermostat neck was used, this could be a tough fit.

There's a lot of interest in using the NB engines in the 1990–1993 cars. For the 1990–2000 engine, this is fairly straightforward. The only trick is that the VICS system will need to be activated, and that can be done with a simple rpm switch similar to those used for modifying the VTEC switch point on Hondas. The 2001–2005 cars cause a greater problem, though. The VVT really needs to work properly in order to make this engine worthwhile. At the time of writing, only a couple of full aftermarket ECUs could do the job. Wiring in the 2001–2005 ECU isn't really an option, in large part due to the factory immobilizers. Nevertheless, it's reasonable to expect that someone will come up with a solution to this eventually.

OTHERS

Those are the big players, but just about anything has been considered and in some cases actually carried out. Rover V-8s are seen in the United Kingdom due to that engine's relatively small size and light weight. The Nissan SR20DET turbo engine has shown up once or twice. A few V-6s have been done, from a Ford Duratec to Mazda's own. A surprising number of Miatas even run on electric power.

Then there are the real oddballs. A Mercedes turbo-diesel? Yup. Motorcycle power? Not yet, but it's only a matter of time. One of the most spectacular is a Jaguar V-12 conversion. It was a stupendous amount of work, and the rear velocity stack is right at the base of the windshield while the hood has essentially been cut in half to clear the intake; but it's been done.

If you have a cool idea and the ability, don't be afraid to forge into the unknown. If it wasn't for that sort of person, there would be no such thing as a V-12 Miata. If you're not quite that brave, the more "common" swaps are still unusual and compelling.

CLOSING

As I said in the introduction, it's not that the Miata is a bad car. In fact, it's so good that people want to make it even better. Whether it's a small tweak to the alignment to sharpen up the handling or a major renovation under the hood, it's possible to make a dramatic difference to Mazda's little roadster.

No matter what you might have planned, good luck. With any luck, the information in this book will help you turn your vision into a reality and let you make your Miata into something truly special.

Index

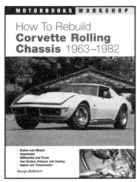

CPSIA information can be obtained at www.ICGtesting.com
Printed in the USA
LVOW02s0453151114

413357LV00006B/7/P